FOCUS

JAMES BROWN AND SAM BROWN

FOCUS

The ADHD Guide to Productivity

& getting stuff done

greenfinch

First published in Great Britain in 2026 by Greenfinch
an imprint of Quercus
Part of John Murray Group

1

A CIP catalogue record for this book is available from the British Library

TPB ISBN 978-1-52944-889-4
EBOOK ISBN 978-1-52944-890-0

Typeset in Sofia by CC Book Production

Printed and bound in Great Britain by Clays Ltd, Elcograf S.p.A.

Papers used by Quercus are from well-managed forests and other responsible sources.

Quercus
Carmelite House
50 Victoria Embankment
London EC4Y 0DZ

John Murray Group
Part of Hodder & Stoughton Limited
An Hachette UK company

The authorised representative in the EEA is Hachette Ireland,
8 Castlecourt Centre, Dublin 15, D15 XTP3, Ireland (email: info@hbgi.ie)

This book is dedicated to every person with ADHD who has known the struggle. We honour the memory of those who are not here to read this, and we thank the community that continues to support, understand and uplift us.

CONTENTS

ABOUT THE AUTHORS ix

WELCOME! AND HOW TO USE THIS BOOK 1

1 WHAT EVEN IS ADHD? 9
It's not just about losing your keys

2 ADHD AND PRODUCTIVITY CHALLENGES 27
Or why productivity is a problem (for people like us)

3 ADHD-FRIENDLY GOAL SETTING 49
Or, the SMART approach to success

4 AUTOMATING LIFE 73
The importance of building routines

5 FINDING MOTIVATION 99
(And keeping it long enough to do a thing)

6 WHICH FIRE TO PUT OUT FIRST? 115
Picking priorities (when everything feels urgent)

7 TACKLING PROCRASTINATION 139
Or why you're vacuuming instead of emailing your boss

8 MANAGING DISTRACTIBILITY 161
Focus, filters and fidgeting

9 TIME MANAGEMENT FOR THE 'TIME-BLIND' 187
Or why a second can feel like an hour and an hour like a second

10 DEALING WITH THE FEELS 204
The emotional side of productivity

11 FORGET ME NOT 224
Working memory and the lost train of thought

12 PROGRESS, NOT PERFECTION 243
(Especially when perfect never happens)

13 WHEN ADHD MEETS AUTISM 261
AuDHD and doing things differently

14 LEARNING TO SAY NO 289
Self-care, boundaries and people-pleasing

15 THE PRODUCTIVITY CRASH 316
Transitions, task switching and getting started again

16 PERMISSION TO BE HUMAN 329

Notes 335
Resources and further reading 341
Acknowledgements 347
Index 349

ABOUT THE AUTHORS

Dr James Brown

James is a biomedical scientist, an award-winning science communicator, a public speaker, an ADHD coach and an author. He was diagnosed with ADHD in 2021, which explained a lot, including his multiple unfinished projects, inability to sit through meetings without doodling and tendency to vacuum when faced with a grant deadline. He is a co-founder of the UK charity ADHDadultUK, co-host of *The ADHD Adults Podcast* and a frequent public speaker on all things ADHD. James's work blends evidence-based science with lived experience, delivered with honesty, humour and just the right amount of irreverence. He has an incredible brain that is thirsty for knowledge and is constantly searching for the latest research on whatever 15 topics have piqued his interest that day so that he can share it on the podcast, social media or with Sam (who pretends she's listening).

When not coaching or writing, he can usually be found playing guitar or impulse-buying new guitars.

Sam Brown

Sam is an executive administrator, writer and researcher with lived experience of both ADHD and autism. Their (current – they have had *many* careers!) professional life involves high-pressure executive support roles, making them a rare combination of systems-thinker and spreadsheet sorcerer, with a deep understanding of how productivity really works (and often doesn't) for neurodivergent people.

Diagnosed with both ADHD and autism in adulthood, Sam has spent years learning how to navigate life with an AuDHD brain in a world not designed for them.

When they're not working (Sam LOVES working!) or hyperfocusing on a new spreadsheet, Sam can be found enjoying whatever their latest hobby is before their interest evaporates and they go into mourning before finding their next fixation.

Sam brings practical magic to this book: their ability to research and build sustainable systems, set goals and focus on the details of a task, while also managing James as he tries to launch 14 new projects before breakfast, alongside their own experience of living with AuDHD, are what help to make this book work.

James and Sam live in the Midlands, write books that they hope they and other people will actually finish, and spend a disproportionate amount of time discussing neurodivergence, bird calls (Sam's current hyperfixation – this may change before they finish writing this book!) and trying to decide which film to watch (or rewatch) next.

Welcome!

AND HOW TO USE THIS BOOK

(Or, read me first, unless you've already skipped ahead)

Welcome! If you're reading this introduction, congratulations – you've already beaten the odds. Many people with ADHD buy books they never read, skip the introduction, or forget they're reading it halfway through and start scrolling on their phone or reorganizing the drawer with the phone chargers. If that's you, we've written this chapter to let you know that we have written this book to help you to accept that that's OK.

Let's start with a seemingly obvious but important note. This is not a book you need to read in one sitting, from cover to cover, in chapter order. In fact, we have designed it *specifically* so you *don't* have to. Some people with ADHD may struggle with the predictability of linear reading, rigid structures, or the concept of 'just follow the steps'. So, we won't ask you to.

Instead, think of this book less as an educational guide or a prescription, more as a menu of options. It's here to help you figure out how to be more productive in a way that actually works for *your* brain, your circumstances and your 'chaos'.

You can start anywhere

So maybe you have started at the beginning, or maybe you've come back to the beginning. Both are fine. Wherever you are on your journey with this book, please know that it's more than OK to start wherever you like. If you're struggling with motivation, flip straight to Chapter 5. If your to-do list looks like a dumpster fire and you don't know where to begin, try the prioritization chapter, Chapter 6. If you're in the middle of an emotional spiral about the fact that you've done none of the things you intended to do today, head to the section on emotional dysregulation in Chapter 10.

There is no gold star for reading this book 'properly'. There is no productivity exam at the end (which Sam is gutted about because she loves a test!). The goal is to help you feel more in control, even if just a little, of the whirlwind that is ADHD and modern life.

You don't need to remember any of the complicated science

Occasionally, this book will use anatomical terms related to the brain and neurology when we describe how the brain governs our ADHD traits. Terms like the 'prefrontal cortex' or the ridiculously named 'anterior cingulate cortex' (which literally translates from the Latin as the 'belt that wraps around the front part of the outside of the brain'). You don't need to remember these terms, and we're not mentioning them to show off or to make you feel stupid. Instead, we're referencing the neurobiology of ADHD to show that the chaos you may experience *has a very real, biological basis.* We think that this is really important as many people with ADHD carry a lot of shame about 'not being able to get shit done'. And that shame tells us that *we lack the ability* to get shit done – that we are lazy, undisciplined, unreliable, etc. Understanding and accepting that there is a biological basis for the challenges of ADHD can help to reduce that shame.

So, you do not have to memorize any of the neurological terms included in this book. Just know this: ADHD often affects how the brain processes attention, motivation, time, emotions and other thinking skills. That's it. Understanding those differences can give you the power, not to 'fix' yourself, but to *understand* yourself.

You don't have to become a productivity guru overnight

Let's be honest: the word *productivity* has been hijacked. Somewhere along the way, it stopped meaning 'getting the important stuff done' and started meaning 'waking up at 5am, running a marathon, replying to two hundred emails, batch-cooking lentil stew and still having time for a sunset yoga session and writing in your gratitude journal'.

That's not what this book is about. Productivity, for many people with ADHD, is not about becoming some kind of hyper-efficient robot.

It's about getting through the day with more wins, however small, looking after yourself as you would a friend or loved one, having fewer meltdowns and trying to avoid burnout. This means **productivity is about doing your work *and* remembering to take breaks to eat or rest**. It can be about replying to the one email that's been haunting you, even if three hundred others are still waiting.

You won't find hacks here that magically turn you into a morning person, or any promises that you'll finally have an inbox of zero (what even *is* that?). You will, we hope, find tools that make life a bit easier and ways of working that fit *you* rather than the other way around.

You can try one thing, fail at it, and still consider that a step forward. You can read one page, forget what it said, and come back next week, and that still counts. This book and the way you choose to use it aren't a structured 'training programme'. Instead, think of the book as a toolkit. You don't have to use every tool. You can see if one or two of them help you to build a version of productivity that doesn't make you want to scream into a pillow.

This book is written with ADHD in mind, which means:

- **Short sections:** No great walls of text. We know your eyes will glaze over.
- **Clear headings:** You can skip to the parts you care about.
- **Stories and strategies:** Because examples help it to stick, and you're more likely to remember a story than a diagram of the brain's reward circuitry.
- **Permission to skim:** Genuinely. There are no rules here. You can jump ahead, read backwards, or leave sticky notes poking out of random pages.

Each chapter is standalone, but they also relate to one another. So, if you read about motivation and suddenly realize your real problem is emotional dysregulation, great! Flip to that chapter. You're not 'getting it wrong'. You're doing it in exactly the right way for *your* brain.

What you'll find in each chapter

Every chapter follows the same basic structure. Not because we're rigid, but because some level of predictability can help to reduce overwhelm (which means that you won't waste precious executive function figuring out where the useful bits are).

Each chapter includes:

- **A real-world example or reflection from us**: sometimes embarrassing, occasionally inspiring, almost always (hopefully!) relatable.
- **A bit of science**: explained clearly, without assuming you did a psychology degree or paid attention in biology classes at school.
- **Practical tools and techniques**: simple strategies you can try straightaway (or ignore and come back to later).

We'll keep the sections short, with plenty of headings, so if you prefer to, you can skim until something jumps out at you. If you forget what you've just read three times in a row, don't worry, same here. Some chapters will speak directly to the stuff you're wrestling with today. Others might feel more 'oh yeah, that's a thing too'. **You don't need to remember everything. You don't even need to finish a chapter in one go. You're not being marked on this.**

This is not a to-do list

Every strategy in this book is an *invitation*, not a *command*. We're not here to give you another check list that stares at you in disappointment from your desk. We've got enough of those.

Instead, we're offering tools. Some could be game-changers. Others might not land for you, and that's fine. The goal is to collect a few that actually work for your brain and your life.

The tools we suggest are grounded in evidence, lived experience and the collective wisdom of many individuals with ADHD who have tried, failed, adapted and tried again. You can:

- **Start with one tool and see how it goes.**
- **Combine or stack tools to try to create routines that feel sustainable.**
- **Ditch anything that makes things harder, more overwhelming, or more boring.**

This is *your* toolkit. You're allowed to make it messy. Add stickers. Use all your coloured pens and highlighters. Swear at it. Just make it yours.

*Final pep talk: you're not broken; you're f*cking brilliant (and possibly tired)*

We want to end this intro with something important: this book is not about fixing you. **You are not broken.**

You've just been trying your hardest to operate in a world that wasn't built for your brain.

Most productivity advice wasn't built for your brain either.

That's why you've maybe felt lazy, chaotic, forgetful, unmotivated, inconsistent or *[insert your shame word of choice here]*. But those words miss the point. The reality is that your brain works differently. That difference brings challenges, yes, but there are ways to free your brain up to do the things you find rewarding, or fun, or the things that play to your strengths and values. All of which makes life feel just that little bit easier.

This book is here to help you stop fighting your brain and start working *with* it. To build systems that support you. To find routines that don't bore you to death. To make room for joy, rest, imperfection and actual progress (even if it's the kind you don't notice until someone else points it out).

If you need to take breaks, take breaks.

If you try something and it doesn't work, try again, or try something else.

And if you do absolutely nothing except read this intro and feel a tiny bit less alone? That's a win too.

Now...off you go. There's no wrong way to read this book. Just start where you're curious, where it hurts, or just pick a chapter at random and see what helps.

Chapter 1

WHAT EVEN IS ADHD?

It's not just about losing your keys

Growing up ADHD for Sam was a constant source of shame. As a child they were beaten for being loud and running around with the boys in their nursery, so they very quickly learned to mask. **Masking is something lots of neurodivergent people do, often without thinking, in order to try to appear neurotypical and not stand out or draw negative attention to themselves.** Sam is naturally externally hyperactive but hid this by twisting their legs together, sitting on their hands and disassociating.

They developed lots of coping mechanisms to mask their ADHD, like:

- Keeping lists of birthdays, along with notes of things that people said they liked, then checking that list at the beginning of every month and posting out cards and presents.
- Making sure they were extra early for everything (but then being aware that it wasn't 'normal' to arrive an hour early, so trying to keep themselves occupied in a nearby shop and then getting distracted and arriving late after all!).

- Digging their nails into their skin to make themselves pay attention when someone was talking to them.
- Setting time aside every day to make sure that they responded to messages within a reasonable time.
- Keeping a list of people that were struggling so they could check in on them regularly.
- Making a note of what was going on in other people's lives so they could remind themselves before meeting them.
- Drinking and taking drugs as a form of self-medication just to help them cope with the overwhelm of a crowded club or party (but then getting so overstimulated they were horrible to everyone or would completely shut down).
- Spending days and days planning things meticulously to make sure that they had thought of every detail of an event or holiday and anticipated every possible issue in advance, only to get distracted and miss the flight, or lose their passport, or not pay close enough attention when booking the flights so they booked both flights in the wrong direction, or going to the wrong venue for a gig, or turning up on the wrong day, or forgetting the tickets, all of which they have done multiple times.

Fast-forward to perimenopause, and they lost all their coping mechanisms and ability to mask and suddenly could not function as a passable human. They forgot birthdays, constantly lost track of time, struggled even more with debt due to impulse spending, became extra forgetful and spent most of the day looking for things they had *just now* in their hand! They were more internally and externally hyperactive than ever and slept less and less due to racing thoughts. They struggled to concentrate on anything because they were distracted by constant mind-wandering and OH MY GOD THERE'S A SQUIRREL!! (Stereotypical, we know, but they do love squirrels.)

All of a sudden, someone who was known for their ridiculously over-the-top organization and impressive work ethic could not organize themselves, struggled to do even the bare minimum at work and did not want to exist. **This was undiagnosed ADHD for Sam.**

What is ADHD, then?

Attention-Deficit Hyperactivity Disorder, or ADHD, is a **lifelong neurodevelopmental condition**. That just means that when your brain was developing in the earliest stages of life, it developed fractionally differently from what we think of a 'typical' brain. That difference in development means that the brain functions fractionally differently from the very start, and it's been that way since childhood, even if you weren't diagnosed until adulthood.

So...what does this mean? The differences in the way the brain works in ADHD affect how your brain manages attention, motivation, time, emotions, impulsive behaviour and so much more.

The big headline 'diagnostic' symptoms of ADHD fall into two groups:

- **Inattention**: Things like being easily distracted, forgetting appointments, starting multiple tasks and completing none, struggling with organization and zoning out mid-task (or mid-conversation).
- **Hyperactivity and impulsivity**: This isn't just fidgeting. In adults, it can often show up more as internal restlessness than bouncing off

the walls. You might feel constantly on edge, feel like you talk too much, interrupt without meaning to, or make snap decisions you regret five seconds later.

A full list of the most recent diagnostic symptoms of ADHD, according to the American Psychiatric Association's handbook,[1] can be found below:

Inattention symptoms

To meet the diagnostic threshold, five or more of these symptoms must be present for at least six months (for individuals aged 17 and older), and they must negatively impact social, academic or occupational functioning.

1. Often fails to give close attention to details or makes careless mistakes in schoolwork, at work or during other activities.
2. Often has difficulty sustaining attention in tasks or play activities (e.g. during lectures, conversations or lengthy reading).
3. Often does not seem to listen when spoken to directly (mind seems elsewhere, even without any obvious distraction).
4. Often does not follow through on instructions and fails to finish schoolwork, chores or duties in the workplace (starts tasks but quickly loses focus and is easily sidetracked).
5. Often has difficulty organizing tasks and activities (e.g. difficulty managing sequential tasks; poor time management; disorganized work).
6. Often avoids, dislikes or is reluctant to engage in tasks that

require sustained mental effort, such as preparing reports, completing forms or reviewing lengthy documents.

7. Often loses things necessary for tasks or activities, such as keys, paperwork, eyeglasses and mobile phones.
8. Is often easily distracted by extraneous stimuli, including unrelated thoughts.
9. Is often forgetful about daily responsibilities, like returning calls, paying bills or keeping appointments.

Hyperactivity and impulsivity symptoms

As with inattention, five or more of these symptoms must be present for at least six months (age 17+) and they must interfere with functioning.

1. Often fidgets with, or taps, hands or feet, or squirms in seat.
2. Often leaves seat in situations when remaining seated is expected, such as in the office or during meetings.
3. Often feels restless or runs about or climbs in situations where it is inappropriate (in adults, may be limited to feelings of restlessness).
4. Often unable to engage in leisure activities quietly.
5. Is often 'on the go', acting as if 'driven by a motor' (may be experienced by others as being restless or difficult to keep up with).
6. Often talks excessively.
7. Often blurts out answers before a question has been completed, finishing people's sentences or speaking out of turn.

8. Often has difficulty waiting their turn, such as in queues or group situations.
9. Often interrupts or intrudes on others, e.g. butts into conversations, games, or activities; may start using other people's things without asking.

This is our first opportunity in this book to point out something fundamentally important: **not everyone with ADHD is the same.** That list you may have just read? **You don't need to have all the symptoms to obtain an ADHD diagnosis.** What this immediately tells us is that if you compare two random people with ADHD, their 'big headline' symptoms will likely be different. Your ADHD is your ADHD, and if anyone tells you otherwise, they are arguing with your lived experience.

So, you don't have to tick every box to have ADHD. Still, if five or more of these symptoms from either (or both) lists have been making life harder for you across two or more different areas (like work, relationships or just managing your daily life), that's when professionals *should* start taking notice.

Many people still view ADHD as a 'disorder of naughty boys', largely due to a lack of societal understanding and the fact that **the actual diagnostic tests for ADHD were designed by studying boys (or more specifically, white, heterosexual, cis-gendered, young boys)** and working out what level of behaviour would be sufficient to be classed as a disorder. Most people with ADHD *do* show signs in childhood, and part of the diagnostic criteria is that symptoms should present before the age of 12, but they're not always picked up, especially if you weren't the 'disruptive' type. People who are *not* cis-gendered, white, straight boys, or who do not behave in the way that the people who developed these tests expect those boys with ADHD to behave, often get missed. They might present with more inattentive symptoms (like daydreaming or zoning out), which can be easier to overlook than hyperactive behaviour. They may also mask (hide their symptoms in order to appear neurotypical), due to societal or cultural expectations and pressures.

Many adults only realize they have ADHD when significant life changes, challenges or an increase in responsibilities or demands (like masking so well you accidentally become a manager at work) **cause everything to start unravelling into chaos, burnout, depression or workplace issues, or when younger relatives get diagnosed and the heaviest penny drops.**

ADHD in adulthood

ADHD symptoms don't magically vanish when you hit 18. They usually persist and often just change shape.

Hyperactivity may evolve into a persistent sense of pressure or mental noise. Impulsivity can become more about emotional reactions or risky decisions. And inattention? That sticks around like a loyal but deeply unhelpful pet.

Adult life is full of demands like emails, bills, family, a never-ending cycle of mind-numbingly boring chores, birthdays to remember, messages to respond to and events to endure.

ADHD can make it feel like you're always struggling to cope with the everyday demands that other people seem to just be able to do without thinking. The symptoms of ADHD can snowball into an overwhelming whirlwind, where everything from missed deadlines, to arguments with people you love, to forgotten commitments and broken promises, to never quite finishing anything can cause disruption, hurt and shame.

Why does ADHD occur?

The reason for ADHD developing in the first place comes down to a mixture of genetics and environment. ADHD tends to run in families because it has a strong genetic basis. **If you have ADHD, there's about a 70–80 per cent chance that it's due to inherited traits.** That's one of the highest heritability rates of any 'psychiatric condition' (although ADHD is a neurodevelopmental difference, rather than a psychiatric condition, it can lead to secondary mental health issues). While there's no single 'ADHD gene', researchers have found that having many minor genetic differences (called variants), each of which play a tiny role, creates the genetic risk of developing ADHD. Most of these genetic variants influence how the brain utilizes brain chemicals known as neurotransmitters, including dopamine, a chemical involved in many ADHD-related brain processes.

Dopamine, and some other brain chemicals, will pop up frequently in this book.

These genetic variations, and their impact on brain chemicals such as dopamine, influence the structure and function of critical brain regions from an early age. Genetics alone are almost never enough to lead to ADHD, though. They are a little like the wood in a bonfire; without a spark you just have a pile of wood.

That spark, which lights the 'ADHD bonfire', usually includes something in the environment that works with the genetic changes to light the fire. Research has identified a wide range of environmental factors, particularly those that are around during sensitive pre-natal and early childhood periods. **These environmental factors interact with our genetics, shaping the brain's development in terms of structure and function.**

Some of the environmental risk factors that have been found to have a robust influence on the development of ADHD include:

- prenatal exposure to smoking, alcohol, or certain toxins, like lead or pesticides
- prenatal exposure to certain medicines, such as some anti-epileptic drugs
- premature birth or low birth weight
- traumatic brain injury
- early childhood adversity, like chronic stress, neglect or trauma.

These factors can affect brain development and how dopamine and other neurotransmitter systems in the brain mature, particularly in the areas linked to attention, impulse control and emotional regulation.

An individual may have a genetic predisposition, but exposure to these environmental factors can act as a catalyst, further influencing brain development in a way that increases the probability and potential severity of ADHD symptoms. No spark, no bonfire.

It's important to say that **this isn't about blame. Many of these factors are outside anyone's control, and none of them explain ADHD in isolation.** It's also important to say that science has historically obsessed over maternal risks while ignoring paternal factors, leaving data biased and incomplete. We need to move past pointing fingers and focus on support.

How developmental differences manifest as ADHD symptoms

With the right mix of genetic and environmental influences, such as the ones we just discussed, the body sculpts a brain that functions differently, leading directly to the hallmark symptoms of ADHD.

At the centre of this is a less efficient brain communication system. This means that the key cells in the brain, neurons, and the chemicals they use to communicate, neurotransmitters such as dopamine, do not work 'typically'. Many of the challenges people with ADHD face, therefore, come down to how areas of the brain communicate.

But there is so much more...We've not yet peeked behind the curtain of the 'non-diagnostic' symptoms of ADHD. More recent research, including brain scanning studies, has suggested that the same differences in how the brain works lead to a wide range of issues that aren't even taken into account in the diagnostic tests for ADHD.

For example, **the emotional issues of ADHD**. ADHD doesn't just affect your focus or fidgeting; it messes with your feelings, too. Emotional intensity, rejection sensitivity, frustration, guilt, shame... these aren't just side effects – they're often core parts of the experience of ADHD. They are covered in detail in Chapter 10.

What does diagnosis actually involve?

If you're **diagnosed as an adult**, it usually means that someone has looked at your life *and* your childhood and spotted a clear pattern. You'll need to **meet criteria around how many symptoms you have** (as we said earlier, whether you have five or more symptoms of inattention and/or hyperactivity/impulsivity), **how long they've been there** (at least six months), **how much they interfere with daily life** and whether they **showed up before the age of 12.** That last one is tricky, so clinicians often rely on **school reports, family interviews, or your best memories** of being the 'kid who never quite got their act together'.

Diagnosis must be made by a trained specialist, often a psychiatrist, following the very tightly defined rules in the fifth edition of the Diagnostic and Statistical Manual of Mental Disorders, known as the DSM-5-TR, or the World Health Organization's own 'book of diseases', the International Classification of Diseases 11th Revision (ICD-11). This is always useful to know when you hear people say, 'It's easy to get a diagnosis of ADHD these days.' It *really* isn't.

Assessment includes lots of filling out forms, even some by family members or those closest to you, and a consultation where the clinician should ask the right questions to make sure they are as certain as they can be that ADHD is the cause of your challenges.

Why do differences in the brain lead to day-to-day challenges?

For those fortunate enough to be able to access assessment and diagnosis, the label of ADHD doesn't really change the reality of day-to-day challenges. Despite some toxic positivity that people with prominent platforms spout about ADHD being a 'superpower', **ADHD can be, and often is, very disabling.** Living with undiagnosed or unsupported ADHD can be exhausting. **It can interfere with your career, relationships, sleep, mental health and self-esteem**. If you've spent years unknowingly developing **coping strategies** just to survive (like overcompensating with perfectionism or relying on adrenaline to meet deadlines), those strategies **can become hard-wired, even if they're not serving you any more.**

At the core of these challenges aren't the 18 diagnostic symptoms, but a series of issues with thinking skills known as 'executive functions'. Let's cover them now.

So, what are executive functions and why are they important in ADHD?

One way to view ADHD is that it is a developmental 'executive function' disorder or condition. **Executive functions are like your brain's**

backstage crew. They don't take the spotlight, but **without them, the show doesn't run**. These are high-level mental processes that help you to plan, resist saying wildly inappropriate things, switch from one task to another, hold information in your head while you do something else and basically keep functioning as an adult.[2]

If ADHD is the problem, executive functions are often the scene of the crime.

> In simple terms, **executive functions are:**
>
> - **'top-down' skills (you don't just react – you pause, think, decide)**
> - **used when you *can't* rely on autopilot or habit**
> - **needed for goal-directed behaviour (doing things *on purpose*, even when you really don't want to).**

They help you to mentally play with ideas (e.g. 'what if I just ran away to a beach house and wrote a book on ADHD and productivity?'), stop and think before acting, handle new or confusing problems, resist tempting distractions, stay focused even when it's boring and so much more.

Three core skills make up executive functioning:

1. **Working memory:** This is **your brain's mental sticky note.** You use it to hold information in mind *and* do something with it. So, if you're reading this book and remembering any of it, that requires working memory. Following a recipe? That involves working memory. Trying to remember why you walked into the kitchen? You get the idea...

2. **Cognitive flexibility (aka mental gear shifting):** This is **your ability to adapt when things change, switch tasks or think about a problem in a new way**. When you get distracted but need to get back on track, you'll need cognitive flexibility. If you realize that a plan was a bit crap, and you need to change course? Same.
3. **Inhibitory control:** This includes **both *self-control*** (not doing something reactively, like replying to an email *right now* just because you noticed it appear in your inbox while you were looking for something related to the task you *should* be doing) **and *interference control*** (tuning out what's task-irrelevant, like your own thoughts, background noise, or YouTube tabs). **It's the ability to resist acting on impulse and delay gratification**, like not eating the biscuit even though you *deserve* it.

For many people with ADHD, all these mental skills can be a bit unreliable at the best of times. Not because they take effort you're not prepared to make, but because the brain areas that coordinate these things (especially the prefrontal cortex) aren't working in the same way that they work in most human brains. We refer to this as '**executive dysfunction**'.

Why it matters: executive dysfunction in real life

If even one of these functions isn't working well, it's like trying to cook with one hob and a broken timer. You *can* do it, but you'll burn things, forget ingredients, and maybe give up and order chips.

Executive dysfunction explains many elements of ADHD, like knowing what to do but still not doing it, forgetting things mid-task (what was I just...?), feeling overwhelmed even by 'simple' tasks and switching mental tabs like a raccoon on Red Bull.

The good news is that these skills are related. At times, this feels like a problem, but it's also an opportunity. **Improving one function** (like using external tools for working memory) **often helps others** (like planning or attention).

Why executive functions go rogue in ADHD

If executive functions are the tools your brain uses to navigate daily life, then ADHD can feel like the toolbox changes every day, is sometimes difficult to open, and the tools might not work as they were intended.

We want to be clear here: **people with ADHD usually *know* what they're supposed to do. They just can't *do* it consistently.** This is what Dr Russell Barkley calls a **performance disorder,**[3] not a knowledge problem, not a motivation deficit in the classic sense and **absolutely *not* laziness.**

You know you need to send that email. Or start a tax return. Or stop doomscrolling. But **there's a gap between *intention* and *action* and ADHD lives in that gap.**

According to models from Thomas Brown and Russell Barkley, **executive dysfunction in ADHD tends to show up across six domains:**

- **Activation:** We can struggle to get started, organize what needs doing or estimate how long things will take.
- **Focus:** It can be challenging to find and maintain attention or shift it when needed.
- **Effort:** It is hard to maintain alertness, stay motivated or process things quickly.
- **Emotion:** Angry tears, emotional outbursts or stewing for hours over something minor.
- **Memory:** Having poor working memory and inconsistent recall.
- **Action:** This involves self-monitoring and impulse control, which can contribute to hyperactivity and impulsivity.

We'll cover further executive dysfunction issues, such as time blindness, in Chapter 9.

So... What?

Having executive dysfunction isn't just about being 'a bit forgetful' or 'bad with time'. **Executive dysfunction can affect academic progress** (missed deadlines, last-minute cramming, failed follow-through), **work performance** (struggling to prioritize, finish tasks, or meet expectations), **relationships** (forgetting plans, reacting emotionally, struggling to stay present) **and mental health** (hello, shame spiral!).

In each chapter, we'll offer tools to help overcome this 'executive dysfunction'. As the **brains in people with ADHD respond differently to motivation and reward**, traditional strategies, like setting goals, making plans, or 'just getting started', often fall flat. Instead, **we often need adapted approaches and external supports to do some of the heavy lifting.** Hopefully many of them will feel familiar to you by the time you finish this book.

Chapter summary

This chapter unpacked what ADHD *really* is (and isn't).

- ADHD is a lifelong neurodevelopmental condition that affects how the brain handles attention, motivation, time, emotion, memory and behaviour.
- The core diagnostic symptoms fall into two groups – inattention and hyperactivity/impulsivity – but not everyone with ADHD experiences both.
- ADHD often presents differently in adults than in children, and many people aren't diagnosed until later in life.
- It's not caused by bad parenting, poor effort or personality flaws; ADHD has a strong genetic basis, influenced by environmental factors during early development.
- The structural and functional differences in the brain in ADHD impact executive functioning – skills like planning, impulse control, emotional regulation and working memory.
- Executive dysfunction explains why people with ADHD often

know what they need to do but can't *make* themselves do it consistently.

- Everyone with ADHD is different. Your experience is valid even if it doesn't match someone else's.
- ADHD can be disabling, especially when unsupported, but understanding the science behind it is the first step toward self-acceptance and practical change.

Chapter 2

ADHD & PRODUCTIVITY CHALLENGES

Or why productivity is a problem (for people like us)

James often calls ADHD 'consistent inconsistency'. What this means is that his *performance* tends to vary, even if he has the *ability* to get shit done. In James's case, one day he will be on fire, getting ALL the tasks done, but the following day, he can struggle even to turn on the laptop, let alone answer one of the emails hanging over him like the sword of Damocles. For James, productivity really does depend on the day; it might depend on how he's slept, or whether his other co-existing conditions have decided to raise their ugly heads, but sometimes there isn't an obvious reason why he's nailing it or functionally useless. And this causes shame. The good days are quickly forgotten, while the bad days linger like cat hair in your carpet: impossible to shift, no matter how hard you try.

What is productivity?

It feels a little bit odd to start a chapter by defining something as seemingly obvious as productivity, but we're going to do it anyway. Productivity is one of those words that gets thrown around *everywhere*. In work meetings, TED Talks, government reports and guilt-inducing Instagram reels by people who have helped to fetishize 'hyper-productivity'.

At its core, productivity is about having something to show for your time. Whether that's gross national product, a company's profit or efficiency, or just doing the washing up... The definition and the pressure shifts depending on whether you are thinking macro or micro.

This book is focused largely on personal productivity, as opposed to macroeconomic or organizational productivity, even though it feeds into the other two. This form of productivity is the version most of us care about: getting through our own to-do lists without imploding or crying in a car park.

Whether at the boardroom or the individual level, productivity follows the basic idea of output vs input, but personal productivity is less about churning out units of work and more about ***how well* we use our time, energy and attention to move towards things that actually matter**. In real life, personal productivity means harnessing your resources, such as focus, skills, energy and motivation, to achieve meaningful results. That could be finishing a report, answering emails, or finally booking that dentist appointment you really need but just haven't been able to pick up the phone and book for the last six months. (Phone calls are SO difficult to make for a lot of us!) It's not just about working harder. **It's about working *smarter*,** and ideally, without burning yourself out in the process.

Why 'time spent' doesn't equal 'value'

In today's world of 'knowledge work', where what you produce is more likely to be ideas, strategies or content than physical objects, the old factory model of productivity doesn't really work for most people. **Sitting at a desk for 12 hours doesn't guarantee results.** In fact, you can spend all day flitting between emails, instant messages and distractions, or you can put in three hours of deep, focused work and create something genuinely brilliant. **The real goal shouldn't be to be constantly busy; it should be to make progress on the things that matter *to you.***

That might mean choosing rest so you can function tomorrow, spending two hours getting one thing done well instead of ten things badly, or letting go of guilt when your output doesn't match someone else's volume or timeline, or even your own previous output. The first of these – rest – often seems like the opposite of productivity, but it's incredibly important to see productivity in a broader context.

If you're exhausted and burned out, you will not be productive. Productivity involves the brain *and* the body. Your mental and physical well-being are not optional extras. They're the fuel that powers everything else.

> **This is why things like rest, exercise, food and even time spent doing absolutely nothing aren't just self-care; they're *essential productivity tools.* You can't pour from an empty cup. And you definitely can't write that grant proposal if your brain is screaming and your body's running on fumes.**

Common barriers to productivity

Almost everyone wants to be productive. But even in the general population, the path is often littered with obstacles. Some of these are external and some are internal. These barriers create friction, slowing you down, draining your energy and making progress feel like wading through glue.

To improve productivity, we first need to understand the two big categories of challenges:

1. the **systemic or environmental stuff** (things around you)
2. the **psychological or personal stuff** (things inside you).

Both matter. And both can be worked on, but only if we name them.

Systemic challenges to productivity

Even the most focused and capable person can be derailed by a messy or mismanaged workplace. These external factors are often baked into the way many organizations operate and can sabotage productivity for everyone.

Poor communication is one of the biggest productivity killers. That includes not having clear organizational goals (so no one knows what matters), receiving vague or inconsistent instructions or feedback from managers, and 'siloed' information (people hoarding knowledge or not sharing across teams). This leads to people wasting time chasing clarity or, even worse, doing the wrong thing well. On the other hand, excessive communication (constant messages, pinging alerts and a culture of instant replies) fragments focus and undermines deep work.

Meetings. How are you supposed to get stuff done when you're constantly in meetings, where you are given even more work to do??? In many workplaces, meetings have become a substitute for progress. You sit through hours of vague discussion without any decisions being made and then get asked why your work isn't done! **Meetings without a clear purpose, agenda or outcome sap energy and time.** They also demoralize teams who feel their actual job has become attending meetings *about* their job.

Next, we have **distracting work environments.** In our opinion, open-plan offices can absolutely get in the f*cking sea. And we're not alone. **A significant body of research consistently demonstrates that open-plan offices, despite their widespread adoption, have a detrimental effect on productivity.** The evidence suggests a range of negative impacts, including increased distractions, a notable decline in meaningful collaboration and adverse effects on employee well-being and health.[1] Initially intended to boost collaboration, instead they often create constant noise, interruptions and overstimulation. Throw in a flood of notifications and emails, and getting into a state of deep focus becomes a rare event.

Research from the University of California found that people who work in an office environment spend just 11 minutes on a task before being interrupted, and it takes over 23 minutes to get back on track.[2] Being sociable at work has many benefits, but **holding boundaries is important.** Setting boundaries in this kind of environment, especially if you're junior or neurodivergent, can feel risky or even rude. However, interruptions are costly, not just for those of us who are neurodivergent, but for everyone.

Unclear expectations are also a barrier to productivity. A Gallup survey of attitudes to work in the wake of the pandemic[3] found that a staggering 49 per cent of workers questioned did not know what was expected of them at work. That's a massive drag on productivity. If people don't know what they're aiming for, they'll guess... and often get it wrong.

What about the internal stuff?

Not all barriers to productivity are external. **Some of the biggest drains on productivity come from within: from our emotions, stress levels and mental habits.** These internal factors can be just as, if not more, powerful than a badly designed workplace.

When people don't feel emotionally connected to their work or their organization, they tend to disengage. They're less productive, less creative and more likely to leave. Another major Gallup study showed that **teams with high engagement are 21 per cent more productive than those without it.**[4]

Burnout and overwork are key issues that often have internal drivers. More hours don't equal more output. In fact, the longer people work without proper breaks or recovery, the more mistakes they make, the less creative they become and the closer they get to burnout. **Burnout isn't just tiredness; it's a full-body shutdown that wrecks productivity and well-being.**

Another barrier to productivity is trying to do too many things at once, or multitasking. **The human brain isn't built for true multi-tasking.** Often, what we call multitasking is really just fast switching between tasks. And **each switch carries a mental cost**. You lose time and increase errors, especially with complex or attention-heavy tasks.

Finally, we have **procrastination**. This isn't just an ADHD issue, but it *is* amplified in ADHD, for both executive dysfunction and emotional reasons. (Anxious about working on something? Do it tomorrow. Let's kick that emotional can down the road a little.)

Delaying a task because it triggers stress, shame, self-doubt or perfectionism is often at the root of procrastination. When you feel like the work *must* be perfect, starting it can feel terrifying. So, you don't.

These internal barriers rarely appear in isolation; they tend to feed off each other.

Let's take this example:

A manager gives unclear instructions. The uncertainty makes it hard to know where to start or how to succeed, so you hesitate and begin to procrastinate. As tasks pile up, your motivation drops and your guilt increases. In a rush to catch up, you start multitasking or working late, self-care falls away, and you head towards burnout.

Now, you're even less productive and even more disengaged. That's the negative feedback loop that so many people get stuck in.

If we want to improve productivity, whether in ourselves, our teams, or our organizations, **we must break that cycle by tackling both external systems and internal load.**

When productivity feels pointless: what are values, and why do they matter?

Your values are the things that matter most to you. Things like creativity, fairness, freedom, honesty, helping others, learning or stability. They're not goals, and they're not morals (although morals and values are interconnected and can influence each other). They're what give your actions meaning. And when your life lines up with your values, everything feels more motivating.

What happens when your values get lost?

For many of us, especially those with ADHD, there can be a disconnect between what matters to us and what we spend our time on. That gap can show up as:

- Feeling bored or drained by tasks that seem pointless.
- Avoiding work, even if it's important, because it doesn't *feel* meaningful.
- A constant low-level frustration that you're not doing what you're 'meant' to be doing.
- Burnout from chasing success that doesn't match the things you care about.

This disconnect is sometimes called **value incongruence** and it has been linked to emotional exhaustion, low motivation, poor performance and even depression.[5]

Real-life examples of misaligned values

- You value **creativity**, but your job is all spreadsheets and rules.
- You value **connection**, but your workload leaves no time for people.
- You value **autonomy**, but your tasks are micromanaged or prescribed.

If you have ADHD, your brain's motivation system is already wired differently. **If a task *also* doesn't align with your values, that can be a double hit, making it even harder to care, start or finish.**

Even if these tasks 'should' be done, they can feel like friction burns on your soul; this discomfort can be a sign that your brain is throwing up a red flag.

How to spot (and use) your values

Research shows that **living in line with your values increases motivation, resilience and well-being.** People who pursue goals that reflect their personal values are more likely to achieve them and feel fulfilled along the way.

Values-based action can help reduce procrastination and emotional distress, especially in people with ADHD and anxiety.

If you're not sure what your core values are, you're not alone. Most of us haven't been taught to look inward; we've been taught to chase grades, promotions or approval instead. But getting clear on your values can be a turning point.

Identifying your values

There are many free, online tools for identifying your values, but you can also try asking yourself:

- What makes you feel proud, even if no one else notices?
- When do you feel most like yourself?
- Think of a time you felt really frustrated or upset. What important thing was missing or being ignored?
- What makes you feel energized, even when it's hard?
- If someone were to describe you at your best, what would you *want* them to say?
- What do you find yourself fighting for, defending, or standing up for (even in your head)?
- What would you still care about, even if it didn't help you earn money or get approval?
- Which three things would you *not* want to give up about who you are?

Once you've got a sense of your core values, use them like a compass. You don't need to overhaul your life overnight; **look for small ways to bring your values into your tasks or routines.**

For example:

- If you value **growth**, frame a boring report as a **chance to practise a skill.**
- If you value **freedom**, block out flexible **'choose-your-own-adventure'** time in your week.
- If you value **helping others**, remind yourself **who benefits from the task** (even if it's 'future you').

What about ADHD? This is a book about ADHD and productivity, isn't it?

So far, we've looked at all the different ways productivity can be derailed: by bad systems, impossible workloads, unclear expectations and emotional burnout. Now it's time to talk about how **ADHD makes *all* of this harder**.

The clinical traits of ADHD, especially the executive dysfunction, aren't just technical terms from a diagnostic manual. They show up in painfully real ways in daily life: missing deadlines, zoning out in meetings, losing track of priorities, missing emails, or starting ten things and finishing none.

This section breaks down how **ADHD directly creates and intensifies common productivity barriers**. The impact isn't mild or quirky; it's measurable. For many people, it can impact career progression, financial security, academic success and mental health.

If you've ever wondered, 'Why can't I just do the thing?' this is where we explain why with clarity and compassion.

Why can't I just do the things I want or need to do?

If you've read Chapter 1, or already have some knowledge about ADHD, then you'll be aware that **ADHD in clinical terms has two sides: inattention and hyperactivity/impulsivity**. Both presentations can create real-world chaos in work, study and everyday life. These traits can be productivity wrecking balls.

Making careless mistakes? If you live with ADHD, you've probably been accused of being careless at some point. But that word, care*less*, is very emotionally charged. It's **NOTHING to do with not caring** (most of the time), and **no one cares *more* about making mistakes than someone who has constantly been berated for making mistakes**. This is about your **brain skipping over details without your permission.**

These small mistakes can seriously damage your credibility at work, and they often take more time to fix than they would have taken to catch in the first place (if your brain had let you!), which adds even more stress to the mix.

Sustaining attention, especially on things that are boring, repetitive or too long, **is one of ADHD's core challenges**. That means:

- You might zone out during meetings and miss key information.
- Reading long documents can feel like climbing a cognitive mountain in flippers.
- You might forget what someone said five minutes ago or that they said anything at all.

This doesn't just make work harder. **It fragments your understanding of what's happening**, which makes planning and follow-through even trickier.

It may not feel like an attention issue, but **poor organization is one of the symptoms of inattention**. Many people with ADHD struggle to manage paperwork, files, emails and even thoughts. **Your workspace might be a mess, not because you don't care, but because the part of your brain that's meant to create order isn't playing ball.**

This can then **lead to overwhelm**, especially if you are someone whose **brain does not cope well with lots of visual clutter** (this can be a particular issue for those of us who are also autistic (see Chapter 13 for more on this). It can also lead to lost materials, missed deadlines, struggling to track the next steps and being late for meetings (or forgetting them entirely). And while you're paddling frantically just to stay afloat, **others may read your chaos as 'not trying hard enough'**. That misinterpretation is incredibly painful and wrong.

There are many more challenges specific to inattention, including challenges following instructions, losing things we need to complete tasks and the dreaded having to finish off something we started. But we think you get the picture now. Inattention brings with it a big box of productivity challenges. But what about hyperactivity and impulsivity?

Hyperactivity and impulsivity: when your brain has no pause button

Hyperactivity and impulsivity might sound like traits that only affect children bouncing off the walls. But in adulthood, especially in the structured, often sedentary, world of work, these symptoms don't disappear. They just change form. And they can still create serious challenges.

In adults, **physical hyperactivity often manifests as internal restlessness.** You might look calm on the outside, but inside, your brain might be jumping from topic to topic at speed. This can make it almost unbearable to sit still through long meetings, focus on tasks that take a long time to complete, or stay in one spot for too long. **Physical hyperactivity in adults is also a very real thing.**

This often shows up as:

- fidgeting or foot-tapping
- getting up and walking around frequently
- needing movement to stay calm and focused.

To others, this can look like you're nervous, impatient, distracted or disengaged. But what's really happening is that **your nervous system is trying to manage a level of internal tension that feels physically uncomfortable** and fidgeting or movement can help to improve focus. Yet it's not always well-received when you are externally hyperactive.

The impulsive aspects of this side of ADHD can be equally challenging. **Verbal impulsivity** is one of the more socially visible symptoms and one of the most misunderstood. If you frequently interrupt people mid-sentence, answer questions before they've finished speaking, or talk more than expected by others in meetings, you'll be painfully aware of this. When the brain fires off a thought, **it can be incredibly hard not to say it *right now* if you have ADHD**. Unfortunately, **this can lead others to see you as dismissive,**

domineering or lacking professionalism, especially in formal or hierarchical settings.

Alongside thinking impulsively, ADHD often comes **with an impaired 'pause' function between thinking and *acting*.** This can lead to snap decisions that feel right in the moment but backfire later. One of the most common ways this shows up is with the word 'Yes'. We can **often take on way too much work by saying yes automatically, without considering the consequences**. Here lies the path to burnout. **Saying no is a superpower, but one you can learn** (we'll cover this in Chapter 14).

Beyond immediately saying yes, **our impulsive actions can also look like sending a blunt email in a moment of frustration or agreeing to a deadline without checking our calendar (or capacity).**

These moments can damage trust, relationships and credibility, even if the intent was never to harm. It may seem reckless, but it's not. It's just that **the brain's internal brakes aren't as strong or consistent as they need to be.**

Put it all together and what have you got?

The daily effort of living and working with ADHD can take a real, measurable toll. Trying to compensate for attention issues, hyperactivity and impulsivity, and executive dysfunction is exhausting. The constant mental juggling, self-monitoring and compensating for mistakes **can often lead to burnout**. Not just 'a bit tired', but real, clinical burnout – physical fatigue, emotional exhaustion and cognitive overload.

Some of us can also be prone to **positive illusory bias**, leading us to make the same mistakes over and over again, because even though we have never previously been able to successfully manage something we have done before within the timeline we have agreed to do it, **we truly believe that this time will be different.**

The career impact is hard to ignore. The numbers don't lie, as brutal as they are: **adults with ADHD are less likely to hold down full-time jobs. They tend to earn less than their peers. They're more likely to be fired or switch jobs frequently.**[6]

A World Health Organization study found that untreated ADHD leads to an average of 22 lost workdays per year.[7] And in one large workplace survey, 87 per cent of adults with ADHD said it had **negatively affected their career.**[8] More than half said it had **cost them a promotion or led to a demotion.**

Beyond the missed deadlines and lost income, the **emotional burden is often heavier. Constantly falling short of expectations despite trying *so hard* can trigger anxiety, depression and a sense of failure.**

ADHD is invisible, so **people often assume the problem is laziness or lack of effort**. And many people with ADHD internalize those labels: *lazy, careless, unmotivated.* Over time, **that can erode self-esteem and fuel a deep, private shame.**

Here's the painful truth: people with ADHD are often working harder than anyone else just to keep up, but that effort doesn't always show in the outcomes.

ADHD obviously doesn't only cause work struggles. But the fallout from those struggles – stress, poor feedback and low confidence – feeds into the condition itself in a cycle.

Here's how the cycle goes:

- ADHD symptoms disrupt performance.
- Poor performance triggers criticism or negative consequences.
- The resulting stress worsens mental health and self-esteem.
- Anxiety, depression and burnout make ADHD symptoms worse.
- Productivity drops again.

And round it goes.

This isn't just a problem with productivity, in the day-to-day workplace sense. **It's a loop that affects career, income, identity and mental health.** Breaking that cycle requires more than just trying harder. It takes understanding, support and new ways of working with the brain you have.

Stop...We have to talk about burnout

Burnout isn't just being tired. It's what happens when you've been running on empty for so long that rest doesn't fix it anymore. **For people with ADHD (and especially AuDHD), burnout isn't just about the effort of meeting expectations at work; it's about the daily cost of living in a world that isn't built for our brains.**

The World Health Organization defines burnout as exhaustion, detachment and reduced performance caused by chronic workplace stress. That's part of the picture, but for neurodivergent people, burnout is 'life-wide' and can be triggered by:

- **Executive overload:** endless decisions, task switching, regulating focus and emotions.
- **Masking and camouflaging:** hiding traits to fit in, which is like running a second job in your head.
- **Sensory and social overwhelm:** lights, noise, unspoken rules and peopling.
- **Chronic mismatch:** living in environments that demand what your brain can't sustainably give.

Symptoms vary widely. Some people feel emotionally numb, others lose skills (like cooking or speaking), and many experience ADHD paralysis, mood swings or shutdowns. It's rarely a neat sequence of 'stages'; burnout is a fluctuating continuum.

Why ADHD makes burnout more likely

ADHD brains already run on limited executive capacity. Add sleep disruption, time blindness and stress, and minor lapses in self-care can snowball into exhaustion. **Research shows adults with ADHD report higher perceived stress, stronger biological stress responses and more reliance on unhelpful coping strategies (avoidance, doomscrolling, overwork).**

You can't take a holiday from your own brain, so avoiding burnout needs a different approach.

The early warning signs of burnout

Burnout often creeps in gradually. Red flags of collapse are usually preceded by subtler 'yellow flags', such as:

- saying yes to everything, starting multiple projects at once
- constant tiredness that rest doesn't fix
- feeling numb, irritable, or snapping more easily
- avoiding even enjoyable activities
- dropping basic self-care.

Learning your own early signs, and asking trusted people to help you spot them, can stop a crash before it hits.

Self-care as essential maintenance, not a luxury

For neurodivergent people, self-care isn't indulgent, it's the oil that keeps the engine running. Sleep, food, downtime and sensory regulation protect against depletion. The cruel irony is that the executive skills needed to maintain self-care (planning, remembering, pacing) are the very ones ADHD makes harder. That's why advice like 'just stick to a routine' often backfires.

Reframing self-care as essential maintenance rather than a reward can be a useful approach. Build in 'nothing time', make reminders to eat and rest and sandwich demanding activities with replenishing ones (such as cuddling pets, moving, sensory comfort, eating safe foods or watching favourite shows).

Prevention and recovery from burnout

When burnout does hit, only radical rest works – physical, mental, emotional and sensory. Think sleep, reducing decisions, stepping back from draining relationships and creating low-stimulation spaces.

For prevention, a few principles help:

- **Pacing:** Alternate demanding tasks with low-load or soothing ones. Energy fluctuates – plan for it.
- **Boundaries:** Say no sooner and more often. Protect your limited capacity.
- **Recharge rituals:** Schedule decompression time after socialising, deadlines or travel.
- **Compassionate self-talk:** Rest is not laziness. You don't have to earn it.
- **Systemic change:** No toolkit will fix a workplace (or relationship) that refuses to accommodate you. Environments that flex to neurodivergent needs prevent repeated burnout.

Burnout is common in ADHD, but it isn't inevitable. Recognizing your warning signs, treating self-care as essential, pacing your energy and seeking supportive environments all make a difference.

Most importantly: you don't need to wait until you're broken to rest. Rest is part of productivity, not the opposite of it.

So...is it possible to avoid burnout and be productive with ADHD?

Yes. Absolutely yes.

We know this chapter has been a bit of a tour through the dark forest of ADHD and productivity. If you've been nodding along (or crying in mild recognition), you're not alone. Everything we've talked about – burnout, procrastination, overwhelm, emotional overload, brain chaos – these are real, exhausting barriers. And **if you've been blaming yourself for not just 'getting it together', we hope you now understand it's not laziness. It's having a brain that was built for a different world.** But this isn't the end of the story.

The rest of this book is where we turn the lights on. You're not stuck for ever. We'll explore practical, ADHD-friendly strategies to help you work with your brain instead of against it. That means tools for motivation, for starting (and finishing) things, for managing time when your internal clock is basically a potato, and for figuring out what actually matters to you, so that your energy goes where it counts.

You won't suddenly become a productivity machine (and frankly, why would you want to?). But you can get to a place where life feels less like survival mode and more like progress – even if it's scrappy, imperfect and powered by snacks and last-minute panic.

So, let's get to it. Throughout the rest of this book, we will look more closely at the challenges we've mentioned in this chapter, explain why they happen and, most importantly, provide actionable tools you can try to start making steps towards 'better'.

You don't need to change who you are. You just need the right support.

Chapter summary

- Productivity isn't about working more; it's about making meaningful progress using your time, energy and focus.
- ADHD symptoms (inattention, impulsivity, hyperactivity) directly disrupt productivity; this isn't a moral failure, it's neurological.
- External factors like poor communication, unclear expectations, too many meetings and open-plan offices also drain productivity.
- Internal barriers such as burnout, perfectionism, multitasking, procrastination and value misalignment further reduce our ability to get shit done.
- These struggles often create a vicious cycle: poor performance > stress > worse symptoms > more underperformance.
- Value misalignment (doing work that doesn't matter to you) drains motivation and increases burnout.
- Breaking the cycle requires understanding, support and practical tools tailored for ADHD brains, which is exactly what the rest of this book provides.

Chapter 3

ADHD-FRIENDLY GOAL SETTING

Or, the SMART approach to success

During his PhD, James often found himself stuck for weeks (sometimes months) without making any progress. Not because he didn't care, or didn't want to work, but because without the right supervision, deadlines or **clear goals**, he simply didn't know what to do next. With no external structure and a brain that couldn't create structure for himself, even deciding which experiment to run became an overwhelming task.

There were whole periods where James would arrive at the lab, turn on the computer, stare blankly at the screen, panic-check emails and then go home having done precisely nothing. There were moments when James very nearly gave up. It felt like failure. Shame. Paralysis. On paper, there was endless freedom to work on a fascinating project. In reality, it felt like being locked in a room with no doors and being told to 'just find your way out'.

The irony, of course, is that James was genuinely interested in his work. But **with ADHD, interest isn't always enough**. The absence of structure, feedback and clearly defined outcomes meant that his brain had nothing to grip on to. Without scaffolding – strategies that support you while you take on new challenges – even the smartest ADHD brains tend to collapse under the weight of their own good intentions.

This chapter will explore the link between ADHD and goal setting; why so many of us struggle to define, prioritize and begin working towards goals; and what makes the usual advice (like 'just break it down') completely useless without context. We'll also share research-backed and ADHD-tested tools to help you to set goals that are motivating, realistic and actually doable...without needing a full supervisory committee to keep you on track.

We'll show you how to:

- **Work with your brain, not against it**, when setting and pursuing goals.
- **Adjust common goal-setting tools** (like SMART goals) to suit ADHD realities.
- **Use external structures and strategies**, like body doubling, gamification and rewards, to actually help you to start and finish what matters.
- **Spot the signs of perfectionism and emotional avoidance**, so you don't set yourself up to fail before you've even begun.

You won't find one-size-fits-all solutions here, because they don't work. What you will find is a practical, flexible approach to goal setting that gives you a better shot at success, even if your brain likes to wander, leap and occasionally forget what the goal was in the first place.

The power of goal setting

The pursuit of meaningful goals is a fundamental driver of human progress, productivity and personal satisfaction. Decades of psychological research have defined the principles of effective goal setting, providing a clear blueprint for translating ambition into achievement. However, this blueprint was largely designed without neurodivergent brains in mind (we'll cover this later).

Setting goals isn't just a productivity cliché, it **is one of the strongest predictors of success across almost every area of life.** Whether it's writing a book, starting a business, or just surviving the week without forgetting bin day, having a clear goal increases your chances of follow-through. Goal setting is a structured psychological process, backed by decades of research that has moved it from fluffy self-help territory into a well-tested science.

One of the most influential models in this space is Goal-Setting Theory (GST).[1] The researchers behind this model studied more than 40,000 people across hundreds of experiments to work out what makes a goal actually do its job and why some goals fall flat. The takeaway? **Goals shape behaviour, but only if they're designed properly.**

Let's look at the five key ingredients that GST says will make a goal more likely to be achieved.

1. Clarity: be specific, not vague

Sometimes, goals like 'try harder' or 'be more organized' can feel like shouting into the wind; they feel noble, but there's nothing to aim at. **Research shows that specific goals can be far more effective for some types of tasks or projects.** A goal like 'Apply for two jobs by Friday and email one person about a reference' is clearer and more doable than just 'Work on job stuff'. **The more precise your target, the easier it can be to measure progress** and know when you've nailed it or at least nudged it forward.

2. Challenge: stretch, but don't snap

Goals should feel like a challenge, but not like a punishment. **If something is too easy, your brain can get bored. If it feels impossible, your brain gives up before you start. The sweet spot? A goal that feels like a push but is still within reach.** For example, 'Walk three times a week' might be a good starting point if 'Run a marathon' makes your nervous system want to hide under a blanket.

3. Commitment: it has to matter to you

You're more likely to stick with a goal if it actually feels important to you. That doesn't mean it has to be life-changing; it just needs to matter to you in this moment. **Goals tend to work better when you've chosen them yourself** (rather than having them dumped on you) **and when you believe you can do them**, even if it's with support. This is where self-efficacy (your belief that you can pull it off) really matters.

4. Feedback: know where you stand

Without feedback, you're basically working blind. Regular check-ins, whether from an app, a coach, a friend, or even a 'ta-da' list (that's a list of all the things you *have* accomplished), can help you to adjust, refocus or just feel encouraged that something's happening. **Feedback keeps the goal visible. It also gives your dopamine-starved brain a little boost from seeing progress, which is critical if you're living with ADHD.**

5. Task complexity: break it down

This one's especially important for ADHD brains. Complex or fuzzy goals ('Launch my business', 'Write my thesis') are overwhelming and easy to avoid. That doesn't mean they're bad goals, but it can help if they're broken down into smaller, more manageable steps. These are called **'proximal goals': bite-sized chunks that reduce mental overload** and help you feel like you're actually getting somewhere. Think of them as waypoints on a very wiggly map.

How goals improve performance

Goal-Setting Theory explains that goals enhance performance through four main psychological mechanisms:

- **Direction:** Clear goals can help to focus attention on what matters, filtering out distractions and irrelevant tasks.
- **Energy:** Challenging goals can boost motivation and effort. People can work harder when the target feels meaningful but achievable.
- **Persistence:** Goals can encourage people to keep going, even when progress is difficult, increasing resilience and follow-through.

- **Strategy:** Goals can prompt problem-solving. When a task is tricky or unfamiliar, people are more likely to plan, adapt and find better ways to get it done.

These effects are consistently backed by decades of research, making **goal setting one of the most effective tools for improving performance, across individuals, teams and entire organizations.**

What about SMART goals? I've heard of them!

Goal-Setting Theory explains why goals work. The SMART framework can help you to figure out how to set one that doesn't immediately make your brain go 'nope'. Coined in 1981 by George Doran,[2] SMART is a simple acronym that breaks an effective goal into five parts. Think of it as a checklist to make some of your goals ADHD-proof (or at least ADHD-tolerant).

S = Specific	Vague goals like 'be more productive' can be hard for the brain to act on. **A specific goal tells you exactly what you're trying to do. It can reduce mental fuzz and make the task feel more concrete.** Example: Instead of 'Get fit', try: 'Go to the gym twice a week'.
M = Measurable	**If you can't track it, your brain can't reward it. Measurable goals let you see progress.** Seeing 'the win' can create dopamine hits and build momentum. Example: 'Write 500 words a day' is better than 'Work on my novel'.

A = Achievable	If something feels impossible, you're likely to freeze or quit. **Aim for the 'challenging but doable' zone.** Example: Not 'Run six miles before breakfast', but maybe 'Walk 20 minutes every other day'.
R = Relevant	Is this goal important to *you*? Not just to your boss, partner, or inner critic. **ADHD brains are often more motivated by meaning than by obligation.** Example: 'Learn coding because I want to change careers' beats 'because someone said I should'.
T = Time-bound	**Deadlines can create urgency. Without them, we tend to forget or endlessly delay.** A time frame can turn a wish into a plan. Example: 'Finish the first draft by 30th July' gives your brain a target.

SMART goals can help to turn 'I should probably do that someday' into 'Here's exactly what I'm doing, and when.' For individuals with ADHD, that structure can be the difference between good intentions and real progress.

BUT... SMART goals aren't always so smart

SMART goals and Goal-Setting Theory have a ton of research behind them. But like many productivity tools, they work best under certain conditions; mainly when the person using them has the brain architecture for which those tools were built.

There's an important distinction in the goal-setting world between two types of goals:

- **Performance goals:** These focus on achieving a target or demonstrating competence (e.g. 'Submit three job applications by Friday').
- **Learning goals:** These focus on building skills or gaining new understanding (e.g. 'Figure out how to use this job site efficiently').

For simple or familiar tasks, performance goals work well. However, when you're doing something complex or unfamiliar, such as learning a new system, building a habit or figuring out how to ADHD-proof your life, **too much pressure to perform can backfire.** You might get tunnel vision, avoid experimenting, or panic and procrastinate.

That's why **learning goals are often better early on**; they support exploration, not just execution.

What about softer, open goals?

Recent research[3] has looked at non-specific goals, like 'Do your best' or even completely open goals such as 'See what you can create.' These fuzzier goals might sound useless from a traditional productivity perspective, but here's the twist: **for complex, creative or unfamiliar tasks, they can *actually work better*.** They've been shown to increase intrinsic motivation, reduce performance anxiety and boost interest in doing the task again.

Non-specific goals, or open goals are particularly relevant for people with ADHD, because they are more forgiving. They don't punish you for not meeting a rigid standard, and **they leave more room for curiosity, autonomy and spontaneous bursts of action, three things ADHD brains often crave.**

The SMART model, like most traditional goal-setting systems, assumes that once you've set a clear goal, the only thing left is effort and strategy. However, **ADHD often disrupts the link between intention and action due to executive dysfunction**. The system expects consistent self-regulation. ADHD doesn't deliver that on demand.

> **So, if you've tried SMART goals and found yourself overwhelmed, paralysed or filled with shame, you haven't failed. The system just wasn't designed with your brain in mind.**

We've talked about how goal setting works, at least in theory. The SMART framework and Goal-Setting Theory (GST) are built on the assumption that if a goal is important enough and clearly defined, your brain will do the rest: plan, prioritize, get started and stay on track.

The open goal technique can help build habits and routines in a more emotionally safe way.

Interest vs importance: the ADHD motivation mismatch

One of the biggest disconnects between traditional goal-setting advice and the ADHD brain comes down to **how we get motivated**.

Most people tend to be driven by importance: 'This is due soon', 'It matters to my boss', or 'If I don't do this, there will be consequences'. That's usually enough to get them started.

People with ADHD, however, have a different motivational wiring. **Our brains run on interest, not importance.** If a task doesn't spark interest, feel novel or rewarding, offer a challenge, or have a built-in sense of urgency, it often doesn't register as something that needs doing, at least not in a way that mobilizes action. This is sometimes called the INCUP model: **Interest, Novelty, Challenge, Urgency = Power**.

This difference is partly neurochemical. **ADHD dysregulation of dopamine impacts reward and motivation** (covered in Chapter 5). In a non-ADHD brain, thinking about a future reward (like a promotion) can give enough of a dopamine signal to help start and sustain effort. But in an ADHD brain that signal is often too weak. Instead, **our brains may respond more reliably to things that give *immediate* stimulation or reward.** This explains why we can hyperfocus on a hobby for hours but still can't bring ourselves to fill out a boring form that takes five minutes.

The key takeaway: if you have ADHD, **making a goal feel 'relevant' or 'important' sometimes isn't enough if it doesn't also feel interesting, urgent or emotionally engaging.**

SMART goals assume that:

Relevance = Motivation

For individuals with ADHD, that isn't always true.

The SMART goal system was built with a 'neurotypical' brain in mind, if such a thing exists. If you have ADHD, you've probably experienced the frustrating reality that **knowing what to do and actually doing it are two very different things.** The next section explains why that gap exists and how it's rooted in the very way our brains process motivation, time and attention.

Where it breaks down: ADHD and the stages of goal setting

Let's walk through how goal pursuit typically works and how ADHD-related executive function challenges can interfere at every stage.

1. Goal formulation and planning

SMART goals start with setting a specific and achievable target. But that's often where ADHD brains hit the first wall:

- **Planning problems:** Breaking down a big goal ('Write a research report') into smaller steps ('Gather sources', 'Write intro') is a core executive function. Many people with ADHD struggle with this. They can end up stuck in analysis paralysis, or perfectionism prevents the smaller steps from being completed. The goal stays fuzzy and overwhelming instead of becoming actionable.
- **Working memory issues:** Even if we manage to plan it out, keeping all the steps in our heads is difficult. We forget the order, lose track of progress, or bounce between tasks without finishing them.

2. Execution and persistence

This stage is where you start doing the thing and keep doing it until it's done. For people with ADHD, several roadblocks tend to show up here:

- **Inhibition issues:** It's hard to filter distractions. A phone ping, a random idea, or an itch to reorganize your bookshelf can completely derail a work session, even if you want to be productive.

- **Time blindness:** Deadlines feel abstract until they're right in your face. Estimating how long things will take is often wildly inaccurate. That can make the 'time-bound' part of SMART goals unreliable for us. A deadline next Friday might as well be next century.
- **Motivation fade:** ADHD brains often start strong but fizzle out fast. Once the novelty wears off, or we hit a frustrating bit, the dopamine dries up and so does our drive. 'I'll do it later' becomes 'I forgot I was even doing that.'

3. Monitoring and self-regulation

This is the stage where we reflect, adjust and keep ourselves on track. Again, this is easier said than done with ADHD:

- **Self-awareness problems:** We might not notice when we've gone off course, or we realize too late that our current strategy isn't working. Without that internal feedback loop, it's hard to course correct.
- **Emotional intensity:** Every goal journey comes with setbacks and boring bits. For people with ADHD, those moments can trigger intense emotional responses – frustration, self-criticism, shame – which can make it feel safer to just give up than to keep pushing through.

The traditional model of goal setting assumes that once we know what we want and why it matters, we'll naturally follow through. **But ADHD interrupts the translation of intention into action at almost every stage.**

This doesn't mean we can't set and reach goals. It means we need different tools and a little more compassion for how our brains work.

Goal setting can be optimized for ADHD

Let's see how this looks in a real-world scenario:

Meet Alex, a 34-year-old with ADHD. Alex wants to:

1. Declutter the office
2. Explore a potential new creative hobby.

Let's see how they might tackle each goal with a different approach to goal setting.

Task 1: Declutter the office

Alex has been meaning to tackle their chaotic home workspace, which is affecting their ability to focus and get anything done. This task is concrete, time-limited and can be broken into steps, perfect for a SMART goal.

SMART goal example for 'Declutter the office'	
Specific	Declutter desk and surrounding area.
Measurable	Clear out three drawers, one shelf and the desktop.
Achievable	Spread it out over three short sessions, with breaks.
Relevant	Improve focus and reduce visual overwhelm while working.
Time-bound	Finish by Sunday at 6pm.

Based on this, Alex's SMART goal is:

'By Sunday at 6pm, I will have cleared my desk, sorted the top shelf and emptied three drawers, doing it in three 30-minute sessions with breaks, to make my workspace less overwhelming and easier to use.'

Why this can work for ADHD:

- Concrete and visual progress (you see the change).
- Breaks it down into manageable chunks.
- Adds a time boundary without being too rigid.
- Creates a meaningful outcome tied to their values (less stress, more focus).

Task 2: Try out a creative hobby

This is exploratory, unfamiliar and potentially joy-driven, so an open goal is a better fit.

Open goal examples:

- 'Spend some time this weekend messing around with digital art and see what I enjoy.'
- 'Explore one or two new creative hobbies this month and notice what feels interesting.'

Why this can work for ADHD:

There's no pressure to 'succeed'. It gives Alex permission to play, follow curiosity and avoid the all-or-nothing trap. Importantly, **it lowers the risk of performance anxiety and increases the chance of actually getting started.**

Let's compare both:

Task	Goal type	Example	Why it fits
Tidy workspace	SMART	Clear out three drawers, one shelf and the desktop by Sunday	Clear, trackable, routine-building
Try a creative hobby	Open	Play around with digital art this weekend	Encourages curiosity, low-pressure

SMART goal or open goal? A recap

- **Rigid goals can work best for simple or well-practised tasks.**
- **When trying something new, creative or emotionally loaded, give yourself permission to set learning goals or open goals.**
- **Experiment with different types of goals based on the task, your energy and what your brain actually responds to.**
- **You are not the problem. The system may need adjusting.**

Using goals to start habits and routines

When it comes to ADHD and productivity, one of the most useful shifts is to build new habits and turn those habits into routines. For ADHD brains, that consistency is often the difference between surviving and actually getting things done with less stress. **Routines save time, mental energy and increase consistency.** In short, habits get you started; routines keep you going. But it can be bloody difficult to start them.

We cover building routines in detail in Chapter 4, but for now let's look at how open goal setting can help with early habit formation.

Is habit-building better with open or SMART goals?

Short answer: both can work, but at different stages and for different brains.

When you're just starting a habit, especially if you have ADHD, low motivation or a rocky history with routines, open or flexible goals tend to work better.

Open goals can:

- reduce performance pressure
- give room for experimentation
- avoid triggering avoidance or shame.

This keeps the bar low enough to actually get started. It invites curiosity and self-compassion rather than demanding consistency.

But once you are underway, SMART goals can:

- help reinforce patterns
- provide measurable momentum
- make it easier to track change.

This works well if the task is already somewhat established and doesn't overwhelm your executive functions.

For starting a routine, the low stakes of open goals can get you started. For habit maintenance - a big issue for most ADHDers - using 'SMART-ish' goals can help. Once the behaviour feels more familiar, and you're trying to make it consistent or automatic, SMART goals can help provide scaffolding and keep you on track.

Strategies for improving goal setting

So now that we've covered how goal setting can go very right, or very wrong, what can you actually do about it?

This section offers practical, ADHD-friendly strategies for improving how you set and stick to goals and bounce back from goals that have not worked for you. Not all of these strategies will work for everyone, or they might work for a short amount of time before you have to choose another strategy, and that's OK. The aim here is to help you build a toolkit that suits your brain and your life.

Strategy 1: Use the right goal for the right task

Remember, different tasks or projects may benefit from different types of goals.

SMART goals can work best for concrete, familiar tasks where structure helps, and **'learning' goals are ideal when you're building a new skill or unsure where to begin,** whereas **'open' goals can support exploration and creativity** and reduce pressure – great for 'see what happens' energy.

If you try to set a SMART goal and it feels oppressive, switch to an open goal or make it smaller. That isn't failing, it's adapting.

Strategy 2: Start small. Really small

ADHD brains often overestimate what's possible in the short term and underestimate how long things will take. Sam frequently thinks they will have the time to completely re-organize their whole life *and* redecorate the house all in one weekend, only to feel completely crushed when all they've managed to do is eat rainbow drops and cry!

Starting small can help you to avoid overwhelm and shame spirals.

- Choose one tiny step, not the whole staircase.
- If it feels too easy, that's probably the right size.
- Let yourself finish something. The dopamine boost matters.

Try this: instead of 'Sort out my finances', go with 'Open the budgeting app'. Your next goal could then be to spend ten minutes on your budgeting app. This might mean literally spending ten minutes or becoming fixated on budgeting for hours. Often, we don't know how things will turn out. If seeing all the steps in a list feels overwhelming, have them in smaller 'groups' of steps, maybe three to four in a group. **Sometimes, setting a small goal that allows you to get started can mean the difference between doing something and procrastinating for hours, hating yourself throughout.**

Putting a load of clean clothes away makes Sam feel like they're being punished for what feels like an eternity. But grabbing one top or a handful of knickers to put away each time they pass the clean piles of washing that mock them daily is much more doable. If it's daunting, start as small as you can possibly imagine and celebrate every handful of knickers (or insert other clothing here) as a big win!

Strategy 3: Make the goal visible (and ADHD-friendly)

Out of sight = out of mind. ADHD brains are notoriously bad at remembering goals that aren't directly in front of them.

You know yourself better than anyone. Do you respond well to electronic systems? Do you like visual and colourful cues? Do reminders just drift silently out of your head? **Knowing how you engage with information can help you pick the best way to make a goal visible.**

As with any strategy you will likely have to change the way you approach this regularly to avoid your brain getting bored or forgetting that the system you just implemented even exists.

Here are some approaches:

- **Make it visual:** Use sticky notes, whiteboards, apps, virtual or physical planners or visual trackers. Make them prominent, colourful and try to build a habit of engaging with them daily. Using static, 'magic whiteboards' that you can put up each week in a different place may fight the object invisibility of the whiteboard that's currently screwed to the wall in your office with a note from 2018 to 'Call Sue'.
- **Create a 'ta-da' list:** Always log what you did, not just what you need to do. For those of you that are oppositional or avoidant, try a 'Things I definitely WILL NOT do today list'.
- **Incorporate tiny rewards:** It could be a cup of tea, five minutes of a favourite song, a colourful sticker on your chart, or texting a friend, whatever works for you. For steps towards your goal, and for each step completed, tick it off.

The trick is to make progress feel real and rewarding.

Sam's master task list system

Sam can struggle massively from overwhelm so they have a series of lists, all online (they use OneNote, which displays the lists like tabs in a planner, and do all of this manually because their brain likes to do it this way, but there are lots of apps that can automate a lot of this for you) so that they can access their lists from their phone, their work laptop, their personal laptop etc.

They have:

- a **work master task list** that has all of the tasks they have to do for work.
- a **'side quest' master list** that has all of the fun tasks they like to do that give them reward, a bit of energy or calm
- a **'done' list**
- **today's to-do list**.

First thing in the morning, Sam scans through their emails, not responding to any of them but putting each task on their work master task list, and they do this again halfway through the day and again at the end of the day. The next part changes often – in the past they have chosen three tasks from the work master task list and three from the master side quest list or one from each, so that they can sandwich work tasks with quick, fun, calming or energy-giving tasks/activities. But currently they choose one big task and one easy win from the work master task list, plus one fun task from the master side quest list.

They might start with an easy win, before having a bash at the big task (it doesn't matter if they don't finish the big task, the objective is just to spend as long as they are able to on it) and finishing off with a fun task as a little reward.

When they've done all three, they move them to a little 'done today' list on today's to-do list page and then they choose another big task (or the same one if they didn't finish and can face doing more), another easy win and another fun task. Some days they might not get all three done. Other days, they might get three, four or even five lots done. Every day is different! Then at the end of the day, they move all of the tasks they've completed from today's done list to their overall done list (this is useful when it comes to appraisal time!), add any new emails that have arrived to their work master task list and switch off ready to start again tomorrow.

Strategy 4: Build in flex points (and recovery plans)

Because life (and ADHD) is unpredictable, it helps to design goals with built-in flexibility and gentle recovery points so you don't feel like you've 'failed' the moment things go off track.

For example:

- **Use flexible goals:** 'Walk two to four times this week' instead of 'Walk every day'. This can be less demotivating: if you hit two, you've still hit your goal!
- **Add a 're-entry point' into your goal:** One small thing you can do to get started again without guilt. Following the walking analogy, 'Getting my shoes on' is a re-entry point.

- ***Try* not to catastrophize** (although we know this sounds ableist): Going off track from a goal doesn't mean you're back at square one; it means you are part way there.

Sometimes it helps to build this into the goal itself: 'If I fall off track, I'll restart by doing X'.

You will drop goals sometimes. That's just ADHD being ADHD. What matters is having a way back. Adding flexibility to goals, at the sweet spot between 'I'll give myself space' and 'I can just sack this off', can be helpful.

Strategy 5: Make use of AI tools

AI tools, like ChatGPT, Google Gemini or voice assistants, can be surprisingly helpful when it comes to setting and managing goals. Think of them less like a productivity overlord and more like a brainstorming buddy who never gets tired of helping you break things down. Here's how AI can support ADHD-friendly goal setting:

- **Break down big goals into tiny steps.** Struggling to figure out where to start? You can ask AI: 'Help me break down "Apply for a new job" into really small, manageable steps for someone with ADHD.' **AI can generate checklists, timelines, or task trees to reduce overwhelm and increase clarity.**
- **Translate vague intentions into SMART goals.** You might have a goal like 'Sort out my finances' or 'Get healthier'. That's too vague for your brain to act on, but AI can help turn 'Get healthier' into

a SMART goal that fits someone who struggles with consistency and motivation. **AI can suggest more specific, measurable and realistic versions based on what you tell it about your needs.**

- **Add structure and time estimates.** If you struggle with time blindness, AI can offer rough time estimates: 'How long might it take to declutter a desk if I work in short bursts?' You can also ask AI to create a simple schedule for you or help you build reminders and routines around your goal.
- **Suggest the right type of goal.** You can even tell it: 'I'm not sure if this should be a SMART goal or an open one. Help me decide?'

AI can walk you through the pros and cons, helping you tailor your goal type to your task and mood. Remember, though, **AI isn't magic. It sometimes gives rubbish advice**; it can be clunky or overly optimistic and using it well can take a bit of practice and training of the AI so that it knows you. And let's be real, not everyone has access to paid versions of these tools or the tech needed to run them smoothly. **If you don't have access to AI tools right now, it's not a failing; it's a resource gap.** This is why we'll always try to offer strategies in this book that don't require expensive tech or subscription fees.

You don't need perfect goals. You need forgiving ones. **ADHD goal setting works best when it's flexible, values-aligned and designed to keep your brain engaged, not punished.**

Whether you're chasing a big ambition or just trying to remember bin day, the strategies in this chapter are here to help you set goals you'll actually want to follow through on. And if you don't? That's OK, too. Goals can be revisited, reshaped and restarted. That's not backtracking, it's learning.

Chapter summary

This chapter covered the importance of choosing the right type of goal for your activity. We looked at how:

- ADHD can disrupt every stage of goal pursuit: planning, starting, sustaining effort and tracking progress.
- SMART goals can be useful for familiar or routine tasks, but they need adjusting to avoid overwhelm or shame spirals.
- Open and learning goals can be more forgiving, especially for creative, complex or emotionally loaded tasks.
- Goal setting works best when it's paired with structure, rewards and tools that reduce mental load.
- You might need to toggle between goal types depending on your task, energy and brain state – and that's not cheating, it's smart.
- Practical strategies that can help:
  - Start small; break goals into steps so tiny they feel silly.
  - Choose the right type of goal for the job: SMART or open.
  - Make goals visible and link them to immediate or emotional rewards.
  - Plan for derailments – build in flexibility and re-entry points so it's easier to restart.
  - Don't chase perfect goals. Chase goals that make sense for your brain.
  - Use AI (carefully) to help you set goals effectively.

Chapter 4

AUTOMATING LIFE

The importance of building routines

Sam has lots of routines that they have to do every day, or they just don't feel right. (Lots of autistic people have rigid routines that they *have* to do.) These routines can become so rigid and evolve into something so complex that they sometimes become a ridiculous burden.

For example, during lockdown, Sam decided to buy James a surprise present of a blow-up hot tub for his birthday. Obviously, they bought the wrong one, so they had to get a special adapter and then build something to keep the adapter and plug dry. They also had to put the heating on repeatedly so they'd have enough hot water to fill it and get in straightaway, but then forgot to turn the hot tub on so that it could keep the water warm, and by the time they remembered the hot tub and got in, the water was stone cold and had to be heated again.

Then the routine building began. They bought all the chemicals and started a daily routine of checking the water and adding chemicals as needed; a monthly routine of emptying, cleaning and refilling the hot tub; and acquired a series of covers, some that they bought, some that they made, some that they adapted, to stop the cats getting their claws through the actual hot tub cover, to help with insulation and to stop rainwater getting into the hot tub. They also had another arduous routine around emptying, cleaning, deflating, drying and packing up the hot tub every winter and then unpacking and cleaning it when they got it out again in the spring. This then became too much for Sam to cope with but because they also couldn't cope with *not* doing it, they agreed with James that they'd just sell/donate the hot tub instead. Of course, it's still in the garage years later because they still haven't managed to actually do that part.

When Sam actually *chooses* to start a new routine, they frequently forget that it exists the day after they started it and generally don't remember it until they try to start the same or a similar routine *again* and feel a nagging sense of déjà vu. They even forgot their whole to-do list system last year (the system we described in Chapter 3, which they've been doing every day for years, and which works really well for them) and felt lost every day for over six months before they accidentally opened OneNote and realized why their life had gone to shit! So, Sam has a difficult relationship with routines. They absolutely need them but find it difficult to stick to them, or even to remember their existence at all, unless it's an intrusive routine that they absolutely *have to do* but usually hate doing.

Why routines matter (even if you've never stuck to one)

If the inside of your brain feels like a browser with 87 tabs open, routines can act like bookmarks: they help you to find your place, stop things from crashing and save you from starting from scratch every single time.

For people with ADHD, life often feels unpredictable. One day, you're laser-focused and getting things done. The next, brushing your teeth feels like climbing Everest. In the middle of that chaos, routines aren't about becoming boring or rigid; they're tools. Tools that reduce decision fatigue, create momentum and make it easier to do the things you meant to do without having to summon heroic levels of motivation each time.

In this chapter, we'll explore why routines can be so powerful for people with ADHD, not because they come naturally, but because they can help us to work around the stuff that doesn't come naturally. We'll examine the science behind routine building, the common ways it falls apart and realistic strategies for creating routines that stick (or at least last long enough to be effective).

You don't need to turn your life into a colour-coded military operation. You just need a few reliable anchors in your day to help steer the ship.

The power of predictability

Think of routines as the scaffolding that holds your day up when everything else feels like it might collapse. Routines aren't about being strict or robotic, they're about creating small pockets of predictability in a world (and brain) that often feels like a whirlwind.

When life gets messy (and it will), routines give us something to hold on to. A morning checklist, a regular walk, even brushing your teeth at the same time each morning/night... these simple things can help to bring order to the internal chaos. For people with ADHD, whose nervous systems are more reactive to stress and change, **this kind of structure can be a genuine emotional safety net**. Psychologist Dr Rachel Goldman puts it simply: 'When we don't have structure, it's easier for our brains to spiral, because there's nothing else to focus on except the noise in our heads.'[1]

But it's not just about emotional stability. **Routines can actually help to regulate your body too.** Getting up, eating and going to bed at roughly the same times each day supports your 'circadian rhythm', the internal biological clock that governs your energy levels, sleep, hormones, mood and many other bodily functions. When that internal clock's running smoothly, you're more likely to feel mentally clear, physically well and emotionally resilient. When it's not, research shows we're more prone to anxiety, irritability and feeling disconnected from others.

This creates a positive cycle that's especially helpful for people with ADHD. **Sleeping well**, which is challenging for around two-thirds of people with ADHD, **boosts focus and emotional regulation, which makes it easier to get moving, eat properly and do daily tasks, all of which help you sleep better the next night**. Read that sentence back, and it is a powerful concept. Sleep well tonight, and you'll have a better chance of sleeping well tomorrow night.

And it's not just adults who benefit. **For children, routines are one of the most powerful ways to create a sense of safety and consistency.** Regular mealtimes, homework slots and bedtimes have been linked to better behaviour, stronger social skills and improved academic performance. One study from 2011[2] even found that children in families with low routine were more likely to develop behavioural disorders like Oppositional Defiant Disorder. Structure doesn't just help kids know what's coming next, it helps them feel safe enough to grow.

Why routines save brainpower (and stop you melting down over lunch)

If you've ever stood in front of the fridge thinking 'What do I feel like eating?' until your brain short-circuited, you've experienced the invisible cost of decision fatigue. Routines exist, in part, to spare us from that.

They're not just helpful, they're one of the brain's most efficient ways to conserve energy. Every time we repeat the same small sequence of actions (get up > wee > make coffee > forget where coffee is > make toast instead), we're offloading mental effort. It's like saving shortcuts to free up mental space. Scientists call this 'cognitive offloading', and it's one of the main reasons routines work so well, especially for people with limited working memory (hello ADHD).

Instead of having to decide every morning what to do, when to do it, and in what order, a routine means your brain can just follow the script. You're automating low-stakes tasks so your executive function can focus on the bigger stuff: work problems, parenting meltdowns, or trying to remember what that urgent email was actually about.

Routines and willpower: the case for being a bit boring

It turns out willpower isn't infinite. You don't start the day with a full tank and glide through choices like a rational productivity god. Psychologist Roy Baumeister's research suggests **self-control is more like a muscle: the more decisions you make, the more tired it gets.**[3]

This is especially relevant if you have **ADHD, where decision-making, impulse control and emotional regulation already cost more effort.** Without routines, you're forced to use that precious energy on things like which socks to wear or whether to reply to that text now or later or maybe never but feel guilty about it all day. Each choice chips away at your mental reserves.

Routines fix this by making a bunch of your daily decisions in advance. And that means when something unexpected does hit – your train's cancelled, your kids are melting down, your inbox is on fire – you still have a bit of brain left to cope.

The Zuckerberg wardrobe hack: less choice, more brain

You've probably heard the story: **Mark Zuckerberg wears the same outfit every day**, a plain grey T-shirt and jeans, not because he's a little short on cash, but **because he wants to make fewer decisions.** In his own words, he'd rather save his mental energy for choices that really matter.

It's easy to mock this as billionaire minimalism theatre, but the psychology behind it is solid. Every choice we make – what to wear, what to eat, which email to answer first – uses up brainpower. So, what Zuckerberg's doing, whether he knows it or not, is a **form of routine-based cognitive offloading**. He's eliminated a recurring, low-impact choice from his day so that his brain can stay focused on higher-value stuff. It's the same reason Barack Obama limited his wardrobe to grey or blue suits and why Steve Jobs famously wore that black turtleneck and jeans combo. They weren't fashion statements. They were strategic habits. James wears a black shirt for every public talk he does for the same reason. That and it hides his muffin top a bit better than a jumper.

Small wins, big impact

There's another reason routines matter: they create wins. Tiny, manageable, quiet confidence-boosting wins. When you do something on autopilot (like taking your meds or unloading the dishwasher without faffing for an hour), your brain gets a little jolt of 'I did the thing!' That builds self-efficacy – the belief that you're capable of doing difficult things. **And for people with ADHD, who often carry a backlog of failure, shame and missed deadlines, those little wins aren't small at all.**

It's a feedback loop: you do a thing, feel capable and become more willing to do the next thing. Eventually, routines stop being just practical tools and start becoming evidence that you can handle your life, even on a rubbish day.

How the brain builds routines (and why they're so hard to stick to)

Building a routine isn't just about remembering to do a thing; it's about literally *rewiring* your brain so that the thing becomes easier over time. That's why routines don't just help with productivity: they are a form of brain-based self-care. But to understand how to build a routine that actually sticks, we need to peek inside the brain and look at what's really going on.

The habit loop: cue > routine > reward

Every habit your brain forms runs on a loop: something triggers the behaviour (**a cue**), then you do the behaviour itself (**the routine**), and then you get something out of it (**the reward**). This cycle is what helps your brain learn: when X happens, do Y, because it feels good or avoids something bad.

Let's take a simple example: washing your hands after using the toilet as a child. The cue was finishing on the loo and being told to wash your hands. The routine was going to the sink and doing it. And the reward? Maybe praise from a grown-up. Or, if you didn't do it, maybe being told off or marched back in to do it properly. Either way, over time, your brain learned: when I do this, I either get approval or avoid something unpleasant.

In ADHD, this learning loop is still there, but we are often blind to the 'cue', or the reward system doesn't always respond the same way. We might need a much more visible or changeable cue, or a bigger or more immediate reward to make the habit stick. And if the routine feels boring or effortful (which it often does), it can be challenging to get started in the first place. However, with sufficient repetition and proper support, the brain can still learn. It may just take longer and require more creative approaches.

From trying to automatic: what happens in the brain

Initially, **starting a new habit can be challenging**. That's **because your prefrontal cortex** (the part of your brain that handles planning and decisions) **is doing the heavy lifting**. It's asking questions like, *Should I really go for that run? Can I be bothered to brush my teeth tonight?*

This is great for thinking things through, but it **requires a lot of mental effort**. And for people **with ADHD, that kind of executive functioning can be unreliable, especially if we're tired, stressed or just overwhelmed.**

But here's the clever bit: **if you do the same thing enough times, your brain starts handing over the job to a more automatic system,** a part of the brain called the basal ganglia. This part of your brain deals with routines, motor skills and habits. **Once the basal ganglia takes over, the habit gets easier to do.** You don't have to think about it as much; it just happens.

Think of it like teaching a new behaviour to a robot inside your brain. At first, you have to show it what to do step by step. But over time, the robot learns to take over, so you don't have to. That's why brushing your teeth or putting on your seatbelt doesn't take much effort now; the robot's got it.

Dopamine: the fuel that powers (and sometimes derails) habits

If routines are the wheels of productivity, dopamine is the fuel. It's the brain's way of saying, 'That was worth doing, let's do it again.' And as you'll (hopefully) already know by this point, dopamine is critical in ADHD.

When you do something that leads to a positive outcome, like ticking something off your to-do list, **dopamine is released in the basal ganglia, which is heavily involved in habit formation.**

This dopamine release strengthens the connection between what triggered the behaviour (the cue) and what you did in response (the routine). Over time, that makes your brain more likely to follow the same path again, without needing as much conscious effort. That's how a habit starts to take hold.

But here's the real twist: dopamine can show up before the reward.

Research shows that **dopamine isn't just released *after* something good happens; it's also released in anticipation**. Once your brain learns that a certain cue (like opening your laptop or hearing a notification ping) usually leads to a reward, it starts firing off dopamine the moment the cue appears. **That's what gives you the little motivational nudge to act.** It's the craving part of the habit loop:

cue > craving > response > reward

So, when your brain sees a cue that used to lead to something satisfying, it gets excited and pushes you to repeat the action, hoping for another dopamine hit. The key is to change cues that usually lead to a negative dopamine loop (like taking your medication in the morning and then scrolling on social media, completely losing track of time and then rushing to get to work) into a positive dopamine loop (like taking your medication and then immediately doing a few stretches, walking the dog, dancing to your favourite song or engaging in your current hobby).

The ADHD factor: why routines are harder for us

It's all well and good to say, 'just build a habit' or 'get into a routine'. But if you have ADHD, you've probably tried that...many, many times. You've probably also wondered why it feels like pushing jelly up a hill. The truth is, building routines isn't equally easy for all brains. And for those of us with ADHD, it's particularly tricky.

The challenges ADHD creates around routines show up everywhere in real life. When we struggle to establish consistent habits, the impact is far-reaching: it affects our school, work, daily life and even our self-esteem.

Without routines, tasks pile up. Deadlines sneak past. Projects stall. And while someone with ADHD might have bursts of brilliant work, those flashes are often drowned out by inconsistent performance. Over time, that inconsistency can lead to negative reviews, stalled careers, job losses and lower lifetime earnings, not because of lack of talent, but because of difficulties managing the boring but necessary bits of work and life.

The consistency tax

'Neurotypical' productivity often relies on doing small things consistently. For ADHD brains, it's more of a stop-start rollercoaster: we sprint, then crash, then scramble to catch up. Every time a routine breaks, it feels like we have to rebuild it from scratch and clean up whatever mess it left behind. That costs energy we could have spent making progress.

This is the hidden tax of living without reliable routines: the cognitive, emotional and time-draining cost of always having to restart. It's one reason why so many people with ADHD, even when they're smart, motivated and hardworking, feel like they're never quite reaching their potential. It's not because we're lazy, undisciplined or disorganized by choice. It's **because the very brain systems that support routine-building, like planning, remembering steps and staying motivated, are the same ones your ADHD messes with.**

This section explores exactly why routines often fall apart for us, and what's going on under the hood when they do.

Executive dysfunction: trying to build a house without tools

As we've already said, to the point where you're probably bored by it, **ADHD is fundamentally a disorder of executive function; the fancy term for the brain's ability to plan, prioritize, start, finish and regulate behaviour.**

Here's how that lack of executive function can impact routines in real life:

- **Starting is hard.** Struggling to start a task isn't laziness; it's a failure in task initiation. If something feels boring, difficult or doesn't offer an immediate reward (like emptying the dishwasher), your brain hits a wall. This makes it incredibly difficult to even begin the routines we want to build.
- **Planning and organization? Also hard.** Creating a routine involves planning steps, determining when and where to perform them, and remembering what you'll need. ADHD makes that whole process feel like assembling IKEA furniture with no manual and three missing screws. Although, to be fair, James can't assemble IKEA furniture even with the manual and extra screws.
- **Working memory fails you.** Your brain's mental sticky note, the bit that holds instructions in your head while you use them. In ADHD, that note either falls off or was never stuck there to begin with. So **even if you want to stick to your routine, you might forget what you were doing halfway through** and end up reorganizing your spice rack instead.
- **Emotion takes over.** Frustration, boredom or overwhelm can quickly derail a new habit. **If something feels difficult or unrewarding, the emotional discomfort can flood your system, and the urge to do *literally anything else* often wins.** The same goes for impulsivity: you might intend to stick to your bedtime routine, but suddenly it's 2am and you're deep into conspiracy videos about otters.
- **Getting stuck or not sticking at all.** Cognitive flexibility, the ability to switch tasks smoothly, is another executive function. **With ADHD, you might get stuck in one step of a routine or be unable to move from one part to the next.** Either way, the sequence breaks.

So, when routines fall apart, it's not because you're not trying hard enough. It's because your brain is operating without the full toolkit most people use to build and sustain habits. But here's the good news: just because you stop doing something, it doesn't mean you can't try again. It's just more difficult if starting again is unrewarding or if you feel like a failure for not keeping the routine going.

Remember the robot learning new actions from earlier? **For people with ADHD, this habit-building process can take longer, and the robot sometimes forgets what it was taught.** We're more distractible, more novelty-seeking and less motivated by long-term rewards. **That means even once a habit is formed, it can fall apart more easily if the cues change** (like being on holiday, or moving house), **or the reward fades** (like when the praise stops).

And because the brain in ADHD often craves immediate feedback, **the habit loop usually works better when there's a quick reward**: ticking a box, earning a sticker, getting a high-five or just feeling slightly smug for doing the thing.

Time blindness: when time stops making sense

Of all the invisible hurdles ADHD throws at us, time blindness (covered in Chapter 9) might be the most frustrating. **Time blindness is a neurological difference that affects how we perceive, estimate and feel time.** And when it comes to building routines, systems that rely on consistent timing can completely derail the plan before it even starts.

Here's how it can show up:

- **You can't tell how long things take.** The warped sense of time passing can mean that a task you think will take ten minutes can eat up an hour. Or something you're dreading might feel like it'll take for ever, so you avoid starting it at all. This makes it really challenging to build a realistic routine, because you're basing your plan on time estimates that aren't reliable.
- **Everything is 'now' or 'not now'.** ADHD brains struggle to connect with the future. **We tend to operate in a kind of time binary: 'now' (urgent, real, emotional) and 'not now' (abstract, distant, easy to ignore).** So, if the benefit of sticking to a routine, like packing lunch the night before, is in the 'not now' zone, it doesn't register as meaningful until it's too late and you're hungry, late and annoyed. (This is also why so many of us procrastinate, even when we want to be better prepared. The future doesn't feel real until it becomes a crisis.)
- **You'd rather have the biscuit now.** Another way ADHD warps time is through something called **temporal discounting**. It's a fancy term for a simple idea: **our brains heavily favour immediate rewards over bigger ones that come later.** That's why the quick dopamine hit of scrolling Instagram often wins over the long-term benefit of doing your taxes or going to bed on time. The future just doesn't feel rewarding enough, so we go for what feels good right now.

It's not just one thing, it's all of it

These time challenges don't happen in a vacuum. They **interact with other ADHD struggles like low motivation** (thanks, dopamine system) **and poor task initiation** (cheers, executive dysfunction).

Together, they form a kind of triple-threat that can sabotage even the best intentions.

- You want to stick to a routine, but you forget when to start.
- You remember to start, but the task feels pointless because the reward is too far away.
- You manage to start, but it takes longer than expected and throws off your whole day.

And then the shame creeps in. You blame yourself. Maybe someone else blames you too. And you start to believe that you're just bad at routines.

You're not.

You're dealing with a brain that processes time, motivation and planning differently, and any solution that doesn't take all three into account is doomed to fail.

The truth is, you *can* build routines. But you'll need to build them in a way that works with your brain, not against it.

Strategies for building routines

For people with ADHD, routines can feel like a double-edged sword: we need them to feel anchored and get things done, but rigid ones quickly become stifling. We spend ages building one and as soon as it fails, we segue back to chaos. Novelty fades, life throws curve-balls and suddenly the whole system feels like a burden rather than a lifeline.

Before we start with strategies, here are three simple tips for creating routines:

1. **Make routines that are flexible enough to not demotivate you.**
2. **Make the cues for routines as visible or loud as possible.**
3. **Aim for consistency, not perfection.**

Strategy 1: Develop a 'meta-routine'

Most productivity advice focuses on doing the tasks: wake up early, exercise, meal prep, clear your inbox, rinse, repeat. But for ADHD brains, the real game-changer isn't building the individual habits; it's engaging with the tools and systems that keep you on track.

Because executive functions (planning, time management and working memory) can be unreliable, the most valuable routine can be the one that checks and maintains your external supports – the planner, lists, timers and cues. Without this daily check-in, even the best-designed systems gather dust and everything feels chaotic again.

Think of it like this: your calendar, lists and reminders are a surrogate prefrontal cortex. They handle the planning and prompting your brain struggles to do consistently. Your job isn't to remember every step of your routine; it's to remember to consult your external brain.

In Chapter 3, we introduced Sam's master task list – her tried and tested way of making tasks visible. Here's how to try it for yourself:

- **Start each day by checking your 'dashboard'**
  Spend 5–10 minutes each morning reviewing:
  - your master task list (and pulling 3–5 priorities to a daily list)
  - your calendar (so you're not surprised by meetings or deadlines)
  - any alarms or reminders you need to set for the day.

  Treat this like brushing your teeth. It's the 'anchor' habit that keeps the rest running smoothly.

- **Build in a weekly review and reset**
  Once a week, spend 15–30 minutes looking over your system:
  - Clear out completed tasks and add them to your 'done' list.
  - Add any new ones you've been holding in your head.
  - Adjust your routines based on what worked (or didn't) that week.
  - Think of this as a system tune-up that prevents the chaos from snowballing.

- **Make engaging with your tools the habit to protect**
  Even if you can't manage every routine perfectly, if you can keep the habit of checking your lists, calendar and timers alive, everything else can be restarted easily. Your 'meta-routine' is your lifeline. It's what might stop a bad day from turning into a bad week.

The 'meta-routine' can also benefit from AI use. Tools such as Notion AI, Zapier and Make can pull everything into a single dashboard each morning, calendar events, identify top tasks, issue reminders and present it in a clean, ADHD-friendly format. AI chatbots can act as a daily stand-up partner, asking: 'What's on your calendar?', 'What 3–5 priorities do you want to tackle?' or 'What reminders do you need?'

Then it can automatically schedule and nudge you throughout the day. AI can even run your weekly review for you, summarizing completed tasks, reminding you of anything overdue and even suggesting tweaks to your routine based on your patterns.

We have added an exercise for you to try when building your own 'meta-routine' in our online resources (see p.343).

Strategy 2: Start small and build gradually

For most people, routines are built step by step, over time, but for ADHD brains, the stakes are higher. Trying to launch a fully-fledged, rigid schedule like 'From now on, I'll wake up at 6am, run 5k, meditate, batch-cook and tackle my to-do list before work' often leads to overwhelm. **The executive function system can't keep up**, and when that mountain of change collapses, it feeds a familiar cycle: 'I've failed again, so why bother?'

Too much change, too fast, often feels like punishment rather than progress, making the brain even less likely to stick with it. Keep changes small and achievable to you can feel the cheering dopamine hit that will keep you going. **(ADHDers also have a lower tolerance for tasks that feel repetitive or boring due to dopamine dysregulation.)**

How to do it:

- **Start with 1–2 simple routines:** (For example, a consistent wake-up time or laying clothes out the night before).
- **Use the two-minute rule:** Make the first step take less than two minutes, so task initiation is easier.
- **Focus on building momentum, not perfection:** Missing a day isn't failure; treat it as a data point and restart.

Strategy 3: The 'Zuckerberg approach'

For those of us with ADHD, mornings are often a minefield: too many steps, too many decisions and not enough dopamine to get through them efficiently.

Routine doesn't mean boring. It means preloading your day with success by making fewer decisions in the moment, so you can make better ones when it really counts.

Pre-deciding what to wear, what to eat, or what time you leave the house doesn't just save time. It **reduces the number of executive function demands before the day even starts**, and fewer demands means less chance of hitting an ADHD wall by lunchtime.

This doesn't mean you need to adopt a cartoon character wardrobe or wear greyscale for ever (unless you want to). But it does mean that **the fewer decisions you have to make about unimportant stuff, the more brainpower you'll have left for the important stuff**, like finishing your work, remembering your meds, or not snapping at your partner because you're overloaded.

Tiny tweaks to steal the strategy:

- **Pick your outfit the night before.** Or rotate between a few go-to combos that always feel right.
- **Plan or batch-cook your meals:** Decide breakfast and lunch for the week on Sunday.
- **Create a launchpad routine:** The same steps, in the same order, every morning before you leave.
- **Automate reminders:** Don't remember what to do, remind yourself.

You'll find a link to an exercise you can use to try the Zuckerberg approach in our online resources (see p.343).

Strategy 4: Externalize everything (because working memory can't be trusted)

Having ADHD means your brain isn't always great at holding on to information in the background. Working memory, the 'mental sticky note' that keeps track of what you were just about to do, tends to be patchy. You might set out to unload the dishwasher, spot a half-drunk cup of tea, end up tidying the living room, and then realize the plates are still in the dishwasher...two hours later.

Relying on your brain to remember routines or tasks is like storing important files on a USB stick that keeps getting lost. **Externalizing – moving the reminders, plans and cues into your environment – can be an effective workaround. It can build a kind of external brain that compensates for what ADHD makes unreliable internally.**

How to do this:

- **Use visual cues as unavoidable prompts**

  Make the reminder something you can't ignore:

  - Stick a neon Post-it on the bathroom mirror (e.g. meds before teeth) and change the colour and position often.
  - Put your gym shoes on your desk chair or on the sofa so you can't sit down without moving them.
  - Keep medication, vitamins, or keys by the coffee maker (or whatever other thing you *do* remember to use).
  - Whiteboards or wall calendars can sometimes work because they're big and visible, not buried in an app, but you will probably have to change their location often to avoid them blending into the background.

- **Set multiple alarms, timers and reminders (yes, even – or especially – annoying ones)**
  - ADHD brains are expert at ignoring one quiet ping. Two or three escalating alarms? Much harder.
  - Use different tones for different purposes (a cheerful sound for breaks, a harsh one for 'wrap up and transition').
  - Smart speakers (like Alexa or Google Home) can announce tasks aloud, which helps if you tend to miss phone notifications, although if you don't do the thing straightaway, it can still be easy to forget.

- **Build a master list as your external memory (Sam's favourite!)**
  - Trying to hold all your to-dos in your head is a fast track to overwhelm and forgotten deadlines.
  - Keep a single source of truth: a notebook, app (Todoist, Notion,

Apple Reminders), or even a big paper list by your desk. Every stray task goes there first. Then, each evening or morning, pick a handful for your daily list so the day feels manageable, not crushing. Let your planner tell you what to do so your brain doesn't have to juggle it.

- **Make your tools frictionless (or you won't use them)**
  - Leave the whiteboard in the room where you actually work, not hidden away.
  - Put your list app on your phone's home screen so it's one tap away.
  - If your reminders live in five different places, your brain will ignore them all. Keep it simple, central and hard to overlook.

You can also try using AI here: Create dynamic dashboards (e.g. Notion with AI integration) that automatically pull in your calendar, tasks and reminders each morning so you don't have to gather them manually. Use AI assistants (like Zapier, ChatGPT or Make automations) to turn emails, texts and notes into tasks automatically and push them into one central list. And smart speakers can become your verbal external brain, announcing routines and even giving step-by-step instructions if you ask ('Alexa, walk me through my morning check list').

Strategy 5: Make cues and rewards obvious and immediate

For many people, the satisfaction of doing the right thing or working towards a distant goal – better health, a tidy home, a promotion – is enough motivation. For people with ADHD, not so much. **The**

dopamine system that fuels motivation is wired differently for us: boring, repetitive or delayed-reward tasks barely register as rewarding. Without a kick of interest or pleasure, your brain treats those tasks like dead batteries; it won't start.

This is why routines, which by nature are repetitive and low-novelty, so often fall apart for people with ADHD. To help make them stick, **you need to hack the habit loop: make the cue loud and unavoidable, and the reward juicy and immediate, so the brain can get the stimulation it's looking for.**

How to do this:

- Use temptation bundling to make the boring feel bearable. **Pair something you want to do with something you need to do.**

  You might:

  - Only let yourself listen to your favourite podcast while folding laundry.
  - Watch a guilty-pleasure TV show while exercising.
  - Save your best playlist for the gym, doing boring admin or cleaning the kitchen.

This works because your brain starts to associate the 'have-to' task with the dopamine hit of the 'want-to' task, making it easier to repeat.

Chapter summary

In this chapter, we explored why routines aren't about becoming robotic or boring; they're about creating anchors that can help ADHD brains to steer through the chaos. Here's what we unpacked:

- Routines can save brainpower. By reducing decision fatigue and automating small, repetitive choices, routines can free up mental energy for the things that actually matter.
- They can help to stabilize your body and mind. Regular waking, meal and sleep times can help to regulate your circadian rhythm, improving mood, focus and resilience.
- They can build confidence. Each small, automatic win (like taking meds or ticking off a task) can help to reinforce the belief that you *can* handle life, even on tough days.
- ADHD makes routines harder. Executive dysfunction, working memory glitches, time blindness and dopamine differences all make starting and sticking to routines more difficult, but not impossible.
- Flexibility is key. Routines that are too rigid break easily; ones with novelty, restart plans and room for fluctuation are far more sustainable.
- The 'meta-routine' is the real MVP. The most important habit isn't any single task, but the daily and weekly habit of engaging with your external brain, your lists, calendar and reminders, which keeps every other routine alive.

We also gave you practical tools to help to make routines stick:

- Start with tiny, easy wins (using the two-minute rule).
- Reduce decisions up front (the 'Zuckerberg approach').
- Externalize everything so your brain doesn't have to hold it all.
- Make cues loud and unavoidable and rewards immediate and satisfying.
- Keep routines flexible and forgiving, so a bad day doesn't derail your progress.

Most of all, remember:

You don't need a perfect, seven-days-a-week schedule to make routines work for you. You just need a few consistent anchors, some external scaffolding and a willingness to treat slip-ups as feedback, not failure.

Chapter 5

FINDING MOTIVATION

(And keeping it long enough to do a thing)

When James was an academic, he used to handle around 150 emails a day and, from the outside, appeared to do so without flinching. This wasn't because he really loved admin (he didn't) or because he had some magical productivity system (he *really* didn't), but because he was **almost entirely fuelled by fear**: fear of letting people down, fear of being thought lazy or incompetent, fear of missing a deadline and fear of the consequences that might follow.

That fear created urgency. It triggered the kind of emotional intensity that can flip his brain into action mode. Emails weren't just admin; they were potential grenades with pins already half out. And because he was constantly reacting, he rarely paused to ask whether any of it was sustainable or even necessary. **Fear can act as a powerful motivator, but it is unsustainable and harmful in the long run**. It often becomes unhealthy in individuals with

ADHD because **it promotes short-term action while undermining long-term, healthy productivity.**

For James, this approach contributed to burnout, mental health crises and eventually led to him leaving academia.

Fast-forward to now, running our own business. James has more control, more freedom...and more unread emails than ever. Some days, James can struggle to answer ten. Not because he cares less about the people who have emailed (he very much cares more), but because the fear has gone, along with the accompanying motivation.

Without fear snapping at his heels, James needs to find new and interesting ways to try and engage with emails in a timely fashion without being left burnt out or ashamed. Some days using 'body doubling' (this is when you are doing something in the presence of someone else and providing accountability; see page 108 for more information on body doubling) or reminders helps, sometimes it 'just happens', which is another reminder that **ADHD can appear like 'consistent inconsistency'**.

Importantly, for James, remembering the impact that not keeping on top of emails has on Sam, who will then almost always take on the responsibility of answering the emails that James isn't able to respond to, can create an **emotional incentive** that can sometimes be enough to motivate him to engage with such a seemingly simple task. But the key word there is 'sometimes'...

Understanding motivation

If you've ever stared at a to-do list, waiting for divine inspiration to strike, and then randomly found yourself cleaning the fridge or your cutlery drawer instead, welcome. You're in the right place.

> **A lack of motivation can manifest as a 'mental brick wall' that stops one from starting or finishing a task, frequent 'side questing' from intended tasks, sometimes even towards less palatable alternatives (like cleaning the fridge or the oven or finally completing your tax return), or even disengaging with a task entirely.**

Motivation, for many people with ADHD, can be troublesome. It often doesn't arrive when you want it to. It doesn't really respond to logic. It sometimes doesn't care about deadlines or consequences. To compound this, **a lack of motivation is often blamed as a moral failing**: 'If you just tried harder...' or 'You just need more willpower, like me.'

NO. And for those who missed it, ***NO!***

In the context of ADHD, motivation isn't about willpower, effort or character. It's about how our brains drive us to engage with a task or activity. Specifically, the brains in people with ADHD work differently when it comes to motivation and reward. **Individuals with ADHD often experience significant challenges with initiating and**

sustaining 'goal-directed behaviour', or to put it simply, starting tasks and keeping engaged with them, especially if they don't find that task rewarding. **This isn't the same as procrastination, although the two are linked.**

So, what is motivation, where does it come from, and how is it involved in productivity?

Motivation: what it is and why it can feel broken

In simple terms, **motivation is what drives us to start, continue, or finish a task.** It's the drive that makes you want to do something, whether it's getting out of bed, studying for an exam, or pursuing a hobby. One way of thinking about motivation is that it is the 'why' behind your actions. Why are you doing this? Motivation provides the answer.

Motivation gives you energy and direction. It fuels your efforts and helps you to stay focused on what you want to achieve, from starting, to keeping going, to completing. When things get tough, **motivation can help people work through challenges with more ease.**

Motivation can be incredibly important for productivity because it acts as the mental battery that drives effective and sustained work. Let's use an example of a fairly typical work task, writing a monthly sales report, to see how important motivation can be.

Task	Without motivation	With motivation
Starting	You might keep putting off starting the report. You might think, 'I'll do it tomorrow,' or find other smaller, less important tasks to occupy your time.	You feel a sense of purpose or obligation to get the report done. You sit down and start gathering the necessary data and outlining the structure without significant delay.
Staying engaged	You may just go through the motions, pulling basic numbers without much analysis or insight. You might feel tired and uninspired during the process.	You're more likely to be willing to dig deeper into the sales figures, identify trends and provide insightful commentary.
Focus and concentration	You might easily get distracted by emails, social media or conversations around you. Your mind might wander, making it difficult to concentrate on the data and writing.	You are more able to block out distractions and concentrate on the task at hand. You can focus on the numbers, the narrative and on ensuring that the report is accurate and well-structured.
Persistence	You might get frustrated if you encounter difficulties, like missing data or a complex calculation, and give up or submit an incomplete report.	You're more likely to persevere in the face of challenges. You might actively seek out missing information, try different approaches to the calculation and ensure that the report is complete.
Quality of work	You might just aim for the bare minimum to get the task done. The report might be rushed, contain errors or lack insightful analysis.	You are more likely to take pride in your work and want to produce a high-quality report that is informative and well-presented. You might even double-check your figures, proofread carefully and ensure the analysis is thorough.

Psychologists often break motivation down into two types:

- **Intrinsic motivation:** This comes from within you. This could be doing something because it's enjoyable, interesting, or personally fulfilling. For example, you might play a musical instrument because you love the feeling of creating music.
- **Extrinsic motivation:** This comes from external factors. It could be doing something because you expect a reward – such as studying hard to get a good grade or working to earn that promotion – or because you want to avoid a punishment or protect someone else from taking on the burden.

As nice and neat as these two types of motivation are, there exists a third state: 'amotivation'.[1] **Amotivation means not feeling motivated at all.** It's when you don't have the drive to do something. Not because you're lazy or don't care, but because **your brain isn't giving you the push to start or keep going.**

This can happen even with things you know are important or things you *really* want to do. You're not choosing to do nothing, it just feels like there's no fuel in the tank.

A theory known as **Self-Determination Theory**, or SDT, can act as a simple way of understanding motivation. SDT states that people are more likely to stay motivated when they feel:

- autonomous (in control of things)
- competent (capable of things)
- connected to others (being meaningfully and positively connected to others).

> This theory suggests that motivation lies in a range, with 'amotivation' at one end, 'extrinsic motivation' somewhere in the middle and 'intrinsic motivation' at the other end. Put simply, the lowest level of motivation is 'practically none', and the highest is 'being able to motivate yourself'.

In essence, then, **motivation transforms 'potential productivity' into 'actual productivity'**. It bridges the gap between having the ability to do something and actually doing it well and consistently. **Whether it's intrinsic or extrinsic, having that drive is a key factor in maximizing your output and achieving the desired results.**

How does ADHD impact motivation?

For people with ADHD, intrinsic motivation is often in short supply. **Research has shown that people with ADHD can have less intrinsic motivation and are more likely to have 'amotivation'.**[2] This means that they often need more support or external incentives to get moving, especially when the task is boring or the reward feels difficult to reach.

> Knowing that **people with ADHD are more likely to struggle with intrinsic motivation and more prone to amotivation** can help you to accept that it is not your fault if you don't find a work task motivates you into action. **You are fighting your brain.**

In ADHD, this can look like **wanting to get started but just not being able to; feeling stuck, even if a deadline is looming; or needing a *really* good reason (or an external push) to get going.** That doesn't mean we're lazy. **It means our brains, particularly the dopamine-based reward system, function differently.**[3]

If we dig into the biology of motivation, it quickly becomes clear why people with ADHD can tend to struggle. Dopamine, (covered in Chapter 1) plays a huge role in motivation, reward and learning.

In ADHD, dopamine is generally less active in multiple parts of the brain, but is particularly inactive in the reward system. This means that **we often need bigger or more immediate rewards to feel the same motivation as people who don't have ADHD.**

Motivation and delayed gratification

A key issue with ADHD is that **we have a reduced ability to delay gratification. This means our brains will direct us to the smaller, more immediate reward *almost every time*.** We're more likely to chase instant rewards, even if they're smaller or unrelated. (Hello, impulsive spending and social media doomscrolling!)

This is because people with ADHD have a delay in their brain's response to rewards. This makes immediate, tangible rewards more effective than delayed or abstract ones.[4]

Research also shows that **ADHD brains often prefer smaller, immediate rewards over larger, delayed ones**, a concept known as 'delay aversion'.[5] Imagine you were offered £10 today or £30 in three weeks' time. Clearly £30 is more money than £10 but for so many people, ADHD or not, the delay of three weeks would cause them to pick £10 now over £30 in the future.

Motivation, then, isn't just about wanting it badly enough. It's about trying to work with a reward system that's often on a different frequency.

It's also very important to state that **motivation is not the same as morality**. Here's a golden truth: **struggling with motivation is not the same as being lazy, weak-willed or self-indulgent. It's neurological.** And, like every other aspect of ADHD, it's something you can work with instead of against.

So... How do you get motivated? Using your toolkit

If finding motivation feels like a struggle, it's not because you're broken. It's because your brain doesn't respond to pressure, reward or motivational talks in the same way as other people's. But with the right approach and support, you can get things done. Not all the time, and not always the 'normal way', but more often, and in the way that suits your brain. There's no one-size-fits-all answer, because everyone with ADHD will have their own unique strengths and challenges.

Before we start, **remember the three key rules:**

1. **Try *one* thing at a time - don't overwhelm yourself.**
2. **It's OK if it doesn't work - failure is a route to success.**
3. **Progress, not perfection - small improvements help to move you in the right direction.**

Strategies for increasing motivation

In this section, we have provided some approaches you may want to try. As before, AI tools can be incredibly helpful for people with ADHD, especially for helping to break tasks down, add structure and even gamify challenges. But the usual caveats apply: sometimes AI is wrong and 'training' is necessary.

Strategy 1: Add accountability with body doubling

People with ADHD often respond better to extrinsic motivation – motivation that comes from external rewards or consequences. (External, social structures, in which you are 'accountable' for your time, can create the urgency, focus and reward that the ADHD brain often struggles to create for itself.) To avoid adding an extra layer of pressure or shame to a task, try to focus on action and progress, rather than achievement. One easy, low-stress way to add healthy accountability to any task is by body doubling. We have had many people tell us that body doubling has been a game-changer for them, allowing them to start the day the way they have always wanted to.

Body doubling is an easy, simple to set up and practical productivity strategy where you complete tasks while someone else, the 'body double', is present. This person, or people, can be physically or virtually present. Their role isn't to help you with the task itself, but to provide accountability and to offer a supportive, non-judgmental presence that can make it easier to focus and stay on track.

Body doubling can be done in many ways:

- Some people team up to do the same, or different activities or tasks, at the same time, in the same space.
- Some people find that watching videos of other people completing activities or tasks gives them motivation to complete their own tasks. (Sam regularly records body-doubling videos for other people to complete tasks or hobbies along to.)
- Some people find that simply messaging someone to tell them what they intend to do (along with pictures or videos to track progress) and having that person check in with them at regular intervals to hold them accountable and encourage them works well for them.
- Some people find that working alongside others online, especially if someone is facilitating a structured session, works really well for them.

It's really important to note that setting achievable and specific goals is part of what makes body doubling work. Aiming to 'Answer some emails' or 'Do some tidying' is vague and difficult to measure, so it may create barriers. Setting explicit and *very* achievable aims can give participants a small win and can help to build on the motivation gained from the accountability of the body-doubling session.

We have an example of how we run online body-doubling sessions in our online resources (see p.343).

Strategy 2: Gamification

Gamification is about making non-game activities feel a bit more like games. Think points, badges, leaderboards and colourful graphs showing progress. Gamification can be against yourself or include others as 'competitors'. It taps into basic psychology to boost motivation and engagement and provides immediate, dopamine-releasing 'wins' that can increase focus and drive. Essentially, it's **tricking our brains into enjoying stuff we'd otherwise find dull.**

James uses gamification when renewing insurance, a fundamentally tedious process. It goes like this:

1. Get the renewal quote.
2. See if there is a cheaper quote on a price comparison website (small win).
3. See if you can still get a cheaper quote with the same cover (another small win).
4. Tell the original insurer what you've been quoted; they'll either match it or not, but either way, James has saved money (another win!).

A word of caution: gamification isn't foolproof. If it's overdone or poorly executed, it can backfire, especially if rewards feel controlling or lose their novelty. To make gamification truly work, it needs to align closely with what users actually care about, providing rewards that feel genuinely meaningful rather than manipulative.

In short, **gamification cleverly uses psychology to turn boring tasks into something more engaging and rewarding**. It won't work for every task or every person, but done right it can genuinely boost motivation.

Strategy 3: Make rewards immediate and visible

Remember, people with ADHD can often have altered dopamine function, meaning rewards often need to be more immediate to motivate behaviour effectively.

Research has shown that behaviours can be changed using immediate reinforcement. One study reported that immediate, performance-based rewards significantly improved task-related behaviours in ADHD youth and adults.[6] So, **by having an imminent and visible reward, motivation can increase.**

So, what can this look like? Here are some possible approaches that might work for you:

- **Structure tasks into shorter segments with immediate, visible rewards.**
- **Use visual tracking systems such as apps, check lists** (ticking things off can give a little reward each time), **or physical tokens** (rewarding yourself with stickers on a wall chart or small items that your brain likes).
- **Pair less motivating tasks with immediate, small, sensory or emotional rewards.** (Sam has a list of fun things to do or rewarding side quests to reward herself with. Things like watching bees or feeding birds for ten minutes, eating or drinking something she loves, doing ten minutes of her latest hobby – but these can be whatever little rewards your brain likes.)
- **Regularly update your visible reward systems to sustain novelty and engagement.** (Whatever system you choose will probably need to be changed regularly to keep your brain interested!).

Strategy 4: Create structure around tasks

Structure can sometimes reduce or even remove the need for motivation. If something is 'automatic', one often does not need so much of the planning, organization and prioritization that can sap our motivation. Creating structure through tools, like calendars, task lists, reminders and visual cues, reduces our reliance on working memory, freeing cognitive resources for task engagement.

So, having a structured routine, that hits the sweet spot between flexibility and rigidity, can help you to get stuff done.

How can this be achieved? Here are some approaches:

- **Have set 'golden hours' for focused work:** People with ADHD often experience peaks and troughs in energy and focus. Identifying your 'golden hours' (when in the day you generally feel 'most functional') and using that time for tasks, not emails or messaging, can help with task initiation and engagement. Sadly, for many people with ADHD, this is often in the evening.[7]

- **Make the start as smooth as possible:** Preparing your workspace, plans, materials and even clothes in advance can **reduce barriers to task initiation** by removing the need to use multiple executive functions, such as planning, decision-making and prioritizing. Basically, it's about cutting down the steps that stand in the way of getting going. Sam has duplicates of everything they need in each bag that they use for each activity. They have a bag for work, a bag for aerial/pole, a bag for when they visit their family, a crafting bag...and they each have at least one lip balm, nail file, sensory toy, antibacterial spray (these are their essential things) along with the items that are specifically necessary for the activity (such as their pass and laptop for work, grip for aerial/pole etc). They lay their clothes out the night before, including underwear, shoes and coat (and have multiple annoying alarms to remind them of this). If they are doing aerial/pole the next day those clothes are laid out too, to wear underneath their day clothes. They need to be able to grab their things and get out of the door before their brain realizes what is happening and starts overthinking and cancelling!

- **Build task rituals:** Establishing consistent pre-task routines (such as a specific drink, a playlist, your clothing) can signal to the brain that it's time to focus. This can work really well with children too. Research has shown that implementing structured routines can enhance executive functioning in children with ADHD, leading to improved management of daily tasks.[8]
- **Use visual task management tools:** Visual tools (e.g. Kanban boards, visual planners) can enhance time estimation accuracy and sustained attention in individuals with ADHD. If you prefer stickers or Post-it Notes on a whiteboard, use them. Whatever your brain will engage with, that's the approach!
- **Pomodoro technique:** Working in structured intervals (e.g. 25 minutes of work followed by a 5-minute break) can help reduce cognitive fatigue, maintain focus and prevent burnout. Completing an energy audit (more on this in Chapter 13) to work out what activities give you a little energy boost can be useful here so that you can sandwich work tasks between energy-boosting activities. These will vary for each person. Some may listen to music, others may step outside to feel the sun on their

face or watch the bees or birds. However, if you find your task rewarding and you are in 'flow', *don't stop!* Task switching can mean it might be hard to start again.

Chapter summary

This chapter unpacked why:

- Motivation is often external for people with ADHD. Intrinsic drive? Rare. We're often fuelled by urgency, consequences, or how our actions affect others.
- Amotivation is real. That weird, stuck feeling where you want to move but can't? That's neurological, not a moral failure.
- Dopamine is involved. Our brains often need immediate or emotionally meaningful rewards to engage with a task. Delayed gratification is not our strong suit.
- Fear-based productivity is a trap. It can make you efficient in the short term but costs you your health and self-worth over time.

We also talked about tools for working with your brain:

- Body doubling to provide gentle accountability and momentum.
- Gamification to add novelty, feedback and a sense of progress.
- Immediate, visible rewards that tap into the ADHD brain's craving for *now*.
- Structure and rituals to reduce the executive function toll and make starting easier.

And remember: you don't need to be motivated all the time to make progress. 'Sometimes' really is good enough.

Chapter 6

WHICH FIRE TO PUT OUT FIRST?

Picking priorities (when everything feels urgent)

In the earliest days of our relationship, when spontaneous sex was possible without having to put ointment on James's joints, an opportunity to prioritize was presented to James, which he could not possibly have got more wrong. Having just moved as a scientific researcher from a lowly ranked university to one of the best-ranked universities in the UK, James had a significant amount of **impostor syndrome** (very common for people with ADHD). This meant that James was convinced that at some point, someone in power would put their hand on his shoulder and say, 'Sorry, why do we employ you?' This imposter syndrome was such a powerful driver of James's behaviour that it led to an episode of completely inappropriate prioritization.

Anyway, back to the throes of spontaneous physical intimacy. One evening after work, about two months into his new job, when the mood was (apparently) right, we began to have sex. As that wonderful (or average, you'd need to ask Sam) experience drew towards something like a peak, James's phone rang, and he could see that it was his new boss. Now, most people would probably be able to ignore the phone or realize that it was not a call that should be taken right *now.* Not James. He immediately cast Sam to one side and, standing proud and naked, answered the phone to speak to his boss like the good employee he was. It's easy to tell this story without shame now, but (without all the naked bits), imagine how well this went down with Sam.

What this tells us is that **the ability to prioritize takes a significant amount of mental effort**, including some of those executive functions we've already mentioned so far, such as cognitive inhibition. In this instance, James was unable to stop the urge to answer the phone, mainly because of the fear that the phone call would be that 'hand on the shoulder' moment, when he would be exposed as a rubbish scientist and be fired. This underlying fear meant that James's initial thought was, 'I need to answer the phone because that makes me look like a good employee!'

Arguably, the thought process *should* have been: 'I'm with the woman that I love, doing something that's actually quite fun, outside of normal working hours. I'll leave the phone for now.' Needless to say, this had a significant impact on Sam's self-esteem, and while many years later she can laugh at this story, there wasn't much laughter at the time (not after the phone call anyway).

Not having a robust system of prioritization has real-world consequences. In this case, those consequences weren't really related to work but were related to our relationship. Having a brain that cuts through any preconceived notions of what is 'important' and what 'should' be done and directs us to do something that feels urgent or important (but in reality, often isn't), makes building and maintaining a prioritization system challenging with ADHD.

This story also tells us that emotional barriers to prioritization are just as crucial as reward or executive dysfunction-based barriers. **If your brain senses anxiety or fear around a task, it'll probably direct you to do something else**, moving that task down the priority list. That fear can often leave Sam unable to make a simple phone call, such as calling her GP surgery to book an appointment, for months. And that can make us feel like we're not proper adults.

This chapter is about exactly that feeling. When everything (or nothing) feels important, and your brain either refuses to pick a lane, or picks one you don't want to be in, things can start to get messy.

James would like to add that he immediately regretted this course of action, but admits that, at the time, if it had happened the following day, he would absolutely have done it again.

What is prioritization?

Prioritization is a cornerstone of an 'effective personal and professional life', whatever that is. It is the mental process of assessing, organizing and then ranking our potential task-oriented activities. Often, this is based on our perception of specific properties of the task, such as its relative importance, urgency, difficulty, potential impact and many other factors.

The reason prioritization is so important is that its purpose is to ensure that the most critical and high-value tasks are addressed first. This optimizes the use of our limited mental resources, as well as time and energy. When you can prioritize well, which, let's be honest, is f*cking hard when you have ADHD, everything gets a little bit easier. You waste less energy doing the 'wrong' things and more of your effort actually *pays off.* That means finishing more stuff, stressing less about the chaos and maybe even remembering to eat lunch occasionally.

Prioritization helps you to focus on what *really matters*, not just what's shouting the loudest. In today's demanding society, the ability to prioritize effectively is not merely beneficial but often essential for success and well-being. Using your time and energy to complete the tasks that really *should* be tackled first is efficient and pragmatic.

Effective prioritization can also give you that rare but beautiful feeling of being on top of things, like you're steering the ship, not bailing out water with a teaspoon. And the knock-on effects are huge: better decisions, improved time management and fewer days lost to chasing your own tail.

But...when a prioritization system fizzles out or is forgotten, life can feel like trying to juggle knives during an earthquake. You may end up spreading yourself too thinly, missing deadlines, completing nothing properly and sinking into low-level panic, sometimes followed by absolute terror. You might find yourself putting way too much energy into the 'wrong' things, like answering every email immediately, jet-washing the drive, framing some pictures or randomly reorganizing your wardrobe, but avoiding the *one* task that matters. Or you might get trapped in firefighting mode, lurching from one crisis to the next with no idea if any of it actually matters.

And here's the deeper problem: if everything feels equally urgent (or equally unbearable), it's really hard to connect what you're doing today with where you want to be in six months, or six years, especially with time blindness. **And when your daily to-do list has nothing to do with your long-term goals or values, those tasks can have less purpose or importance in your brain, and work, or life in general, can start to feel pointless.** That's not just bad for productivity; it's bad for your well-being, motivation and sense of fulfilment.

So, how do people prioritize?

Most people, in general, tend to **prioritize based on two factors: urgency and importance** (and we've included this approach towards the end of this chapter). Urgency is all about time pressure. A task might be considered urgent if it:

- has a looming deadline
- involves someone waiting on you
- comes with immediate consequences if it's not done.

Urgent tasks demand attention *now*, regardless of their significance in the broader context. These are the classic 'squeaky wheel' tasks. And just as the saying 'The squeaky wheel gets the grease' goes, we will often deal with them above all else.

The second factor that is most used to help prioritize is importance. This, as we'll cover later, is where many people with ADHD hit a mental wall, because what does 'important' *actually* mean? It's contextual. Important to whom? Important why? In the context of prioritization, important *should* refer to the value or significance of a task in the long term. So, a task is important if it:

- contributes to a major goal
- aligns with your core values
- has a meaningful impact on outcomes (for you or others).

Unlike urgent tasks, important tasks often don't shout for attention. They sit quietly on the back burner... *until they become urgent.*

But here lies a trap: **urgent stuff gets your attention *right now,* but it's not always important. And the important stuff? That usually needs calm, consistent effort. The kind of effort that ADHD brains find harder to summon.**

How does the brain decide what to prioritize?

Biologically, the brain uses many of the same areas we've already mentioned to assess the urgency and importance of tasks, such as the prefrontal cortex, which is involved in managing the executive functions that allow us to prioritize: planning and organizing, holding important information in mind (working memory), inhibiting distractions or impulsive responses, and managing attention based on what matters most.

This is known as 'top-down attention', where **focus is directed towards goals rather than whatever catches your attention in the moment**. Prioritization depends heavily on this ability to stay focused on what's important, not just what's urgent or interesting.

Deeper in the brain, **the basal ganglia** regulate actions and habits, suppress unhelpful impulses and decide when to act and when to hold back. In the context of prioritization, this system **helps sort through options and push the right one into action**, rather than jumping to whatever feels easiest or most tempting.

The cerebellum works alongside these other brain areas to help with timing and rhythm, sustained effort and coordinating mental and physical actions. This **supports the timing side of prioritization**, like estimating how long something will take, or pacing your effort to get through a task without burning out.

And, importantly, the emotional aspects of prioritization are governed by the emotional areas of the brain, known as the limbic system. Your brain doesn't prioritize tasks in a vacuum. Emotion and motivation play a huge role, and that's where the limbic system comes in. This system contains the amygdala, which helps process emotional salience (how strongly you feel about something), and the hippocampus, which connects tasks with memories and emotional context. **If something feels boring, overwhelming or threatening, your limbic system may nudge you to avoid it, regardless of its importance.**

Lastly, alongside the brain areas, brain chemistry also plays a part. For these brain areas to work smoothly together, the right balance of brain chemicals is vital, especially dopamine and noradrenaline. **Dopamine supports motivation, reward processing and learning.** It helps you to stay interested in tasks and feel good when you make progress. **Noradrenaline helps with alertness, attention and filtering out distractions.** Both are crucial for keeping the brain areas needed for effective prioritization working at their best. If their levels or activity are too low, the system can start to crumble, like a house of cards built in the wind.

Why is prioritizing such a challenge in ADHD?

If what we've covered so far feels familiar, you're not alone. **Prioritization issues are one of the most common ADHD productivity traps**, often leading to 'reactivity' (responding instinctively to whatever feels most urgent or emotionally charged in the moment), rather than strategy (which involves stepping back, assessing options and making deliberate, goal-based choices). Learning how to spot what *really matters* (even if it's not shouting at you) is a skill worth building.

As **prioritizing tasks requires the brain to use its executive functions** and as **the brain in ADHD loves to disrupt executive function**, prioritizing life's day-to-day activities can sometimes feel like a 'mental assault course'. You might end up spending all your energy on the supposedly urgent but unimportant tasks (like replying to emails you could have ignored) and not enough on the slow-burning, life-changing stuff (like working on your side project, fixing your finances or finally going to therapy). This is usually not a conscious choice – it's driven by how our brains work – and yet it can still lead to shame, self-chastisement and criticism from others.

Prioritization is also a component of what psychologists call 'cognitive control'. **Cognitive control plays a key role in regulating our behaviour in response to changing environments and allows us to concentrate on 'actions despite distractions'** (which is so catchy it should be on a T-shirt).

It requires:

- **Goal setting:** Identifying which outcomes matter most.
- **Inhibition:** Resisting distractions or competing temptations.
- **Cognitive flexibility:** Adjusting your plan as new tasks emerge.

Maybe unsurprisingly, **there is robust evidence that cognitive control can be a common issue in ADHD.**[1] When the brain doesn't have 'typical' executive functions, most tasks, even simple ones, add up to build 'cognitive load'. Think of this like adding more and more weights to a barbell that your brain must lift. Studies have shown that **under high cognitive load, people are more likely to revert to habitual behaviours,**[2] which means that, without active prioritization, **we can default to doing what feels easiest or most familiar,** even if it's not the best use of our time.

Imagine you finally get home from work on a hot day, exhausted and sweaty, and all you want is a shower before you go out to meet friends. You head upstairs, grab the last clean towel and, just as you turn on the water, your phone rings. It's your boss with an important call you've been waiting for all week (this sounds familiar). You pause. Do you shower first and miss the call, or answer now and risk running out of time to shower?

Now imagine that as you're deciding, the smoke alarm starts beeping downstairs. You don't smell smoke, and it *could* be a battery issue...or something far more disastrous. Suddenly, your priorities shift again. Shower? Call? Check for fire?

This is what ADHD prioritization often feels like: you start with a plan ('I'll shower'), then something more interesting or urgent pops up ('The phone call!'), and then another thing hijacks your attention completely ('SMOKE. SOMEWHERE'). **Deciding what to do first isn't just difficult with ADHD; it can be *paralyzing*.** When *everything* feels urgent, the part of your brain that's supposed to filter and sort the tasks we need to engage with just throws its hands up and says, 'Mate, good luck. You're on your own.'

Why is the brain in ADHD less able to prioritize?

The brain systems involved in prioritization are the same for everyone. The difference for people with ADHD lies in how these systems work together and how efficiently they support processes such as decision-making, attention and motivation.

In ADHD brains:

- The **prefrontal cortex functions less efficiently** or shows weaker activity **during tasks that require focus and self-control.** This can mean:
  - Long-term goals feel less 'real' or motivating.
  - It's harder to filter distractions and stick with a chosen task.
  - You may jump into action on something urgent (or interesting) instead of what's important.

  When the prefrontal cortex is weaker, you're more likely to react to whatever's loudest, shiniest, or most stressful. In short, **urgency wins over strategy.**

- The **basal ganglia**, the group of smaller brain areas that help you start useful actions and stop unhelpful ones, **may be smaller or less connected to other brain regions.** This can cause 'signal errors' in the decision system, making it harder to:

  - Pause and think before acting.
  - Stick with a plan once it's made.
  - Avoid impulsively choosing easier or more stimulating tasks over what matters most.

  Imagine trying to drive through a busy junction where the lights don't quite work. Everything still functions, just not as smoothly or safely.

- **The cerebellum may not work optimally**, meaning you might:
  - Underestimate or misjudge how long things take.
  - Struggle to pace yourself across a task.
  - Feel restless or uncoordinated in how you start and stop tasks.

  That's part of why you might feel 'behind' before you've even begun or burn out quickly once you do begin.

- **The limbic system might be more reactive, and its communication with the prefrontal cortex can be disrupted**, meaning:
  - Boring or stressful tasks can feel unbearable, even if they're important.
  - Negative emotions like shame or overwhelm may derail your focus.
  - You might be drawn to tasks that feel rewarding right now, even if they don't serve long-term goals.

In other words, **emotion tends to drive decision-making more strongly in ADHD brains**, and that emotional 'filter' can warp our sense of what actually matters.

Add to this the **lack of typical dopamine and noradrenaline activity, important for prioritization**, and the whole system starts to glitch.

What this tells us is that, when people with ADHD choose the most novel or immediate option, it isn't about 'wanting' or 'choosing' to prioritize things that others might not see as a priority. It's that they are led **by a brain that itself doesn't quite understand what our options are and in what order we should approach them.**

It's a bit like trying to navigate a busy city using a satnav that only highlights the most exciting tourist attractions, not the quickest or most essential routes. You might *know* you need to get to the pharmacy before it closes, but your internal GPS keeps pointing you toward the shopping arcade or that café with massive doughnuts. It's not that you're ignoring the important task, it's that your navigation system is wired to prioritize novelty and dopamine, not deadlines and logic.

Prioritization also involves other thinking skills which are challenging in ADHD. **Time blindness** (covered in Chapter 10), which is an underappreciated but central aspect of ADHD, plays a part. If you **can't accurately judge how long something will take or how close a deadline really is, then, of course, you'll struggle to rank your tasks**. Everything is now. Everything is later. Everything is both.

Time blindness can be especially difficult if you also tend to have a positive illusory bias, which lots of us with ADHD do. This can lead us to misremember previous experiences with a positive bias. We can feel absolutely *certain* that we can *definitely* complete a task in five minutes *maximum*, even if that task almost always takes us a minimum of half an hour to complete. The combination of not being able to accurately judge how long something will take, even if you do that thing every day, along with a positive illusory bias, so that even if you're aware of how long it usually takes, 'this time will be different!' has repeatedly led to James thinking that he has enough time to have a poo four minutes before a meeting starts and then realizing, three minutes in, that he may have misjudged this AGAIN.

We haven't finished (yet). There are further aspects of how the brain works in ADHD that can make prioritization challenging. **Poor working memory can mean that we very quickly forget key information that can inform decisions around prioritization.** Issues with task initiation can mean that, even if we decide, 'I'll do that task first', **if it's not the right task, time or environment for your brain, it's more difficult to avoid defaulting to something rewarding.**

Common prioritization pitfalls in ADHD

Before we get into some practical prioritization tools, let's briefly acknowledge the traps we often fall into:

- **Urgency panic:** Reacting to the loudest alarm instead of the most important task.
- **Over-scheduling:** Filling every hour of the day without accounting for transitions, breaks, or unexpected events.
- **Positive illusory bias (or magical thinking):** Believing that tomorrow you will be a completely different person (one who finally 'has their act together' and is able to get shit done) or that *this time, it WILL be different.*

These pitfalls can feel insurmountable, but with the right strategy and tools for you, they can be avoided, even if just for some of the time.

Prioritization strategies that actually work (even if your brain is on fire)

As usual, we'll start by reminding you that **no single system works for everyone** and that it's OK to try something and for it to fail. We learn more from something failing than we do from it working the first time. So, if you want to improve your prioritization skills, pick one approach and try it out. Record how it goes. Adapt it to better suit you if you need to. There is no right or wrong route to developing new strategies.

Strategy 1: The 'master task list'

We really hate to roll out the tired old 'make a list' trope, but sadly, before you can decide what to do first, you need to know what you're choosing from.

That's where a master task list comes in (see Sam's version of this in Chapter 3). Think of it as the map before the route, or the brain-dump that stops your actual brain from exploding.

When everything lives in your head, your brain can become the list, constantly distracting you with thoughts of urgent things that need to be done, especially as you're trying to fall asleep, and that's a fast track to stress, forgetfulness and mental gridlock. A master task list is simply one central place where all your current tasks, ideas and obligations are stored. Its location might be a notebook, an app, a whiteboard or even a pile of sticky notes, whatever works for your brain. However, each of those methods has its obstacles (for example, keeping it on paper and forgetting to take it to the office will be...interesting). **This is why we usually recommend having a digital master task list, accessible from any devices you have, so that you know you can add to it, wherever you are, whenever your brain starts throwing up things that you need to get done.**

Without a master task list, prioritizing becomes a guessing game. You can forget tasks until they become urgent, important but non-urgent things can get lost in the fog, and your brain keeps holding everything in working memory, which is exhausting.

A master task list gives you a stable foundation to build on. A master task list isn't a daily to-do list (that comes after), something you need to check every five minutes, or a productivity shame list of everything you've failed to do. It's just your brain's external hard drive. Somewhere to store all those reminders that keep popping up in your brain. The beauty is: **once it's out of your head and on to the page (or screen), you're already halfway to making a plan.**

Sam also has a **master side-quests list**, where she lists things she enjoys doing, which might help to get her started, keep her motivated or give her a bit of energy when she needs it. This ranges from actual tasks that need doing that she finds rewarding or enjoyable, to random things that make her smile, feel good, stimulate her or help her to feel calm.

As we described in Chapter 3, she chooses three tasks from her master task list and three tasks/activities from her master side quest list for her daily to-do list. If she completes them all she chooses another three. You might just choose one, but she **really likes** the number three.

Deciding which of those tasks to choose first is where prioritization comes in and the following tools can help with this.

Strategy 2: The task matrix approach

One of the most useful prioritization tools available is the **Eisenhower matrix**, which may sound like a spy thriller but is actually a simple square grid. It can help you to sort your tasks by key factors. The most common combinations of factors used are urgency and importance, and impact and difficulty.

- **Urgent** = screaming at you (like deadlines, notifications or other people's panic)
- **Important** = actually matters (like your goals, health, relationships, values)

OR

- **Impact** = has a positive outcome for your personal goals or targets if completed
- **Difficulty** = the level of effort, time or cognitive load required to start and complete the task.

See our our online resources for an example of how to use the task matrix method (see p.343).

Strategy 3: The MoSCoW method

Another simple but powerful tool for deciding what to do (and what can wait) is the MoSCoW method. No, it's not Russian. It's an acronym that helps you sort your tasks into four categories:

- **Must have – absolutely essential:** Without this, things break, people shout or deadlines are missed.
- **Should have – important, but not critical:** Still worth doing – but maybe not right now.
- **Could have – nice to do, but low stakes:** Only attempt if you've got time, energy or a gap to fill.
- **Won't have (this time) – not happening today:** Maybe later. Maybe never. That's OK.

This method is great for ADHD brains because it cuts through the overwhelming 'I have to do everything right now' feeling and **gives you permission to not do things.**

The MoSCoW method is less about urgency or effort and more about scope. It helps you protect your time and energy by **identifying what's essential for today and what's not.** That can be a lifesaver if you're overwhelmed, exhausted or stuck in perfectionist mode.

It also creates a healthy boundary: some things won't happen today, and that's part of the plan, not a failure.

See our online resources for an example of how to use the MosCow method (see p.343).

Strategy 4: The ABCDE method

This system helps you quickly sort tasks by how important they really are and what can be either delegated or deleted entirely. It's especially helpful if you struggle to see the difference between 'I could do it' and 'I must do it'.

Here's how it works. Each task gets a letter:

- **A = Absolutely must do.** Critical to your goals, with serious consequences if ignored.
- **B = Should do.** Still important, but the world won't end if it's delayed.
- **C = Nice to do.** Feels productive but has no real consequences.
- **D = Delegate.** Someone else can (and probably should) do this.
- **E = Eliminate.** Doesn't matter. F*ck it off.

The golden rule? ***Never do a B task until your A tasks are done.*** This method forces you to zoom out and ask: 'Does this task actually matter?' It can be especially useful if you're drowning in small, low-value activities that crowd out the important stuff. The brain in ADHD often finds it hard to work out what's 'important enough', and the ABCDE framework can give that much-needed structure.

Each of these methods can inadvertently create a decision: **what if two options are equally urgent and important?** In this case, exploring the consequences of each choice can help nail down what to do first. **If there are more consequences to not doing one of a set of options that feel equally urgent or important, then start there. If there are no differences in the consequences of doing or not doing any competing tasks, then it doesn't matter which one is tackled first.** Toss a coin, pick one at random, and see how it feels to think: 'I'm starting here.'

For an example of how to use the ABCDE method, go to our online resources (see p.343).

Strategy 5: Use AI to help you prioritize

When your brain is convinced that everything is urgent, or equally unbearable, AI can be a genuinely useful sidekick (with the usual caveats mentioned in previous chapters). It's not going to fix your executive dysfunction, but it can help you make sense of the chaos, especially when prioritizing feels like trying to herd fog.

Think of AI tools (like ChatGPT, Microsoft CoPilot, or Google Gemini) as a non-judgemental thought partner: someone who won't roll their eyes when you say, 'I have 20 things to do and no idea which one to start with.'

AI can help with prioritization in many ways:

- **Turn a mess into a plan:** If you dump your full task list into an AI and say, 'Can you help me figure out what I should do first?', it can categorize tasks by urgency, importance or impact. Even seeing things grouped that way can help break the decision gridlock.

Try: 'Here's my task list. Help me prioritize using an Urgency–Importance matrix.'

- **Build a daily plan from your master task list:** If you've created a master task list (go you!), but feel stuck turning it into a daily list, AI can help.

Try: 'Based on this list, suggest 3–5 tasks to focus on today. Make sure they're a mix of short wins and high-value tasks.'

- **Add time estimates or flag hidden difficulty:** AI can estimate how long tasks might take, or point out which ones will drain your energy, even if they sound easy.

Try: 'Which of these tasks are likely to be most mentally tiring or time-consuming?'

- **Create a decision framework:** Feeling stuck between two equally urgent tasks? Ask AI to walk you through the potential consequences, impact or required effort of each.

Try: 'Help me choose between finishing a grant application and replying to 30 urgent emails. Which should I do first and why?'

- **Tailor your approach to your energy:** Some days you can Eisenhower like a champ. On other days, you need the ADHD version of flipping a coin. AI can adapt.

Try: 'Help me use the MoSCoW method to sort this list, but I'm low on energy and motivation today.'

Strategy 6: The traffic light system

This is a simple way of prioritizing tasks. Once you have your master task list, go through it and colour code each task (you can highlight them or move them into coloured or labelled boxes, whatever works for you) depending on priority:

Red:	These are the highest priority tasks, urgent tasks that need to be done immediately.
Amber:	These are medium priority tasks, still important but not urgent *quite yet* (but could be very soon).
Green:	These are low priority, not important, not urgent.

Theoretically you should do the red tasks first, then the amber, then the green. But you could sandwich amber and green tasks that you know you will find enjoyable in between red tasks to help keep you motivated.

Strategy 7: Just choose one

Now, this one may feel like a cop-out, but it can help. If sorting all your tasks is too big an ask right now, scan through your tasks and mentally or physically highlight the ones that will have the most impact, or the smaller steps that will move you towards a bigger goal, or the most urgent and important ones and **pick one to do now**. You can choose one at random, or number them and roll a die, or get AI to choose one for you – whatever works best for you.

If that's too much, just choose one task that you'd be happy doing first and do that one. Once you get started you might be able to do more, or you might not. Doing *something* is better than doing *nothing*, so just do what you can, when you can, and don't beat yourself up too much if you can't do much today. Just try again tomorrow.

Strategy 8: Two-minute win

Another one for when you're struggling, because we all have those days when our brains refuse to cooperate. Choose a two-minute win like:

- **Send an unblocking email:** Is there a task you haven't been able to start because the instructions were unclear, or you need a decision or action from someone else? Send the email that could help you to unblock that task. If you're stuck on how to word the email, get AI to help.
- **Take a tiny first step:** Was there a task on your mind last night that stopped you from getting to sleep? What is the first teeny tiny step you could take towards getting that task done? Take it.
- **Do the smallest possible action that could make another task easier:** It could be opening a document, organizing some files, clearing dirty plates or rubbish off your desk (or is that just us?), washing one dirty mug, comparing calendars to find time for a meeting, creating a template for a task or email, whatever you can bear to do *right now* that could make a bigger task easier to do in the future.

Once you've done your two-minute win, celebrate! You did it! Can you do another? If so, great! If not, try again later.

We've now seen different ways to tackle a pile of tasks: by urgency, importance, impact, difficulty, or whether they even deserve your time at all. And each system can give you different answers.

A task that's low urgency might still be high impact. Something that feels 'nice to do' might eat up half your day. Depending on how your energy, mood and brain chemistry are behaving, a different method might work better on a different day.

And that's OK. You're not doing it wrong.

What matters most is **finding an approach that works with your brain, not against it.**

Importantly, abandoning the method halfway through and starting again tomorrow is also valid. **Progress, not perfect prioritization is the aim at this stage.**

Ultimately, these frameworks are just tools, not rules. **The goal isn't to get it perfect. The goal is to get moving. Even deciding what not to do is a form of progress.** So, try them out. Tweak them. Forget them and come back later. The point is not to obey a method, it's to make space in your brain so you can do the stuff that matters to you.

Chapter summary

This chapter explored why prioritizing is so hard, what's going on in the brain when we try (and sometimes fail) to do it, and how to start building a system that works for you.

We covered:

- What prioritization actually is – deciding what to do first, not just what to do eventually.
- Why it's hard with ADHD – thanks to time blindness, poor working memory, emotional interference and a brain wired for urgency and novelty.

- The role of the brain – including the prefrontal cortex, basal ganglia, cerebellum and limbic system, plus the dopamine and noradrenaline chemistry so crucial to task management.
- Common traps – like urgency panic and believing your future self will somehow be a different person.
- The master task list – because your brain was never meant to hold it all.
- Four practical tools you can try: the Eisenhower Matrix (Urgent vs Important, when you are up against a deadline or Impact vs Difficulty when energy is low); the MoSCoW Method (helps when you're overwhelmed); the ABCDE Method (good for cutting the crap); the traffic light system.
- Alternately, if you are overwhelmed, just choose one task or take a tiny first step for a two-minute win.

Most importantly, we reminded you that:

- There's no perfect system.
- Some methods won't work (or won't work today), and that's OK.
- Just making a decision, even to do one thing, is progress.

You don't need to get it all right. You just need to start somewhere.

And if the first fire you put out turns out to be a scented candle? It's still a win.

Chapter 7

TACKLING PROCRASTINATION

Or why you're vacuuming instead of emailing your boss

Procrastination is a huge issue for Sam, and writing this book was a big reminder of this! James is magically able to just sit and write chapters from scratch, whereas Sam's brain tried to avoid writing at all costs, even though it was really enjoyable when they actually managed to get down to it. Sam is someone who is always doing something, so procrastination for them almost always involves them keeping themselves busy doing anything other than the actual thing they're supposed to be doing and, in a lot of cases, it's usually a much worse option than the one they are avoiding. They took a week off work on three occasions so that they could get their bits of the book done.

The first week, they managed to do their tax return (something they *really hate* doing! This was *not* a fun day), they started reorganizing all of their clothes drawers, but a couple of them were broken, so they went to fetch some tools, but ended up moving things around in the garage instead. Then, before they finished this, they went to put something in the shed, saw their gardening gear and started mowing the lawn, but the mower ran out of battery, so they went inside to charge it, and the drawer that the charger was in was such a mess! So, they started tidying the drawer but they felt crumbs under their feet, which nearly sent them over the edge, so they went to get the vacuum cleaner, saw all the dishes in the sink and couldn't cope with that, so started emptying the dishwasher so that they could then refill it...We could carry on, but we think you probably get the idea! Before they realized what was happening, there were part-finished projects going on everywhere they looked, inside and outside of the house, and they still hadn't managed to get any writing done.

The second week was similar and they realized on the second day of the third week that their brain still thought that it would be completely fine to do all their writing the day before the deadline, despite the fact that they had never written a book before and had never in their life managed to produce a written piece of work, like an essay, in one sitting. The positive illusory bias was strong!

They finally managed to push themselves further and further into crisis mode as the third week progressed and obviously – because you are reading this book – managed to finish eventually, although the AuDHD chapter had to be trimmed down considerably from the 12,000 words they initially wrote! In the process, they realized that some parts of their procrastination were actually useful. They saw that were putting themselves under a lot of emotional pressure. They had never written a book before, so it was a big deal to them, and they wanted to get it right. So, they kept delaying getting started because they were afraid they would get it wrong. That part wasn't useful (!) but the thinking they did during the procrastination was, so during the final week they used their procrastination time to give themselves space to think, when needed, while they were doing something else. Of course, they now swear that if they ever do this again...next time will be different! Will it actually be though? Probably not!

Procrastination: everyone does it

Let's be honest, everyone procrastinates. Whether it's leaving laundry until the only clean thing you have left is a Halloween costume, or dodging an awkward conversation by suddenly deciding the fridge must be cleaned, **humans are built to avoid discomfort and chase reward**. Delaying tasks is a universal habit, and around 95 per cent of us do it sometimes. But for people with ADHD, procrastination isn't just an occasional bad habit. It can be a daily battle.

Some of you might actively procrastinate because it's become a part of your process for getting things done and it works for you. If so, great! This chapter probably isn't for you. This chapter is about the kind of procrastination that doesn't just make you miss a deadline but makes you question your entire ability to function. It's the email you still haven't replied to after three months, the project that's too big to start, the admin task that somehow feels emotionally radioactive.

The infamous **'intention–action' gap is where procrastination lives**. And for many of us, it's also where guilt, shame and anxiety start.

What is procrastination, really?

Before we can tackle procrastination, we need to get clear on what it actually is and what it isn't. It's not just bad time management. It's not that you can't be bothered. And it's not fixed by colour-coding a to-do list and hoping for the best.

Psychologists define procrastination as voluntarily delaying something important that you intended to do, even though you know the delay will make things worse. This isn't about waiting for the right moment; **it's about putting things off in a way that hurts and doing it anyway.**

That definition matters, because it helps us separate procrastination from things that might look similar on the surface but are driven by very different brain processes.

Let's break it down.

1. It's a delay driven from within

No one's stopping you. You've got the time, the tools and even the intention. But you're still not doing the thing. You want to reply to that email, submit that form, start that project...but somehow, you just don't.

That's different from external delays (like waiting for someone else's input) or healthy postponement (like deciding to sleep on a decision so you can think clearly).

2. You actually want to do the task

We're not talking about things you never meant to do in the first place. This is stuff that matters to you, maybe even deeply. This is not the stuff you're avoiding because you don't care. Quite the opposite. **You care so much that it's emotionally hard to start.**

That's one of the biggest differences between procrastination and laziness. **A lazy person might not be bothered either way, but a procrastinator is often in emotional agony about the thing they're not doing.**

3. You know it's going to backfire

Procrastination is irrational but not because you're unaware of the consequences. You are aware, often painfully so. That awareness often adds a layer of shame or guilt to the delay, creating an emotional loop where avoidance becomes even more likely.

> **Procrastination is a failure of self-regulation, not of values or willpower.**
>
> **You're not avoiding the task because you don't want to succeed.**
>
> **You're avoiding the feelings that come up when you try.**

So, what isn't procrastination?

- **It's not prioritizing.** Choosing to do one important thing before another is just good planning. Procrastination is when you skip both and scroll Instagram instead.
- **It's not a strategic delay.** Sometimes waiting is wise, like holding

off until you get a key bit of info. That's not procrastination. That's preparation.

- **It's not laziness.** Laziness implies indifference. **Procrastination is active avoidance of something that we know is important by choosing to do something else, often something easier or more rewarding in the short term.**

The most painful part of procrastination isn't the task you're not doing. It's the mental battle playing out in the background. You *should* be doing the thing. You *want to be* doing the thing. But you just...aren't.

And that internal conflict? That's where the guilt, anxiety and frustration come from. Procrastination doesn't feel like switching off. It feels like being stuck in your own head with the volume cranked up.

Emotions alone can stop us from doing the thing

One of the biggest shifts in how psychologists understand procrastination is this: **it's not really about poor time management. It's about managing emotions.**

More specifically, **procrastination is often a short-term strategy for feeling better, not a character flaw**. When we put off a task, we're usually trying to avoid the way it makes us feel, not the task itself.

Think about a task you've been dodging. Maybe it's boring. Maybe it's confusing. Maybe it feels loaded with pressure, or like a trap waiting for you to fail. **Those uncomfortable feelings of boredom, anxiety, frustration and self-doubt are the real problem.**

And **your brain, like all brains, doesn't enjoy discomfort. So, it finds a way out.** It offers you a quick dopamine boost: scroll your phone, tidy the kitchen, rewatch that one YouTube clip again. **Suddenly, the pressure's gone. You feel better...for now.**

This is what researchers call 'mood repair'. You're not avoiding the task because you're lazy. You're avoiding the emotion it brings up. And that temporary relief? It's powerful. So, your brain learns: that worked, let's do it again next time!

The problem with 'feeling better'

That little boost is short-lived. The task is still there. And now, you feel even worse because you still haven't done it. Welcome to the cycle:

Stress > avoid task > brief relief > guilt >
more stress > even harder to start

Over time, this can build up into a crushing loop. Studies show that procrastinators might feel better at first, but as the deadline looms, their stress, anxiety and shame can skyrocket. And this stress can affect their sleep, health and self-esteem.

The worst part? **The more you avoid something, the more emotionally charged it can become.** What was once a mildly annoying chore can become a mountain of shame and fear. So, you avoid it more. The cycle feeds itself.

This isn't a failure of logic; you know you need to do the thing. **It's a clash between two parts of your brain:**

- **The limbic system** (your 'emotional brain') wants to feel good right now.
- **The prefrontal cortex** (your 'planner brain') knows about deadlines and goals and long-term consequences.

When procrastination happens, the emotional brain wins, not because of weakness, but because emotional discomfort is hard to sit with.

The psychological drivers of procrastination

The urge to procrastinate is not random. It is reliably triggered by specific psychological factors and task characteristics. These drivers create the negative emotional states that individuals seek to escape through delay.

1. Task aversion

At the most basic level, **people are highly likely to procrastinate on tasks they find overwhelming, daunting or unattractive**. Research has identified six key attributes that make a task a prime candidate for procrastination. Tasks might be perceived as:

- boring
- frustrating
- difficult
- unstructured or ambiguous
- lacking in personal meaning
- or lacking in intrinsic rewards (i.e. it is not fun or engaging).

The more of these qualities a task possesses, the stronger our impulse to postpone it. It is important to note that our 'aversion' might not necessarily be to the work itself – in fact we might really want to do this work – but to the negative feelings we think it will provoke. Often that fear is massively exaggerated (ever found a task surprisingly interesting once you are underway?) but in procrastination terms, the damage is done because the psychological barriers/ emotional resistance feel insurmountable.

2. Fear-based avoidance (fear of failure, criticism and success)
Fear is a potent driver of procrastination. A deep-seated fear of failure, of not meeting expectations, of being judged negatively or of being criticized, can be psychologically paralyzing. In this context, the task itself becomes a threat, representing a potential public or private confirmation of one's perceived inadequacies. To avoid this painful possibility, the individual avoids the task altogether.

This dynamic often leads to self-handicapping, a key psychological insight into the behaviour. **By procrastinating, an individual creates a ready-made excuse for potential poor performance.** If they fail after rushing at the last minute, they can attribute the outcome to a lack of time or effort rather than a lack of ability, thus protecting their fragile self-esteem.

Less commonly discussed but still relevant is the **fear of success. Achieving a goal can establish a new, higher standard of performance, creating an ongoing pressure to maintain that level of success.** The anxiety associated with this new expectation can, paradoxically, lead to procrastination as a way to avoid the burden of future success.

3. The perfectionism–procrastination paradox

Perfectionism, covered in Chapter 12, far from being a driver of timely, high-quality work, **is one of the most significant causes of chronic procrastination**. This connection creates a destructive and self-perpetuating cycle. The perfectionist sets unrealistically high, often unattainable, standards for their performance. **The immense pressure to meet these impossible standards generates intense anxiety and a profound fear of failure, which in turn triggers the emotional-avoidance response of procrastination.**

The delay can lead to a frantic, last-minute effort, which can result in work that is rushed and subpar. This outcome can then reinforce the perfectionist's core belief of inadequacy, fuelling the perceived need for even more stringent, flawless standards on the next task, thus locking them into the loop.

This paradox is maintained by cognitive distortions, particularly all-or-nothing thinking (also known as **dichotomous or 'flourish or fail' thinking**). In this mindset, **an outcome is either absolutely perfect or a complete failure; there is no middle ground for good enough.** The very concept of submitting work that is simply complete but flawed is anathema to the perfectionist, making avoidance seem like the only safe option.

4. Analysis paralysis and decisional procrastination

Procrastination is not always about avoiding a specific task. Sometimes it is about avoiding the decision of what task to do. **Analysis paralysis (or choice paralysis) describes a state of cognitive and emotional shutdown that occurs when an individual is faced with too many options or a particularly weighty decision.** The process of overthinking and overanalysing every possibility can become so overwhelming that it can lead to a state of inaction or stuckness.

This paralysis is often triggered by a fear of making the wrong choice, which connects directly back to the drivers of perfectionism and fear of failure. The perceived stakes of the decision can be so high that the mental load required to evaluate all options and potential outcomes becomes excessive. This can lead to **decisional procrastination**, where the inability to decide which path to take results in taking no path at all. **The individual avoids the anxiety of the decision by postponing it indefinitely.**

What procrastination does to productivity (spoiler, it's not great)

When procrastination becomes a pattern, not just a one-off, it can start to take a serious toll on your ability to get stuff done. Not just on paper, but in real-life consequences: missed deadlines, last-minute chaos and the creeping dread of being written off as 'the unreliable one'.

Whether you're a student, a freelancer, or managing a team of people who all think you have it together, **chronic procrastination can quietly wreck your performance**. Tasks get left until the last possible moment, which usually means they're done in a panic, rushed, error-prone and rarely your best work.

In workplaces, this can ripple outward:

- Colleagues might have to pick up the slack.
- Trust gets eroded (will they actually deliver this time?).

- Group projects or shared goals fall behind.
- Morale tanks – yours and everyone else's.

And long term? **Chronic procrastination doesn't just stop you from being productive now, it can stall your career.** You might avoid taking on more challenging (and rewarding) work, miss opportunities to learn new skills, or stay stuck in survival mode instead of growing. It's exhausting, demoralizing and a recipe for burnout.

But I work better under pressure! (Do you, though?)

Lots of people with ADHD say they need pressure to get started. That looming deadline triggers a cortisol-dopamine cocktail that finally gets you moving. **This idea is sometimes called active procrastination, delaying on purpose because you believe you'll perform better in a time crunch.**

But while a bit of deadline stress can sharpen focus for some people, the research is clear: **genuine procrastination generally leads to worse performance, not better**. Creativity doesn't flourish under panic. Details can get missed, and the emotional toll (guilt, self-criticism, anxiety) isn't exactly a motivational masterclass.

The busy loophole: when having too much to do actually helps

This bit is weirdly hopeful. Some studies show that **being busy can reduce procrastination in certain situations**, particularly after you've already missed a deadline.

Why? **Because of how we explain failure to ourselves.**

If you miss a deadline and you've only had one task to do, it's easy to think, 'I'm lazy. I'm just shit.' That internal shame spiral makes it even harder to re-engage.

But if you've got loads on your plate, your brain can say, 'Well, I've been swamped. No wonder that didn't get done.' **That external reason softens the shame and makes it easier to get back on track.**

This doesn't mean you should overload yourself to avoid guilt; that's just another route to burnout. However, it does demonstrate the power of self-talk and self-compassion.

Blaming yourself fuels avoidance. Giving yourself grace can open the door to getting started again.

ADHD and procrastination: it's not just putting things off

We've talked about how procrastination happens for most people, as a mix of emotional avoidance, faulty thinking and the lure of short-term rewards. But in ADHD, procrastination is something deeper, harder to shift and often more painful.

For adults with ADHD, procrastination is baked in. Not because of laziness or a broken moral compass but because of how the ADHD brain is wired. As we have already discussed, **differences in brain structure, function and chemistry mean that the systems responsible for getting started just don't work the same way**. So, while the outcome might look similar from the outside (why haven't you done it yet?), what's going on under the hood is very different.

Let's look at this in more detail.

Feature	General procrastination (neurotypical)	ADHD-driven procrastination
Root cause	Learned habit of avoiding discomfort or effort	Hardwired differences in brain function, especially in the prefrontal cortex and dopamine system
Emotional experience	Guilt, mild anxiety or stress about unfinished tasks	Overwhelm, shame, panic and sometimes a total mental shutdown (ADHD paralysis)
Mental effort	Often involves choosing to avoid a task	Involves fighting internal resistance with exhausting effort and often losing the fight
Time perception	Prone to underestimating time or over-relying on pressure	Experiences time blindness, struggles to *feel* the future or prioritize in real time
Thinking patterns	Perfectionism, waiting for the right mood, short-term reward-seeking	All of the above, plus dopamine dysfunction makes future rewards feel irrelevant

In short, procrastination in ADHD is not always helped by standard time-management advice. **This kind of procrastination is a neuro-biological issue**, one that can't be out-organized or tough-loved into submission.

Understanding this shift is key. It means **the solutions** need to go beyond colour-coded planners and motivational quotes. They **need to include support for emotional overwhelm, tools for executive dysfunction and, for many people, treatment that targets the brain's chemistry itself.**

Why procrastination hits hard in ADHD

We've mentioned executive dysfunction so much now (especially in Chapter 1), you probably know more about it than we do. In ADHD, these mental skills don't work as they should, which makes procrastination a daily struggle rather than an occasional hiccup. Issues with ***planning, prioritizing and organization, task initiation, working memory, time blindness, motivation and emotional regulation*** together create a perfect storm:

> Starting the task feels bad > a more fun option appears > impulse wins > you feel better (for now) > you forget you intended to work on the task > you procrastinate.

In addition, two potent emotional states, **overwhelm and task aversion**, frequently trigger procrastination in the ADHD population.

Overwhelm: The subjective experience of being overwhelmed is a common and powerful precursor to all procrastination, but in ADHD often leads to a state of **'ADHD paralysis'**. This feeling can be **triggered by the perceived size or complexity of a task, the sheer number of competing responsibilities or ambiguity about how to proceed.** For an individual whose executive function deficits already make planning and task decomposition exceptionally difficult, the prospect of tackling a large or ill-defined project can frequently seem too daunting and emotionally loaded to begin.

Task aversion: While we might all feel a degree of task aversion when faced with **tasks that are boring, tedious, repetitive, overly challenging or lacking in personal meaning**, if you have ADHD there's an additional factor. To the ADHD brain, tasks that fail to provide adequate stimulation or reward **can feel almost physically uncomfortable or even painful to endure**. In this situation, **procrastination**, which often involves shifting to a more novel or stimulating activity, **kicks the emotional can down the road so we don't have to deal with it now, providing immediate relief.** This relief powerfully reinforces the avoidance behaviour through negative reinforcement, making it more likely to occur in the future.

If you add to this the toxic cocktail of anxiety, fear of failure and perfectionism, you create the optimum conditions for ADHD procrastination to flourish.

The ADHD procrastination ripple effect

Chronic procrastination in ADHD isn't just annoying, it is one of the biggest reasons adults with ADHD struggle in daily life.

Procrastination at work or in education leads to missed deadlines, last-minute scrambles, lower performance and a reputation for being unreliable. In the home and relationships, delaying chores, errands and paying bills creates chaos and financial strain. In relationships, forgotten plans and broken promises are often seen as carelessness, leading to conflict, resentment and loneliness. Repeated failures to follow through chip away at confidence and self-worth. **Guilt, shame and harsh self-judgment set in, fuelling anxiety and depression and making procrastination even harder to escape.**

Studies show that higher ADHD symptoms and more procrastination are strongly linked to a lower quality of life, including worse sleep,[1] poor self-care[2] and even greater risk of substance misuse.[3] **Procrastination isn't a side issue, it's central to how ADHD affects adult life. Tackling it can unlock real improvements in health, functioning and happiness.**

Strategies to tackle procrastination

Procrastination with ADHD is often about overwhelm, emotional discomfort, or a brain that struggles to translate intention into action. Making a start helps. Here are some ADHD-friendly strategies to reduce the friction and get things moving.

Strategy 1: Break tasks down to reduce overwhelm

Big, vague tasks can feel overwhelming and overwhelm shuts down initiation. Breaking a task into tiny, concrete steps makes it more doable and gives your brain a quick dopamine hit for each step completed. **Procrastination often occurs when *starting* feels harder than *not starting*.** Making it easier to start than to avoid can flip this by reducing the friction of beginning.

Instead of 'Write the report', try:

- 'Turn laptop on', then

- 'Open the document', then
- 'Write the title', then
- 'Draft bullet points'.

Keep each step small enough that it feels like no big deal and cross things off as you go. It reinforces progress.

There is a 'Break it down' exercise in our online resources (see p.343).

Strategy 2: Shrink the commitment

A little like breaking tasks down, 'shrinking the commitment' can help with starting, which (if we're lucky) can actually lead to finishing! We often avoid tasks because they feel endless or impossible. Telling yourself **'just five minutes' can lower the psychological barrier** and activate the brain's reward loop once you get going.

How to try it:

- Set a 5-minute timer and agree you can stop when it's done.
- Tell yourself, 'I'm just going to do five minutes. That's it.' The goal isn't to finish, it's to begin. Once the timer ends, you can stop guilt free... but often you'll find the hardest part (starting) is already over.
- Use 'just one thing' lists.
- Instead of writing 15 overwhelming tasks, write just one. One email. One plate washed. One phone call. Your brain sees it as doable and once you tick it off the reward loop kicks in.
- Celebrate the micro-win: tick a box, say 'nailed it', do a little dance, or tell someone. Tiny celebrations can help to retrain your brain to associate starting with something positive, and that can make it easier next time.

- Have a *second* 5-minute task ready if you're in flow.
- You don't have to plan on doing more, but if the dopamine hits and you're rolling, ride the wave. Just don't make it the expectation. The real win is starting, not grinding.

Strategy 3: Add accountability (when internal motivation is unreliable)

Many of us don't feel enough pressure when working alone. Our brains don't always register internal deadlines as real or urgent, especially when a task feels boring, overwhelming or emotionally loaded. But **involving another person, even just passively, can create the right amount of just-start-it energy.**

Sometimes, this can feel a little embarrassing. But it's not about being watched or shamed, it's about feeling supported, seen and slightly more responsible for following through. A little external accountability can spark just enough urgency to help you get started and stay on track.

How to try it:

- **Accountability partners:** Share your goals or progress with someone you trust: a friend, coach, partner, colleague or online buddy. Tell them what you're working on and ask them to check in at a specific time. Knowing someone's expecting an update can make a huge difference.
- **Body doubling:** This ADHD-favourite strategy (see more in Chapter 5) involves working alongside another person while you both do your own thing. It can be in person, over video call, or in

a virtual body-double group. You don't even need to talk, just the quiet presence of someone else can help to lower the emotional weight of starting and create a sense of structure and calm.

It works best when you:

- Say out loud (or type) what you're about to do.
- Start at the same time as your body double.
- Check in afterwards, even briefly.

If your brain resists doing the task itself, start by setting up the body double or sending a check-in message. Often, just that one action can get things moving.

Strategy 4: Workspace optimization

Your environment can either support your focus or sabotage it completely. With ADHD, external clutter provides enough internal noise to become a barrier to making a start. A well-structured, low-distraction space doesn't have to be Pinterest-perfect, it just has to **reduce the number of things competing for your brain's limited focus fuel so you can begin**. See Chapter 8 for more strategies on how you can tame your environment.

Strategy 5: Identify the emotions

Sometimes it's not the task that's the problem; it's how the task makes you feel. Many ADHDers procrastinate not because they're disorganized or forgetful, but because the task stirs up discomfort: fear of failure, shame, perfectionism, boredom, or feeling overwhelmed.

If we don't spot those emotions, we can end up trying to solve the wrong problem (like making another to-do list when what we really need is a moment of self-compassion). This can be difficult for those of us with alexithymia (difficulty identifying, understanding and describing emotions), but if you can, you might try the following:

- **Pause and ask: 'What am I feeling about this task?':** Are you anxious you'll get it wrong? Embarrassed you've left it too long? Annoyed you even have to do it? This one-minute pause can surface what's actually going on underneath the delay.
- **Name it to tame it:** Putting your feelings into words – 'I'm scared I'll mess it up' or 'I feel guilty for leaving it so long' – can activate the thinking brain and reduce the emotional sting. You don't have to fix the feeling right away. Just recognizing it can make it easier to work with your brain instead of against it.
- **Try a compassionate internal script:** When you catch yourself avoiding something, pause and say (in your head or out loud): 'This is hard because it feels [*insert emotion*], not because I'm lazy. It's OK to feel that way, and I can still take one small step.'
- **Ask yourself: 'What would make this feel safer to start?'** That might be giving yourself permission to do a rough first draft, or simply naming the discomfort out loud.

If you've got a backlog of avoided tasks, don't just organize them, empathize with yourself about them. Understanding the why can help to unstick the how.

Chapter summary

Procrastination is often mistaken for laziness or bad time management, but for adults with ADHD, it's something deeper: a neurobiological and emotional barrier that makes starting and finishing tasks incredibly difficult.

This chapter explored:

- why we avoid the things we actually want to do
- how procrastination becomes a loop of guilt and anxiety
- why typical advice like 'just get organized' doesn't work for ADHD brains.

We unpacked the emotional drivers behind procrastination, including fear of failure (and success), perfectionism, overwhelm and task aversion, and showed how they interact with core ADHD traits like time blindness, executive dysfunction and motivation issues. We also examined the toll this takes across every part of life, from work and relationships to health and self-worth.

But there's hope. Tackling ADHD-driven procrastination is about working with your brain, not against it. Strategies like task breakdown and external accountability, when paired with emotional tools like mindfulness and self-compassion, can help to break the cycle of avoidance and make forward movement possible, even if it's just one small step at a time.

Chapter 8

MANAGING DISTRACTIBILITY

Focus, filters and fidgeting

It's difficult to think of a time when either of us has not been distractible, but for James academia was a tornado of distractions. Even with a bold, laminated 'Do Not Disturb' sign on his locked office door, people came, saw and distracted him. The sign might as well have said, 'Please knock and ask if I've got a minute.' People did. Constantly. Students. Colleagues. Even other academics who were technically supposed to be in their own offices, doing their own work. The result? A workday punctuated by interruptions that felt urgent to them but utterly derailed him.

It wasn't just the people, of course. There was also the endless ping of emails and instant messages (all of which were, of course, catastrophically urgent to the sender), the flickering of Twitter (back when it was still Twitter) and the panicked awareness that somewhere in the building, biscuits were being eaten without him.

Back then, James would tell himself he was 'multitasking' or 'being responsive'. What he was actually doing was task-switching himself into exhaustion. ADHD doesn't come with an internal PA to tell you when to say, 'Not now.' So, if someone knocked, he beckoned them to come in. If a thought popped up, he followed it. If an email notification popped up...you get the idea.

Now, self-employed and mostly working from home, the distractions look different, but they're still there. James will start writing, pop downstairs to grab a drink, notice the dishwasher wasn't emptied from the previous night, empty it, reload it before spotting several dirty mugs he didn't add to the load, see a delivery van drive park outside and stand frozen thinking, 'What have I bought now?' and then spend 20 minutes Googling whether his afternoon crash is caused by dehydration or existential dread. The email? Still half-written. The drink? Never even poured.

Sometimes, the consequences are low stakes (a delayed reply). Sometimes, not so much, like the time he drove to the wrong university to give a talk, having confused Surrey with Sussex in a rush of 'I'll just whack it into the satnav.' Or the time he missed a flight entirely because he, Sam and a friend were distracted by the baguettes in the departure lounge restaurant.

Distraction can also show up in less amusing ways. Such as in mid-conversation, when James picks up his phone to check something he swears is relevant...only to completely miss what Sam just said, which can make him look like he's not interested. (He's working on it.)

What helps? Sometimes, a clean digital landscape. The phone is on silent. Notifications are off. Email apps are closed. Working early in the morning, before the world wakes up and starts waving shiny things in his face, was a game-changer. As were noise-cancelling headphones – at least the sixth pair he bought, as he'd lost the previous five (which of course he found as soon as the sixth pair arrived).

But even with all of that, distraction still happens. That's not a failure. That's ADHD. **The goal isn't perfect focus, it's enough focus, directed in the intended direction, for long enough to get through the important bits.** Some days, that means deep work. Some days, it means answering two emails and remembering to eat lunch. And honestly, sometimes that's good enough.

Filtering out what is and isn't important

Imagine your brain has a bouncer at the door, keeping out irrelevant thoughts and noises. When the bouncer is doing their job, maintaining focus is easier. When they step away for a bit, random customers (or in this case, distractions) can, and do, get in. The frontoparietal network, including the brain areas covered later in this chapter, effectively works as that bouncer, managing the constant distractions trying to get in order to allow your brain to focus.

Neuroscience helps us to understand distractibility as being more than just 'not paying attention'. It's really about the brain struggling to hold on to the information we need in the moment, like what we're doing, why we're doing it and what comes next. **When distractions strike, they don't just gently tug us off task. They actively mess with our executive functions, especially working memory and self-control.**

Distractions tend to fall into three categories:

- **Visual:** Something catches your eye, and suddenly you're looking at your phone instead of a spreadsheet.
- **Manual:** You take your hands 'off the task', like reaching for your phone while mid-conversation.
- **Mental:** Your mind drifts off, even if your eyes and hands are still doing the thing.

The trickiest one? Mental distraction. You can spot someone looking at their phone or fiddling with a pen, but it's much harder to notice when someone (or you) is mentally a million miles away. To make things more complex, **visual and manual distractions usually come with a side order of cognitive distraction, too. If your hands or eyes leave the task, your brain probably already has too.**

Distractibility, or the tendency to be pulled 'off task' by internal or external stimuli, is a universal common human experience, not just an ADHD trait. People can differ substantially in their vulnerability to distraction, and situation, environment and emotions all play a part, but most people struggle to maintain focus at times, especially in our overstimulating, digital-first environments.

How the brain regulates attention

If you've ever felt like your attention has a mind of its own...well, you're not wrong. It turns out **attention isn't managed by one single part of the brain** – there's no 'focus button' hiding somewhere in your head. Instead, **attention comes from several large-scale brain networks working together** (and sometimes arguing with each other). These brain areas work to maintain attention by filtering out distractions when they arise.

Ready for some boring (though not for James) neuroscience? Let's meet those brain areas.

First up is the **dorsal attention network (DAN)**, which is a little bit like your brain's taskmaster. **The DAN is in charge when you decide to focus on something**, like trying to read this book without checking your phone. We talked about 'top-down' attention in Chapter 6: when you choose a goal and pursue it. **The DAN helps your brain aim at it like a spotlight.**

The key parts of this network sit around the top and sides of your brain, including areas called the intraparietal sulcus and frontal eye fields (don't worry, there's no test, remember). **The DAN works to keep your attention on the task and to filter out distractions.** Well, at least it tries to.

Next, we have the **ventral attention network (VAN)** and the **salience network (SN)**. While the DAN keeps you locked onto your goal, **the VAN and SN are always scanning the environment for anything more important – or more interesting**. This is called 'bottom-up' attention, and **it kicks in when something unexpected grabs your focus** (like a sudden noise or a notification ping).

- **The VAN acts like a circuit breaker.** It notices something important and interrupts what you were doing.
- **The SN is your brain's switchboard and priority filter.** It helps decide *what* is important by weighing up sensory, emotional and cognitive input. Is it new? Is it urgent? Is it relevant?

A little bit like this:

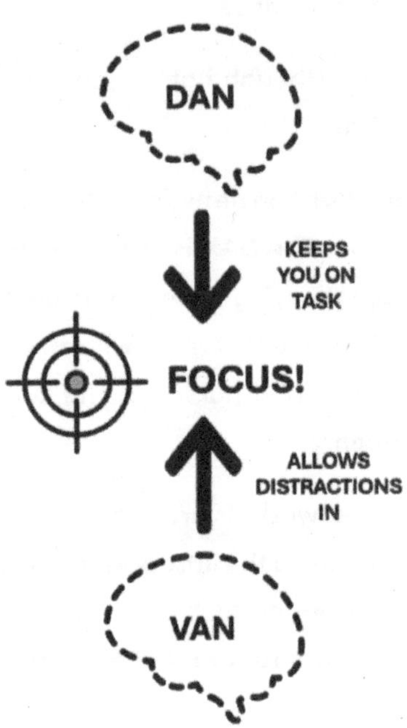

Together, they make sure you're not so focused on reading a spreadsheet that you miss the fire alarm going off. But, as you might suspect, **in ADHD these networks can be a bit overenthusiastic**, jumping in before the task-focused parts have had a chance.

The **frontoparietal network** of the brain also plays a key role. **When you need to hold complex thoughts, switch between tasks or solve tricky problems, the frontoparietal network steps in.** Sometimes called the 'central executive network', it's the one that **manages mental multitasking (not the fake kind), working memory and flexible thinking.** It's also a sort of command centre, linking up with other networks to adapt your brain's settings depending on what's needed. For example, when you switch from writing an email to figuring out how to fix your printer, the frontoparietal network helps to reroute your attention.

Finally, we have the **default mode network (DMN). When you're not focused on anything in particular**, like when you're staring into space, remembering an embarrassing thing you did ten years ago, or thinking about that lasagne you had last week, the DMN takes over. **It's the home of self-reflection, imagination, planning and the kind of deep, drifting thought that we call mind-wandering.** Originally, scientists thought of this as the 'task-negative' network (since it's what the brain reverts to when you're not focused on a task), but that's a bit unfair. **The DMN is doing important behind-the-scenes work, like helping you understand yourself, imagine future events or process emotions.** It's just not great at cooperating with the networks that want you to finish your expense report.

Why does this biology matter? **Understanding that distractibility is a *purposeful* universal human function governed by dedicated brain areas, and not just an ADHD symptom, can help reduce shame.**

Why focus isn't just about trying harder

As we have discovered, **sustained attention**, the ability to stay focused over time, **doesn't come from a single part of the brain. It's actually the result of several big brain networks constantly talking** (and sometimes shouting) over each other.

To stay focused and avoid distractions, your brain needs to maintain a balance among these networks. The real skill isn't just

focusing; it's managing the internal noise, so the right networks stay in charge at the right time.

In a 'neurotypical' brain, when the brain areas for focusing attention are active, the brain dials down the default mode network (DMN), the system behind mind-wandering, daydreaming and internal chatter. **So when the task-focused networks ramp up, the DMN shuts up.**

This quietening down is essential for attention. If the DMN keeps piping up while you're trying to work, it's like trying to write a report while someone keeps narrating your entire life in your ear.

So, who or what decides when it's time to focus or let your mind wander? That's the job of the **salience network (SN).**

The SN is like a switchboard operator, constantly scanning for anything important, whether from the outside world (like a loud noise) or from within your mind (like 'Did I forget to email my boss?'). If it finds something that matters more than what you're currently doing, it can flip the switch from task mode (FPN/DAN) to introspective mode (DMN), or vice versa.

Meanwhile, remember, the VAN is standing by, constantly rumbling on in the background,ready to yank your attention away if something unexpected pops up. If everything is working well, the VAN only kicks in when something genuinely important appears. **But if the VAN is a bit too jumpy,** your focus can be pulled towards every stray sound, thought or email ping, whether it matters or not.

So, what actually is distractibility?

Being distractible is, remember, part of a *purposeful* way in which the brain can make you aware of important internal and external things. It's when the elegant choreography between all these networks – focusing, filtering, switching, suppressing – is slightly off its axis, meaning that the 'bottom up' warnings of internal/external events shout louder than they should.

What's different in ADHD?

Remember the bouncer from earlier? In ADHD, the bouncer is often on their phone, half-asleep, or has just popped out for a cigarette break. This means that the bouncer still exists; they just don't do their job as intended.

In ADHD, the brain structures responsible for managing attention still exist; they just work differently. This affects how well we can filter distractions, switch focus and stay on task, especially when a task is boring or effortful. This isn't just an observation from everyday life; in controlled laboratory research studies, these kinds of distractions disrupt performance more for ADHD brains than for non-ADHD ones,[1] especially when the task is already a bit boring or difficult.

In ADHD, this system of attentional control breaks down in a few key ways:

- **The DMN can stay too active during tasks**, flooding your mind with unrelated thoughts.

- **The VAN might overreact to irrelevant distractions**, dragging your attention away from tasks.
- **The SN might struggle to switch gears** smoothly between focus and introspection.
- **The DAN and FPN might lose their grip on the task at hand.**

In short, distractibility isn't one broken part. It's a glitch in the group project. And if you've ever been in one of those, you know how that goes.

As there are two main types of distractibility that affect people with ADHD, internal and external, let's look at them individually.

External distractibility: when the world pulls your attention

The chances are, you are already very familiar with external distractions. **External distractibility is the tendency to be easily pulled away by things happening *around* you.** For people with ADHD, the outside world can feel like it's constantly banging on the door of our attention. Sounds, sights, movement, clutter, even the temperature of the room, any of it can sneak in and take over our focus.

Examples of external distractions could include:

- a sudden noise, like a door slamming or someone talking nearby
- something moving in your peripheral vision, like a squirrel outside a window
- a cluttered desk with lots of interesting things to look at
- the temptation to check your phone whenever it buzzes.

The study of distractibility in ADHD has largely focused on this particular type of distraction.[2]

The fact that these distractions are, erm, distracting you, isn't about being weak-willed or lacking discipline. It's about how our brains are wired. The brain structures listed earlier might find it harder to filter out these external stimuli. Even small background distractions, like a flickering screen or a distant noise, can seriously disrupt our performance. And as external distractibility is driven by our environment, it can feel unpredictable.

But here's the good news: **once we understand what kind of distractions we're most vulnerable to, we can start putting supports in place.** Later in this chapter, we'll help you to spot your external triggers and build tools to keep your focus safe from sensory ambushes.

Internal distractibility: when your own mind distracts you

Internal distractibility, as the name suggests, comes from *inside* your own head. It's when your **thoughts, feelings and internal sensations pull your attention away from what you're trying to do.**

Here are some examples of common internal distractions:

- having racing thoughts that jump from one idea to another
- getting stuck on a worry or a problem that pops into your head
- daydreaming or getting lost in your own imagination
- feeling restless or fidgety and having the urge to move
- remembering something important you need to do later.

For many people with ADHD, their own thoughts can be even more distracting than the things happening around them.

These distracting thoughts have different flavours too. **The most interesting (and annoying) ones are mind-wandering, racing thoughts and intrusive thoughts.**

Mind-wandering

Mind-wandering is when your brain wanders off without express permission, thinking about dinner, your ex or whether penguins have knees (they do, by the way). When this is planned, such as when you're relaxing by watching a really dull episode of that show you've been streaming for six hours, it can be useful. It allows for lots of self-reflection. But, when it occurs when you are trying to focus your attention on the thing that you're 'supposed' to be doing, it can be a problem. **Everyone's mind wanders sometimes, but with ADHD the volume and frequency of spontaneous mind-wandering is dialled way up.**

ADHD brains are especially more prone to this unintentional mind-wandering when the task at hand is boring or low in stimulation. This can feel like constantly losing your place in the conversation, forgetting why you walked into a room or 'coming to' and realizing you've spent ten minutes arguing with someone in your head.

Although it can look like rudeness from the outside, spontaneous mind-wandering isn't a sign of disinterest or a moral failing. It's an attention regulation issue. Our ADHD brains are less able to inhibit irrelevant thoughts because the DMN is active when it should be at rest.

Racing thoughts

Racing thoughts are like having a turbocharged engine for a brain, constantly revving even when you're desperate for a bit of quiet. It's more than just a wandering mind; it's a relentless torrent of mental chatter, a motorway of ideas, worries and what-ifs with no exit road in sight. While this surge of thinking can sometimes feel exhilarating, sparking bursts of creativity or energy, it often leaves you feeling utterly drained, as if you've run a mental marathon without ever leaving your chair.

Imagine your brain as a web browser with countless tabs open simultaneously. Each tab is playing a different video at full volume; one is replaying a conversation from yesterday, another is stress-testing a dozen future scenarios, and a third is simply narrating your every move. **This mental cacophony makes it nearly impossible to focus on a single task, turning simple decisions into complex calculations and leaving you feeling overwhelmed.**

This experience can be common for those of us with ADHD, but especially for those who have ADHD and co-existing anxiety-related conditions. For someone with ADHD, racing thoughts can feel like a form of mental hyperactivity, a restless brain that jumps from one shiny new idea to the next without pausing for breath. In anxiety, these thoughts often take a more worrying turn, creating a feedback loop of 'what if' scenarios that can spiral into catastrophic thinking, making it hard to feel safe or relaxed.

The torrent of thoughts often picks up speed during times of stress or significant life changes. It's as if your brain's processing speed gets cranked up to deal with the extra load, but without a filter to manage the flow. And when you finally try to wind down for the night, the silence of the room can amplify the noise in your head. The mental chatter that was a background hum during the day can become a deafening roar, keeping sleep just out of reach as you lie there, an unwilling audience to your brain's chaotic late-night show.

This can make it difficult not only to fall asleep but also to stay asleep, leading to fatigue that can fuel the cycle of racing thoughts the next day.

Intrusive thoughts

Intrusive thoughts are the uninvited guests of your mind. They are the **thoughts, images or urges you don't want but can't seem to stop**, and they often show up at the most inconvenient times. These thoughts can be startling, ranging from sudden bizarre impulses (like the urge to shout in a quiet library) to deeply upsetting or scary ideas that feel completely out of character.

It's important to know that almost everyone experiences a strange or unwanted thought now and then. Our brains are creative, chaotic organs that generate all sorts of mental noise. **However, for individuals with conditions like OCD, anxiety or ADHD, these thoughts can become 'sticky'. They feel more frequent, more vivid and far more distressing**, making it difficult to dismiss them as random neural firings.

These aren't daydreams or intentional ponderings; they feel like they come from out of the blue. The 'spam email for your brain' analogy is spot on. They pop up, unrequested and often inappropriate. Your natural instinct is to shove them away, mark them as junk and hit delete. But funnily enough, **the harder you try to fight or suppress them, the more persistent they become.** This is because your brain interprets your struggle as a sign that this thought is important and dangerous, so it keeps it on high alert, paradoxically bringing it back to your attention again and again.

The most crucial thing to remember is this: **having an intrusive thought does not make you a bad person**, nor does it mean you secretly agree with the thought or are likely to act on it. **A thought is just a thought.** Think of it as a momentary glitch or a weird pop-up ad in your consciousness. **The presence of the thought is not a reflection of your true beliefs, values or intentions.** The real measure of your character is that you recognize the thought as intrusive and unwanted in the first place. **You are the observer of the thought, not the thought itself.**

The third way: The 'd-factor'?

Of course, distractions are rarely as simple as 'internal' and 'external'. A recent study[3] looked at distractibility and found that **while internal and external distractions are distinct, they are also strongly linked and can be explained by a single underlying trait called 'general distractibility', or the 'd-factor'.** (Is it just Sam that was distracted by thinking the d-factor was something related to a penis?) The same study found that **people who are more 'externally distractible' tended to have a greater number of ADHD symptoms.** Still, once the 'd-factor' is accounted for, external distraction alone does not add much explanatory power about ADHD beyond that.

What the same authors found *particularly* interesting was that distractibility can vary, even in the same person, due to their level of 'cognitive demand' or the amount of work the brain has to undertake. Put simply, **the more complex a task is in terms of what the brain is required to do, the lower the levels of distractibility, and vice versa**. So, if you are engaged in a task that doesn't require a lot of mental energy, you may be more distracted.

Does it matter where the distraction comes from?

Understanding the difference between internal and external distractibility is important for a few reasons. Firstly, it helps us understand the challenges people with ADHD face: it's not just about 'not caring' or 'putting your phone away'. **Our brains are wired differently, making it more challenging to maintain control of our attention.**

Also, **knowing whether someone is more affected by external or internal distractions can help tailor strategies to help with focus.** For example, someone highly sensitive to external noise might benefit from a quiet workspace, while someone struggling with racing thoughts might benefit from mindfulness techniques.

By understanding the neurological basis of these challenges, we can be more empathetic and less judgmental towards individuals with ADHD.

Strategies for managing external distractibility

Strategy 1: Tame your environment

Your environment can either work with your brain or against it, and for ADHD brains, that's a big deal. Because when every sound, flicker of light, or tempting notification feels like a neon sign flashing 'look at me!', setting yourself up to focus means engineering fewer traps to fall into.

We can't always control the world around us, but we can make tweaks that reduce the noise, literally and figuratively.

- **Block the noise**

If background sounds hijack your attention or stress you out:

  - Noise-cancelling headphones are a lifesaver in shared or noisy spaces.
  - Try white noise apps like Noisli or Coffitivity to create a gentle, predictable audio backdrop.
  - If sound is a major issue, try low-level background noise (like rain sounds or lo-fi music) to compete with sudden noises.

These can help mask unpredictable sounds that otherwise derail your focus.

- **Manage visual distractions**

Too much visual clutter can make your brain feel just as messy as your desk. Try:

  - Facing a blank wall while working, rather than a window or open space.

- Using desk dividers, plants or shelves as visual boundaries (these act like blinkers for your brain).
- Clearing surfaces of anything not essential for the task at hand. The more stuff in your field of vision, the more places your attention can wander.

- **Tweak the lighting**

Lighting affects both mood and focus. However, those with photosensitivity may need to approach this carefully:

- Natural light is ideal: it boosts alertness and well-being. Try working near a window (ideally in a way that doesn't cause you to get distracted by every passerby!) during daylight hours.
- If that's not possible, opt for soft, indirect lighting rather than harsh overhead bulbs, which can lead to eye strain and sensory overload.

- **If you can, make it yours (but not too much)**

A workspace that feels pleasant or comforting can help you settle in. Just don't turn it into a playground for procrastination.

- Keep one or two motivational or calming items nearby (like a favourite object or framed quote).
- Avoid decorating your desk with things that you know you'll end up fiddling with for 45 minutes instead of working. Equally fidget tools, textured objects, weighted lap pads or chewing gum can give your brain stimulation without pulling you off task.

You'll find a link to a 'Workplace optimization' exercise you can try in our online resources (see p.343).

Strategy 2: Think 'frictionless focus'

Ask yourself: 'What normally distracts me here?' Then reduce the pull, or friction, that it causes. That might mean:

- Moving snacks or your phone out of reach.
- Turning off push notifications.
- Closing unused browser tabs.
- Putting your phone in another room if you're not using it for work.
- Establishing a way to signal to others that you are not to be disturbed. (We both have a 'Do not Disturb' sign on our doors and if the door is closed it reminds the other not to enter.)

Strategy 3: Block digital distractions

Let's be honest: our phones and laptops are not neutral tools – they are dopamine slot machines. And for brains that are already wired to chase novelty, switching between tabs or checking a notification doesn't feel like a distraction; it feels like relief.

That's why we need to protect ourselves from our tech. Not with shame or superhuman willpower, but with external boundaries that make focus more likely than scrolling.

If you find yourself typing 'YouTube' before you've even realized what your fingers are doing, it's time to put digital walls in place. These digital walls, which can take pre-planning and Zen-like commitment, include:

- **Freedom** blocks websites and apps across multiple devices – ideal if you're tempted to switch from your laptop to your phone.

- **Cold Turkey** lets you lock yourself out of distractions with no mercy (perfect for deadline mode).
- **StayFocusd** (Chrome extension) limits your time on specific sites before shutting them down for the day.
- **One Sec** (which gets James's prize for the most amazing, simple idea) an app that makes other apps load more slowly, creating enough friction to make your brain less interested.

These tools create just enough of a barrier to pause your autopilot and give your brain a chance to make a better choice.

Strategy 4: Set up a 'launchpad' for focus

Ever sat down to start something and then spent 20 minutes looking for a charger, a pen or the file you swore you saved yesterday? That's just the ADHD brain needing better scaffolding to get going.

Creating a 'launchpad' isn't about perfect organization. It's about reducing the energy needed to start and removing distractions before they become a problem.

- **Gather before you begin**

Starting a task with missing ingredients is like trying to bake a cake without checking if you've got eggs.

- Spend 2–5 minutes gathering everything you'll need: notes, documents, charger, water, fidget tools, snacks, noise-cancelling headphones.
- Check your environment for 'silent saboteurs': things that seem harmless but will pull your attention later (e.g., your phone, a half-finished crossword or that weird notification from a shopping app).

- Create an 'ADHD station' for any environment where you work: all your essential items, (usually) stored in one place.

Having everything in reach means fewer excuses to get up and drift away mid-task.

- **Clearing the runway**

Before a plane takes off, the cockpit is prepped and the runway cleared. You can do the same for your brain:

  - Declutter your workspace, even if it's just pushing things to the side.
  - Close browser tabs or open windows that aren't needed for the task at hand. (All of them. Even the one with the ADHD memes.)
  - Take 30 seconds to set an intention: 'What do I want to do next – not forever, just next?'

This 5-minute ritual is like telling your brain: 'We're landing here now. This is the task.'

- **Use a visual or physical cue**

Some people find it helpful to have a physical or visual anchor that signals 'focus time'. That might be:

  - Putting on headphones or a specific piece of clothing.
  - Lighting a candle or using a particular playlist.
  - Using a sticky note with the current task written on it and placing it in your line of sight.

These cues can act like a mental on-switch, helping you associate certain sights, smells or actions with focused work. Some of them can also indicate to others that you are not to be disturbed.

Strategies for managing internal distractibility

Remember, **sometimes, the loudest interruption is inside your own head**. Racing thoughts, spirals of anxiety, half-finished mental conversations, or sudden ideas for a podcast episode that needs made right now...popping into your head five minutes into your focused work session.

Managing internal distractions isn't about silencing your brain (that rarely works). **It's about making space for thoughts without letting them hijack your attention.** Here's how to try to do that.

Strategy 1: Externalize your brain

Your brain is for having ideas, not storing all of them. If you try to hold everything in your head, ADHD will happily drop the whole tray.

Keep a 'parking lot' notebook or open document next to you while working. When a thought pops up ('Email Chris!' or 'Buy WD-40'), jot it down and keep going. You're not ignoring it, you're saving it for later. Voice notes can work just as well, or adding them to your master task list. The key is to create a catching system for stray thoughts, so they don't keep pinging around like rogue satellites.

Pro tip: if your to-do list or app feels overwhelming today, jot your idea down on paper or a single Post-it Note or whatever your brain will let you use. Make it as frictionless as possible.

Strategy 2: Use time-blocking to contain attention

When you've got ten thoughts at once, telling yourself to 'just focus' is about as useful as shouting 'just swim' at someone who's drowning.

- Use time-blocking to give your brain a temporary boundary. Set a timer (e.g. 15 minutes) and tell yourself: 'I don't have to do this forever; I just need to focus until the timer goes off.'
- The Pomodoro technique (25 minutes focus, 5 minutes break) works well for many, but some ADHD brains prefer longer 'focus sprints' – 45, 60 or even 90 minutes if you're in flow. Sam loves working like this and tends to sandwich difficult work tasks in between quick wins and fun tasks, using Alexa or a gravity timer to help them pace.
- During your focus time, don't aim for perfection. Just aim for presence. The break is coming. You can think about cheese or existential dread then.

Strategy 3: Interrupt the mind-wandering loop

Sometimes, your attention just...drifts. You find yourself rehashing an awkward conversation from 2007, or suddenly you're deep into a Wikipedia article about vending machines.

Instead of trying to force your mind back, gently call it home:

- Ask yourself:
    - 'What am I doing right now?'
    - 'Is this where I want my attention to be?'

These simple mindfulness prompts can act like mental bumpers: they don't criticize, just redirect.

- If your mind is spiralling, use grounding tools like the 5–4–3–2–1 technique:
  - 5 things you can see
  - 4 things you can touch
  - 3 things you can hear
  - 2 things you can smell
  - 1 thing you can taste or are grateful for

This can re-anchor your attention in your body and surroundings, like reloading your mental browser. It doesn't matter if you can't remember how many things you're supposed to see or hear. Sam often just tries to focus on *anything* they can see, hear, touch/feel, smell, taste until they feel like they're back in the room and can move on.

Strategy 4: Reduce cognitive overload

Your susceptibility to distractions/distractibility increases when your working memory is overloaded.

- To reduce the load, make the object of your focus smaller, e.g. rather than 'Write the report', try 'Open document' or 'Write title.'

Ridiculously small wins matter. They can generate momentum and reward.

Strategy 5: Support emotional distractions

Sometimes the thing derailing your focus isn't your inbox, it's your internal monologue. **Emotions are distractions when they're unacknowledged.**

If you're spiralling, try naming the emotion out loud:

'This is anxiety.'

'I'm feeling overwhelmed.'

Naming it can help to create distance. You're not the feeling; you're the person noticing the feeling.

Give yourself permission to pause. Take a short break to move your body, breathe, cry, scream into a pillow or just lie down for a minute. **Processing feelings isn't a waste of time; it clears the mental clutter so you can focus again later.**

Remember, you don't have to win *every* battle with distraction. You just need tools that help you stay in the game.

Chapter summary

This chapter unpacked why:

- Distractibility isn't a failure of willpower. It's a neurological trait that shows up more intensely in ADHD due to how our brain networks filter – or don't filter – incoming information.
- Focus isn't one single skill, but a group project between multiple brain systems. In ADHD, this coordination often deviates from the norm.
- Both external and internal distractions are valid, and for many of us the internal ones (thoughts, feelings, mental spirals) can be just as disruptive as noisy environments or phone pings.
- Mind-wandering, racing thoughts and intrusive thoughts are common in ADHD. They're not signs of laziness or bad character, just further examples of how attention regulation gets tricky.
- We covered a toolkit of approaches to try to better manage distractions, including: taming your environment, blocking digital distractions, creating a launchpad for focus and externalizing your brain using sticky notes, voice memos or your master task list.
- Internal distractions can be tamed with grounding exercises, mindfulness cues and self-check questions like 'What am I doing right now?'

The goal isn't perfect focus. It's enough focus, for long enough, to do what matters.

Chapter 9

TIME MANAGEMENT FOR THE 'TIME-BLIND'

Or why a second can feel like an hour and an hour like a second

Time management is something Sam *really* struggles with. They are completely unable to ever accurately estimate how long *anything* will take them to do, even if they've done that thing almost every day of their life. They will almost always *under*estimate how long something will take to do. However, there are also times when they magically manage to do 15 things in 2 minutes! But unfortunately, that only happens for them rarely. They will frequently think that they'll be able to respond to 50 emails in an hour and then spend an entire hour on just one email, leaving them feeling emotionally dysregulated and full of self-hatred afterwards.

In their fully masked days, when they tried to pass themselves off as an organized human being that had their shit together, they put themselves under an immense amount of pressure and would get wherever they needed to be early. They would frequently get to an interview for a job at least an hour early and would try to pass the time somewhere close by so that they didn't turn up too early (they also have a chronic fear of getting anywhere early because that's generally when the most awkward small talk happens), then they'd lose track of time and end up being late. In some cases, over an hour late. In one case, they still managed to get the job! They were also late for almost every aerial/pole class because, although they made that journey twice a week, every week, they failed to accurately predict how long it would actually take every time.

As mentioned previously, they also thought that leaving the bulk of the writing they needed to do for this book until six days before the final deadline was completely fine, even though they'd tried and failed to sit down and write *so many times* before that, because they always truly believe that even if none of the conditions have changed at all, this time will be different! Once they did start, time ceased to exist. They didn't shower, only ate and drank when James brought food/drinks up to them and stopped only when James, or complete exhaustion, forced them to.

Knowing what we should do, doesn't mean that we'll always be able to do those things. We're all just doing our best to work with our differently wired brains and that means that things don't always (or even, rarely!) go to plan. Accepting this and going easy on ourselves when things don't go the way we want them to can be one of the most effective things we can do. Try it...!

Why time management matters (more than you think)

When most people talk about productivity, they focus on what you're doing: ticking off tasks, meeting deadlines, achieving goals. But under the surface, *how* you use time is often the invisible skill that connects it all.

Imagine trying to cook a meal with no idea what time dinner will be, how long things take to prepare and cook, or whether your oven is even on. That's life without time management. **Productivity doesn't just mean getting shit done, it means getting the *right* shit done at the *right* time, in a way that doesn't completely fry your nervous system.**

Effective time management can:

- Reduce anxiety and overwhelm.
- Make it easier to start and finish tasks.
- Give you a more accurate picture of your workload.
- Help you to spot when you're doing too much (before you burn out).
- Give you the freedom to say no or not today.

At its core, productivity is about getting stuff done efficiently and effectively. And that depends heavily on time-related skills, including:

- Estimating how long tasks will take.
- Planning and prioritizing based on deadlines.
- Starting and switching tasks at the right time.
- Sticking with something long enough to finish it.
- Leaving enough time for rest and recovery.

In workplace settings, poor time management predicts lower job performance,[1] higher stress levels and more task-switching inefficiencies.[2]

In academic contexts, it's even more pronounced. **Time management skills are among the strongest predictors of academic success, even placed above intelligence in some studies.**[3]

For people with ADHD, this link is even tighter. One large-scale study found that **time management difficulties were one of the top correlations between ADHD symptoms and underachievement at school and work.** In other words: poor time management doesn't just make life chaotic, it can directly disrupt your ability to be productive, hit goals and feel competent.

But it's not all doom and missed meetings. The same studies show that **when people improve their time management, through coaching, external tools, routines, or accountability, their productivity improves too.**[4] Often dramatically.

So, while better time management might sound like one of those generic self-help tips, it's much more than that. It's a powerful way to reduce overwhelm, increase self-efficacy, and build a more functional day-to-day life.

Time management: how the brain uses time wisely

Time management sounds like it should be simple. Set some priorities, follow a plan and voilà, a productive day achieved. However, the truth is that managing time well depends on a complex set of invisible processes working smoothly together behind the scenes.

At its core, **time management isn't just about scheduling. It's about *perceiving* time accurately, *estimating* how long things take, *organizing* tasks around those estimates and *regulating* your own behaviour so that you actually follow through.** That's a tall order for any brain, let alone one that's also dealing with stress, distractions or unpredictable energy levels.

Time itself isn't something we passively observe, like watching sand fall through an hourglass. **Our experience of time is constructed from a mix of sensory signals, attention, emotion and memory.** That means time can feel like it's dragging or racing, depending on what we're doing or how we're feeling. **A boring meeting can feel endless. A scroll through social media can make two hours vanish without warning.**

And because our perception of time is so subjective, planning and managing time well often depends on tools that go beyond just trying harder. It requires strategies that account for how human brains actually work, not how we *wish* they worked.

Time isn't just a clock: why time management is trickier than it looks

Time management often gets framed as a matter of organization or willpower. Plan better, try harder and be on time. But the ability to manage time well is rooted in something far more complex: our brain's internal experience of time itself.

This might sound abstract, but it's something we rely on constantly. From getting out of the door in the morning, to estimating how long dinner will take, to deciding whether there's time to write one more email – it's all based on a behind-the-scenes mental process that isn't visible but which shapes nearly every part of our lives.

And this process isn't identical for everyone. **Just as some people are more sensitive to sound or temperature, some people have a very different relationship with time itself.** Time can feel like it speeds up, slows down or vanishes entirely, not just now and then but consistently. For these individuals, managing time isn't just a challenge. It can feel almost impossible without the right tools or support.

Understanding that time perception is subjective and that managing time relies on complex brain functions, not just effort, is key to changing the way we think about time management. Issues with the perception of time passing go well beyond being forgetful or disorganized. The way your brain understands time doesn't care about your experience, or your deadline; it just does what it developed to do.

How the brain tells time (without a clock in sight)

Time might feel like something outside us – ticking clocks, changing light, calendar reminders – but your brain doesn't actually *hear* time passing. It doesn't even have a dedicated time-sensing organ, unlike the organs it has to sense sight or smell. Instead, **time perception is something your brain *constructs*, moment by moment, using a complex system that's still not fully understood.**

Rather than originating from a single 'time centre', **our sense of time is stitched together by multiple brain regions working in tandem, some involved in movement, others in attention, memory**

or decision-making. These networks coordinate to help us estimate how long something will take, remember when things happened and plan what to do next.

The key brain regions involved in time perception are:

- **Cerebral cortex:** handles higher-level thinking, planning and attention
- **Cerebellum:** involved in fine-tuning movements and potentially precise timing
- **Basal ganglia:** crucial for processing sequences and estimating duration
- **Prefrontal cortex:** the part that helps with focus, impulse control and decisions
- **Hippocampus:** keeps track of when things happened (temporal memory)
- **Insular cortex:** ties in awareness of bodily states and feelings over time.

Think of it like an orchestra. Each section playing its part, coordinating in real time to produce your subjective experience of time passing. But if the conductor has gone AWOL or one instrument plays out of sync, it can throw off the whole performance.

ADHD, time blindness and future amnesia

Most people's internal clock is ticking away in the background. They just feel when ten minutes have passed, know roughly how long something will take, or can sense when they're cutting it fine for a meeting. But if you have ADHD, that inner clock? It's probably unreliable, or simply missing.

Time blindness (sometimes called time **agnosia**) is more than just poor timekeeping. It's a **neurological difference that makes it genuinely hard to feel the passage of time, estimate how long something will take, or know how long ago something happened.**

Time blindness shows up in all sorts of frustrating ways:

- **Underestimating or overestimating how long things take.** You might think something will take five minutes and it takes an hour, or you put off a task for weeks, assuming it'll eat up your whole day...and it takes 20 minutes.
- **Always running late (even for things you care about).** Wanting to be on time doesn't help when you have no intuitive sense of time passing.
- **Getting stuck in 'waiting mode'.** You've got something happening later, so you feel like you can't start anything now. Except later is three hours away.
- **Forgetting routines.** You look up at 3pm and realize you forgot to eat, drink, take your meds, or shower. Again.
- **Losing track of what happened when.** Last week feels like yesterday and yesterday feels like last year.
- **Hyperfocus.** That magical-but-messy state where you lock into something and lose all sense of time. And sometimes your bladder.
- **Procrastination.** Putting off tasks because you can't quite grasp how long they'll take or how soon they're due.
- **Work pacing issues.** Rushing through jobs or taking far too long, with no consistent rhythm.

Why is time blindness an ADHD thing?

ADHD brains are wired differently, in ways that deeply affect how time is experienced and managed. For example, almost all the brain areas involved in time perception, but particularly the prefrontal cortex and the basal ganglia, works differently in ADHD. Add to this the roles that the neurotransmitters dopamine and noradrenaline, which we know work differently in ADHD, play in time management and we have a recipe for time blindness.

Research shows that people with ADHD experience very real, measurable differences in how they process time estimation, time reproduction, time sequencing and duration discrimination.

And to further complicate matters, **these problems are worse when the task you are trying to focus on is one that does not provoke strong emotions for you.** So, you might be great at tracking how long your favourite game took but lose hours staring at an admin task you are unable to start.

How time blindness wrecks your day (and sometimes your life)

Time blindness isn't just an occasional inconvenience. It can impact almost every part of life. **When you can't sense how time is passing, it becomes incredibly difficult to keep routines, meet deadlines, or even just show up when you said you would.** That ripple effect spreads out to your relationships, work, mental health and day-to-day functioning.

Let's look at how this plays out in real life:

A day in the life (with time blindness)

Let's walk through a typical day for an adult with ADHD who works in an office. Not a crisis day. Not a holiday. Just a typical Tuesday with time blindness quietly sabotaging everything.

Morning. The race begins (late)

You wake up...and just lie there. Not because you're lazy – although you might also be lazy (we definitely are sometimes!) – but because your brain hasn't figured out *how long* you actually have. Getting up *feels* early enough. Until it isn't.

You plan to shower, eat and leave by 8:15. But suddenly it's 8:14 and you're still in your pyjamas, Googling 'Does coffee count as one of your five a day?' You rush out the door with wet hair, no breakfast and the sinking feeling that you're late (again).

Mid-morning. The to-do list black hole

You arrive at your desk flustered, already behind. You know you've got a 10am meeting but it feels abstract and far away. You start clearing your inbox, just a quick tidy-up, and next time you look up, it's 10:08. Your heart drops. You've missed it. Again.

You're not scrolling Instagram. You weren't even procrastinating. You just...lost time. Because without that inner clock, the brain doesn't automatically remind you when 10 minutes have passed...or 50.

Lunchtime. What even is a routine?

You meant to go for a walk at lunch or eat something with a

vegetable in it. But you've been stuck waiting for a response to an email, so you didn't want to start anything. You were ready to spring into action, but the email never came.

This waiting mode makes everything else feel untouchable, even if it's hours away. You end up doing...nothing. And then eating half a packet of biscuits at 3pm because you forgot lunch happened.

Afternoon: the mental flow trap

You finally get stuck into a report that interests you, and you nail it. A state of mental flow. Beautiful formatting. Everything just works. Until you realize you were supposed to pick up your children, or join a call, or leave work half an hour ago to meet a friend.

People can often mistake this for hyperfocus, but really, it's another form of time blindness. Though like hyperfocus, you didn't choose to focus that intensely. You just couldn't switch away. The result? Missed transitions, skipped breaks and another mini-disaster to explain.

Evening. The domino effect

You leave work late, meaning dinner is late, which pushes back the one task you meant to do this evening. But now you're too tired. Or maybe you try anyway and underestimate how long it'll take. Suddenly it's midnight, and you're Googling how long you can survive without sleep and eating Nutella straight out of the jar.

The guilt creeps in. You feel disorganized, unreliable, maybe even ashamed. But none of this was a conscious choice (except maybe the biscuits...and the Nutella).

This is what happens when your brain doesn't feel time the way other brains do. An ADHD brain very likely can't plan, track or use time in a linear way, unless you build those structures externally.

Strategies for tackling time blindness

There are many ways to support or improve your time management skills. As usual, AI tools can act like a supportive assistant, one who remembers things for you, summarizes your plans and gently nudges you back on track. But remember **the AI is only as good as its training.**

Here are some other approaches you might try:

Strategy 1: Make time visible

Because time can feel so slippery to us, one of the most effective strategies is to make it visible. That means externalizing it by turning the invisible, abstract idea of time into something you can see, feel and (sometimes) remember exists.

Here are a few ways to try to make time visible:

- **Visual timers:** Unlike digital clocks that only show the time now, visual timers show how much time is left. They provide a real-time countdown that you can actually see.

  This taps into our brain's craving for immediate feedback. **Research shows that people with ADHD respond better to tasks**

when the delay between action and reward is shortened, and a visual timer gives you a clear, ongoing cue that something is happening now, not later (which might as well be never).

- **Use the right clock for you:** Analogue clocks show time passing, not just time displayed. That's a surprisingly big deal. You can see half an hour slip by as the minute hand moves. You can glance up and realize it's been 40 minutes since you opened TikTok just to check something.

  Equally, using a digital clock which is very noticeable and, preferably, has changing colours to help to keep it visible, can also be very effective.

  Tip: Put a clock in every room. Yes, even the bathroom. In fact, especially the bathroom. And if you can, move it often because, no matter how bright it is, it will become invisible to you eventually. Sam sticks everything to the walls with Command Strips to make it easy to move things around.

- **Visual schedules:** Make time visible with:
  - Wall charts. Try big, bold weekly planners that live where you can't miss them.
  - Colour-coded calendars. Use colour to group tasks together (e.g. admin = blue, fun = yellow, social = red). This works well on Outlook/Google calendars too.

- **AI planners:** Tools like Reclaim.ai, Clockwise or Notion AI can auto-schedule your day based on energy levels, task length and existing commitments. You can also use AI to turn a messy brain dump into a tidy, colour-coded to-do list.

Strategy 2: Use tech to outsource time management

Smart speakers like Alexa, Google Nest or Siri can be more than music players or dolphin fact dispensers. For ADHD brains, they can act as an external executive function, especially when it comes to managing time.

Ways to use them intentionally:

- **Cue transitions out loud:** 'It's 9:45, you said you'd stop now.' Spoken reminders can break through hyperfocus better than silent ones.
- **Hourly check-ins:** 'Are you doing what you're meant to be doing?' These prompts can support time awareness and self-monitoring.
- **Start alarms, not just stop alarms.** Try setting a 'Start winding down' alarm at 4:30pm, to help with the transition from work to home, and then a 'Stop work' alarm at 5pm.
- **Custom routines:** Your 'start work routine' could adjust the lighting, play focus music, and start a timer, all in one command.
- **Record a reminder in your own voice.** (For example, 'Don't leave the presentation till midnight again!')

Tip: Make announcements *really* annoying on purpose. Your future self will be annoyed, but annoying announcements are more difficult to ignore.

Other tech approaches that can help include:

- **Task managers:** Apps like Todoist, TickTick or Trello can help to organize your to-do list and break down bigger projects.
- **Time trackers:** Tools like Toggl or RescueTime show you where your time actually goes. (Warning, you might not like the answer.)
- **Smart reminders:** Use recurring alarms, location-based nudges

('Remind me to email X when I get to work'), or cascading reminders to support memory and transitions.

Strategy 3: Build routines with factored-in wiggle room

Routines can give your day shape, but only if they're not so rigid that they snap. ADHD brains need flexibility and structure.

- **Morning/evening anchors:** Start and end your day with consistent routines. Brushing your teeth before doomscrolling counts.
- **Buffer time:** If something takes 30 minutes, schedule an hour. Add time between appointments to recover, help with transitions, snack or stare into space.
- **Plan backwards:** Instead of planning from now forward, plan backwards from when something is due. This can help you to spot all the hidden steps ahead of time.

Strategy 4: Get to know your patterns

Time blindness isn't just about forgetting the time, it's about losing time to distraction, hyperfocus or low dopamine. Self-awareness can help you to spot the traps.

- **Identify time sinks:** What pulls you in and makes hours disappear? TikTok? Reorganizing kitchen cupboards? Name your nemeses so you can set limits.
- **Schedule your golden hours:** Notice when you feel most alert or focused. If you've got a sweet spot (e.g. 10am–noon), guard it fiercely.
- **Use rewards:** ADHD brains often need external motivation, so build in little dopamine hits – treats, breaks, praise, whatever works for you.

Strategy 5: Support your brain, not just your schedule

Time management doesn't start with a planner; it starts with your brain being in a vaguely functional state.

- **Getting enough rest** helps with memory, attention and time perception. It's hard to fix time blindness when you've lost Tuesday.
- **Moving your body** can help to boost dopamine, reduce stress and improve focus, all of which support better time use.
- **Learning to pause** and notice the moment might sound like hippy nonsense, but it can help you to develop a better sense of time passing.
- **Eating foods that support dopamine** (like protein, B6, or omega-3s) won't cure ADHD but they might help your brain to work a bit more smoothly.

Above all, start small – one tiny change at a time.

Chapter summary

Time management can feel impossible when time blindness exists.

This chapter unpacked:

- Why time feels weird: your brain doesn't have a built-in clock. It cobbles together time using attention, memory, emotion and body signals, all of which are affected by ADHD.
- What time blindness looks like: running late even when you care, losing hours to distractions or hyperfocus, putting

things off because the timing feels...unknowable.

- How ADHD brains struggle with time: from differences in brain structure (hello, prefrontal cortex) to dopamine quirks that mess with motivation and reward, ADHD sets us up for time trouble.

But here's the part that matters:

Time management is still possible, *if* you stop trying to manage it all in your head. External tools and scaffolding can stand in for your internal clock.

We've shared a toolkit of strategies you can dip into:

- Make time visible (clocks, timers, alarms).
- Break tasks into bite-sized chunks.
- Build flexible routines with buffer time.
- Use technology to track, block and remind.
- Learn your own patterns. (Hello, golden hours!)
- Support your brain and body (sleep, snacks, movement).

You're not bad at time. Your brain just tells time differently. And that's OK, because now you can try to *work with it*, not against it.

Chapter 10

DEALING WITH THE FEELS

The emotional side of productivity

Recently, when times were financially rough, James decided to sell some of his long-accumulated, impulse-purchased tech to raise money. After a bad experience once in selling a computer (the buyer scammed James by pretending the computer was broken and threw it away, and James just accepted this without getting the proof needed to claim the money back from the couriers), he made absolutely certain that this computer was well packaged and would arrive in perfect condition. To doubly ensure this was done correctly, James had help from a lovely friend called Kirsty, who was staying with us as a guest. After nearly two hours of setting up the box, adding packing, putting the large screen in the box, taping it up, adding more packaging through the box handles, taping up again, the job was done.

Only it wasn't. Scanning the room, James noticed that he hadn't added the charging cable to the contents of the box. A simple mistake. We all make them. Immediately, the overwhelming sense of 'THE WORLD HAS JUST ENDED' hit, and without explanation, James quietly went upstairs and lay on a bed crying for several hours. When Sam (eventually) came upstairs to see what was happening and saw James collapsed in tears, Sam, now also crying, did their best to calm the situation down, being very aware that the lovely Kirsty was still sitting downstairs, now alone. Asking James if he could come downstairs, James said, 'I think it's best if I just leave you. I'm such a burden, you're better off without me.'

A charging cable. A box that could simply have been reopened and resealed. A disappearing spouse, a confused guest and an offer to separate and dissolve our marriage. This might sound like a scene from a poorly scripted comedy film, but this is what emotional dysregulation can look like. Intense, prolonged and wildly inappropriate emotional responses to life's events.

Luckily, Sam didn't accept James's kind offer of splitting up, and, after about three more hours, James came downstairs, sheepishly, carrying with him a slightly heavier amount of shame than normal. The next morning – and this is a true gift of ADHD – it was as if none of this had ever happened.

This chapter will guide you through emotional regulation and emotional dysregulation and how they can impact productivity. Then we'll offer some approaches which are backed by research and experience to try and dial these moments down a little (or help you get over them more quickly).

Emotions and how we regulate them

When people talk about ADHD, they often focus on the obvious stuff, like forgetting where you put your keys or accidentally doom-scrolling instead of replying to emails. But **one of the most powerful and least talked-about parts of ADHD is emotional dysregulation**: when your feelings hit like a freight train and your reaction seems way bigger than the situation 'should' warrant.

To better understand this, it is helpful first to understand what emotions are and what emotional regulation entails.

Come off it, we all know what emotions are, don't we?

Emotions aren't just 'feelings'. They're full-body, full-brain reactions to how we interpret the world around (and inside) us. At their core, emotions are your brain and body's way of answering the question: 'Is this good or bad for me right now?'

They're made up of several 'parts' working together (not always smoothly):

- **Cognitive:** thoughts, judgments and meaning-making ('This is dangerous!' or 'This feels nice')
- **Subjective:** your felt experience ('I feel scared' or 'I feel calm')
- **Physiological:** body reactions (heart racing, sweating, relaxed breathing)
- **Movement:** actions or impulses (running away, smiling, freezing, punching a cushion).

These reactions can be triggered by external stuff (like a barking dog or a message from your boss) or internal stuff (like a memory, a gut feeling or hunger). Sometimes, we *know* why we feel something; sometimes, we don't. And that's OK.

All emotions start with a quick behind-the-scenes judgment: 'Is this helping or hurting me right now, based on what I want or need?' This 'valuation' process happens automatically and is shaped by our current goals or needs (e.g. safety, connection, approval), personal experiences and learning, and built-in survival instincts.

So, a raised eyebrow from a stranger might seem neutral to one person but feel threatening to another, depending on their past or current mental state.

Emotions unfold like a mini story:
trigger > reaction > action.

But the parts of that story (thoughts, feelings, body sensations, behaviour) don't always line up neatly. You might *feel* calm but still have a racing heart. Or *know* you're safe but still want to run. That's normal.

If you're the type of person who likes to know where words come from, you might be interested to know that the word *emotion* comes from the Latin *emovere*, meaning 'to move out'. This tells us something. ***Emotions exist to prepare us to take action***: to protect ourselves, connect with others, or repeat things that please us. Thinking about emotions this way often makes sense. Fear = run or freeze. Anger = stand your ground or defend. Joy = keep going, do that again!

This is why some scientists describe emotions as a 'Perception–Valuation–Action' sequence:

1. Perceive what's happening (inside or outside).
2. Judge its meaning or value.
3. React in a way that moves you towards feeling more OK.

In other words, **emotions are your brain's way of helping you to survive, get your needs met and make decisions**, even if they don't always show up at the most convenient time.

Emotional regulation: controlled emotional response to events

With what we've learned (or skipped past if you started this chapter here) about emotions so far in this chapter, let's now move on to how we control or 'regulate' them.

This process often happens in the background, without the need to consciously 'regulate' ourselves. In essence, **emotional regulation is your brain's ability to:**

- notice what you're feeling
- understand why you're feeling it
- choose (ish) how to respond
- recover when the emotion has passed.

Emotional regulation isn't just about pushing your feelings down or pretending everything's fine when it isn't. It's about how we notice, manage and respond to our emotions in a way that (ideally) helps us cope with life without imploding, snapping at loved ones or crying in the toilet of a shopping centre. If emotions exist to prepare us to take action, then emotional regulation exists to help us recognize and manage the emotions so that we can take the most appropriate action.

Several key areas of the brain work together to help regulate our emotions. When we experience an emotion, a number of brain systems become activated.[1] Some of them are ancient and shared with other animals. These are the fast-reacting parts of the brain that helped our ancestors survive.

Here are the leading players:

- **The amygdala:** This is your brain's early warning system. It quickly detects anything that might be a threat (like a snake or an angry email) and prepares your body to respond rapidly.
- **The ventral striatum:** This part is all about motivation and reward. It helps you decide if something is worth chasing (like cake) or avoiding (like criticism).
- **The PAG (periaqueductal grey):** Deep in the brainstem, this region coordinates basic survival responses, like freezing, fleeing or fighting.

It's crucial to note that **these brain areas kick in automatically, *often before you even know how you feel.*** But that's not the whole story.

Humans also have newer and more developed brain areas, which help us think about our feelings, make sense of them and (hopefully) respond in a socially appropriate way.

It is these more evolved areas of the brain which have a key role in effective emotional regulation, especially after the emotions start to be noticeable.

These brain areas include:

- **The anterior insula:** This helps you to tune into what's going on inside your body, like your heartbeat, breathing or that sinking feeling in your stomach.
- **The anterior cingulate cortex (ACC):** Your brain's conflict monitor. It helps you weigh up emotional demands and competing priorities, like: 'I'm angry, but I'm also in a meeting, so maybe don't shout right now.'
- **The hippocampus:** This links emotions to memory, time and place, such as remembering that a particular street makes you anxious because something bad once happened there. Or feeling scared? Well, you're watching a horror film at home, but the house is locked and you have a dog, so you're probably safe.

OK, but what is emotional regulation and how can I do it?

Emotional regulation involves both internal processes, such as self-talk or reframing a situation, and external ones, like stepping away from a conversation before you say something you'll regret. **Done well, emotional regulation helps us to stay connected to people,**

manage stress, focus at work and bounce back when things go sideways.

There is a helpful model of emotional regulation, proposed by James Gross.[2] **Gross's model separates emotion regulation into five stages: situation selection, situation modification, attentional deployment, cognitive change and response modulation.** Importantly, it suggests that emotional regulation occurs at different points in the emotion-generating process.

Here are those five stages, separated into 'before' and 'after' an event:

Before the emotion fully arrives:

These are things you might do *ahead of time* to reduce the intensity of an emotion or steer it in a more helpful direction.

1. **Situation selection:** Choosing to avoid or go towards a situation based on how you expect it will make you feel. For example, leaving a noisy party early if you find it overwhelming.
2. **Situation modification:** Changing something about the situation itself to affect how it feels. This can be as simple as cracking a joke during a stressful meeting to lighten the mood.
3. **Attentional deployment:** Shifting your focus to something less upsetting or more manageable. Putting on music or scrolling memes to distract yourself from spiralling thoughts deploys our attention elsewhere.
4. **Cognitive change (reappraisal):** Reframing how you *think* about the situation, so that it feels less upsetting. So, instead of 'They're ignoring me,' you might think, 'They're probably just busy today.'

After the emotion has hit:

The final stage comes into play *once you're already feeling something* and trying to manage your reaction.

5. **Response modulation:** Trying to hide or reduce the emotion you show on the outside, even if it's still roaring away on the inside. If you've ever held back tears in a meeting or put on a brave face when you're upset, then you have suppressed your emotions.

We can put each of these stages into a 'real-world example':

1. **Situation selection:** You know that team meetings often leave you feeling overstimulated and snappy by the end, especially if they're over an hour. So, you arrange with your manager to attend just the first half and catch up on the rest asynchronously.
2. **Situation modification:** You're stuck in the first half of the online meeting, but it's dragging, so you turn off your camera and grab a fidget toy, or start doodling while listening to regulate your agitation without disengaging entirely.
3. **Attentional deployment:** After the meeting, you check your email and see a vague and slightly passive-aggressive email from a colleague who was in the meeting with you. You feel the rejection burn. Instead of replying straightaway, you deliberately switch to watching a funny video or sorting your Spotify playlist – something that buys time and soothes the emotional storm.
4. **Cognitive change (reappraisal):** Rather than interpreting the email as 'they're annoyed with me', you challenge that thought: 'Maybe they're just rushed or having a bad day. It probably isn't personal.'
5. **Response modulation:** During a frustrating follow-up meeting

where the email sender is present again, your heart's pounding and you want to snap. But you take a deep breath, make a note to raise it privately later and keep your tone calm until the meeting ends.

This is what emotional regulation could look like in practice, with each stage of a challenging emotional situation being met with a healthy coping strategy to ultimately keep you calm (and still in a job).

There are many other theories and models of emotional regulation and they largely follow similar themes. To avoid overcomplicating the issue, let's now examine how this helps support productivity.

The link between emotional regulation, executive function and productivity

It might not be the first thing people think of when they hear the word productivity, but **emotional regulation plays a pivotal role in how we start, sustain and complete tasks.**

Healthy emotional regulation helps us to buffer against the internal storms that make tasks feel harder than they are. It does this by supporting the brain's executive functions, including:

- **Task initiation:** Managing the emotional discomfort that often precedes starting something boring, complex or overwhelming.
- **Cognitive flexibility:** Adapting when things don't go to plan, rather than catastrophizing or abandoning ship.
- **Sustained attention:** Reining in intrusive thoughts or emotional distractions to stay focused.

- **Self-monitoring:** Being aware of how you're doing without tipping into harsh self-criticism or spirals of shame.
- **Impulse control:** Resisting the urge to react emotionally or divert attention to something easier or more rewarding.

In other words, **learning to regulate emotions doesn't just make you feel better, it can help you do better.**

> **Productivity isn't just about achieving goals or having the right tools. It's also about how we feel while doing it – and understanding whether those emotions help or hinder our ability to act.**

ADHD and emotional dysregulation: when 'the feels' get in the way of getting shit done

We often think of ADHD in terms of distraction, forgetfulness or being 'bad at time'. But **for many of us, the real daily struggle isn't attention, it's emotion.**

Emotional dysregulation was actually considered a core part of an ADHD diagnosis back in the day, ranked even above attention issues in some early descriptions. But when the diagnostic manual DSM-III came along in 1980, it stripped out the emotional side of ADHD and labelled it an 'associated feature' instead of a defining trait. This might sound like admin, but it has shaped decades of how ADHD has been diagnosed and treated, meaning that the emotional side has been largely ignored.

Fast-forward to now, and researchers, clinicians and a whole lot of lived experience are all pointing back to the same thing: if you have ADHD, **emotional dysregulation isn't an optional extra, it's often *the* core issue.**

For many people with ADHD, it's the out-of-proportion emotional responses, mood swings and intense rejection sensitivity that derail their lives more than distractibility ever could.

Researchers have proposed three models to explain how emotional dysregulation fits into ADHD:[3]

1. **It's baked into ADHD:** Emotional dysregulation is part of the condition, not separate from it.
2. **It's a subtype:** A specific group of people have both ADHD and high emotional reactivity.
3. **It's a parallel issue:** ADHD and emotional dysregulation are separate but overlapping challenges.

Whichever model you go with – and we strongly go with emotional dysregulation being 'baked into ADHD' – there's a growing consensus: **emotional dysregulation *matters*. It affects how ADHD shows up and how severe it feels.**

Without emotional regulation, we're more likely to:

- Avoid tasks that trigger difficult emotions like anxiety, fear of failure or shame.
- Struggle to start tasks because emotional overwhelm shuts down our ability to prioritize.
- Abandon goals at the first sign of frustration or perceived criticism.
- Feel paralysed by perfectionism, guilt or self-doubt.

- Get stuck in emotional loops, such as rumination, that take up mental bandwidth.

Let's say you're about to send a report to your manager. But you suddenly feel a wave of anxiety and start thinking, 'What if it's not good enough?' That emotional discomfort might lead to avoidance (putting off sending it), distraction (checking your phone instead), or even redoing the whole thing from scratch. **Emotional regulation strategies like cognitive reappraisal** ('It's OK if it's not perfect – it's a draft') **or mindfulness** ('Notice the anxiety without acting on it') **can help you to override the emotional blockade** and send the report anyway.

People with ADHD often experience emotions like they're happening at full volume. This isn't being dramatic or 'over-emotional', it's neurobiology.

Why is emotional dysregulation such a feature of ADHD? In people with ADHD the brain areas involved in emotion regulation, mainly the amygdala (which spots emotional threats) and the prefrontal cortex (which calms things down), don't always work in sync as they are poorly connected. The amygdala is often overactive, causing us to feel intense fear and anxiety which is often disproportionate to the situation. Meanwhile the prefrontal cortex is often underactive, which makes it less able to moderate the intense emotions coming from the amygdala.

This mismatch is part of the reason ADHD brains struggle with things like impulsive outbursts, difficulty calming down, and going from zero to 'I've ruined my life' in 30 seconds.

Studies using brain scans back this up: **adults with ADHD often show less activation in parts of the prefrontal cortex when they're trying to regulate emotional responses under stress.**

And because emotion regulation and executive functioning share brain resources, problems with one can exacerbate the other. In other words, **struggling to plan and organize your day is a lot harder when you're also overwhelmed by a storm of emotions.**

Rejection Sensitive Dysphoria (RSD): the pain you can't explain

One form of emotional dysregulation is so intense it's been given its own name: Rejection Sensitive Dysphoria, or RSD for short. It's not officially in the diagnostic manuals, but if you've ever felt **intense shame or despair after what seemed like a small criticism**, avoided doing something in case someone thought less of you, or overreacted to feeling ignored, dismissed or excluded...then you've probably experienced RSD.

RSD can feel like social pain turned up to 11. For those who haven't experienced it, it can come across as attention-seeking or overreacting. But, in reality, **it's a brain wired to experience rejection as a threat to identity.** And it's exhausting. Over 90 per cent of people with ADHD report experiencing RSD symptoms.[4] For around a third, it's the single most difficult part of living with ADHD.

RSD can lead to people avoiding asking key questions that then become barriers to getting shit done, avoiding meetings with certain people and even leaving jobs. James once left a job at a pub after someone else was praised for something James had never been praised for. So, he instantly quit, citing 'a virus, they don't know which one' as the reason. Imagine the shame? You probably don't have to.

Of all the manifestations of emotional dysregulation in ADHD, RSD sits as king of the hill, atop a pile of broken relationships, projects that never got off the ground and the ghosts of past jobs quit too early. **For most of us, this part of ADHD, which isn't even an official 'thing' in psychology/psychiatry, is the most unbearable part.**

Strategies for getting on top of ED

If you've ever felt like your emotions have their own remote control (and you're not the one holding it), then much of what we've presented in this chapter will feel familiar. **Emotional dysregulation is one of the most frustrating parts of ADHD, not just because the feelings are so big, but because they can feel like they hijack your day, your relationships and sometimes your confidence.**

The good news? You don't need to turn into a Zen monk or master every therapy skill to get a handle on it. Instead, there are a handful of practical, evidence-based strategies you can experiment with that take the edge off, build resilience and stop a bad five minutes from becoming a bad day. **You won't need to do them all at once** (no one can, especially with ADHD), **but you can try one or two at a time and see which tools actually help your brain calm the chaos.**

Strategy 1: Coaching and therapy

Firstly, we have to acknowledge that these services are often not free, and therefore, privilege and financial status can impact access to them. **Emotional dysregulation in ADHD often improves when you build awareness and learn practical coping tools, and both therapy and coaching can sometimes help here.**

- **Coaching focuses on the present and future:** It can help you to spot emotional triggers, create strategies and use accountability to practise new habits (like pausing before reacting). Coaches often help you to use tools like thought-challenging worksheets or structured routines so you're not relying on willpower alone.

- **Therapy can dig deeper into unhelpful thought patterns or trauma responses:** ADHD-informed Cognitive Behavioural Therapy (CBT) or Dialectical Behaviour Therapy (DBT) in particular can help with ADHD-based emotional dysregulation. DBT, for example, teaches distress tolerance, emotional regulation and interpersonal skills, especially useful for rejection sensitivity and big, fast mood swings.

Many people can benefit from both: coaching for day-to-day action plans, and therapy for underlying issues and skill-building.

Strategy 2: Mindfulness and grounding

Mindfulness isn't about 'emptying your mind' (which is impossible for most of us), **it's about noticing what's happening in your body and environment before you spiral.** Here are some approaches that can help dampen down the emotional cyclone:

- **Grounding techniques can interrupt emotional surges by anchoring you to the present.** Quick examples:
  - **The 5-4-3-2-1 method:** Notice five things you can see, four you can touch, three you can hear, two you can smell, one you can taste.
  - **Box breathing:** Inhale for four seconds, hold for four, exhale for four, hold for four.
  - **Tuning into one sense:** You might focus on touch, e.g., running cold water over your hands or paying attention to the feel of your feet on the floor.

Evidence suggests that mindfulness can reduce amygdala reactivity (your brain's 'alarm system') and help you respond rather than react. For ADHD, short, practical practices (two to five minutes) are more sustainable than long meditations.

Strategy 3: Label feelings and challenge (DESC)

Many people with ADHD act on feelings without naming them first, which can make emotions feel like facts. **By labelling the feelings** – if you are able to, not all of us can – using a tool like the DESC method (Describe, Express, Specify, Consequences), **we can begin to challenge thoughts and feelings that are misaligned with reality.**

Step 1. Pause and label: Literally stop and name what you're feeling ('I'm anxious', 'I'm frustrated'). This starts to shift the emotion from a full-body takeover into something you can observe.

Step 2. Challenge: Use the DESC method (Describe, Express, Specify, Consequences) to assert what you need to handle the situation:

a. **Describe what's happening** ('When the meeting runs over by 30 minutes...').
b. **Express how you feel** ('...I feel stressed and overwhelmed').
c. **Specify what you need** ('I need to leave at the agreed time').
d. **Consequences – outline the positive outcome** ('...so I can focus better later and meet deadlines').

This can help you to stay grounded, communicate clearly and can stop emotions from turning into explosions or shutdowns.

Strategy 4: Opposite Action

Sometimes our emotions tell us to do things that make the problem worse, like avoiding a phone call when we're anxious (which only builds more anxiety), snapping when we're angry (which usually leads to guilt or conflict), or disappearing when we feel ashamed (which can deepen the shame).

Opposite Action is a skill we've stolen/borrowed from DBT (Dialectical Behaviour Therapy) that helps to break this cycle by asking us to act in opposition to the way the emotion is pushing us.

It's a simple idea, but it can feel anything but simple in the moment. **You're deliberately doing the thing your brain is screaming not to do, which can feel awkward or even unnatural at first.**

Examples:

- If you're sad and want to isolate, call or text someone – even if it's just a quick 'hi'.
- If you're angry and want to lash out, soften your tone and slow your speech.
- If you're anxious and want to cancel, go to the event but plan a polite early exit if needed (so you feel safe).

Why bother? Because emotions are a bit like bullies: they can shrink when you don't let them run the show. Each time you practise the opposite action, your brain will hopefully learn that the feeling isn't as dangerous as it feels, and the intensity may drop faster next time.

The key is to start small. Pick one opposite action to experiment with each week. Even tiny changes (like sending a two-line text instead of full-on socialising) can shift how much power those intense feelings have over you, and over time, the fallout from emotional surges starts to shrink.

Chapter summary

Emotional dysregulation, those 'big feels' that show up uninvited, is one of the most overlooked yet disruptive parts of ADHD. This chapter explored what emotions actually are (beyond just 'feelings'), how the brain typically regulates them, and why for ADHD brains the volume knob often feels stuck on max.

We looked at how emotional regulation supports productivity by helping with the emotions around task initiation, flexibility, focus and impulse control, and how dysregulation can derail us into avoidance, shame spirals, perfectionism or quitting entirely. Emotional dysregulation, including Rejection Sensitive Dysphoria (RSD), isn't just an add-on to ADHD; for many, it's the biggest obstacle to staying on track.

We also suggested practical tools that can take the edge off when emotions threaten to hijack your day. These included:

- Coaching and therapy – to build awareness, develop action plans and learn emotion management skills like distress tolerance.
- Mindfulness and grounding – quick, realistic practices, like the 5–4–3–2–1 method or box breathing, to calm emotional storms.
- Labelling feelings and challenging them (DESC) – naming emotions and communicating needs assertively, so they don't run the show.
- Opposite Action – using the DBT-inspired technique of acting opposite to your emotional urge (like reaching out instead of isolating) to retrain the brain over time.

The key takeaway? Emotional dysregulation might make you feel like your life's been hijacked by a tiny trigger (hello, forgotten charging cable), but you're not completely powerless. By understanding the brain's role and experimenting with one or two strategies at a time, you can start to reduce the fallout, recover faster and keep moving forward, even when your feelings are loud.

Chapter 11

FORGET ME NOT

Working memory and the lost train of thought

James has always assumed that most people don't forget where they've put their phone while still holding it. Or leave the kitchen in a panic because they've lost their keys, only to realize they're in the fridge, right next to their phone, actually.

Working memory should be the glue that holds productivity together, except James's is more like a glue stick left in a hot car: dry, crumbly and completely useless when you actually need it. The ability to hold things in mind just long enough to do something with them turns out to be quite important if you're trying to live a functional adult life.

Being able to remember your childhood phone number or recite obscure facts but not keep the 'must call the GP' thought in your head for longer than four seconds can be demoralizing.

This invisible short-circuit has derailed even the best-laid plans. James might walk into a room with purpose and leave it three minutes later having done five unrelated tasks, none of which were the one he went in for.

Eventually, he tried creating physical 'anchors'; creating an 'ADHD station' and buying a bumbag to carry the essentials: phone, keys, wallet, earbuds, lip balm, fidget cube, spare fidget cube. It worked. For a while. Until he lost the bumbag.

So, he bought another one. And lost that too. To this day, there's a mystery bumbag in his house or office or possibly another dimension, quietly humming with uncharged devices and expired ibuprofen. And while the idea was solid – externalizing memory by creating a physical, always-accessible storage system – the execution faced the classic ADHD problem: things only work if you remember to use them.

The point here isn't that external aids don't work; it's that **ADHD brains need multiple systems (and often multiples of the same system). Because working memory lapses aren't rare glitches. *They are the operating system.*** James now has visual reminders, audio reminders, app-based nudges and, occasionally, Sam yelling 'PHONE?!' across the house like it's a weird domestic game show.

Your working memory won't magically improve. But by building better scaffolding, external cues, habits and backup plans, we can stop dropping quite so many mental spinning plates. And maybe, just maybe, find the bloody phone before it rings.

What is working memory?

Before we dive fully into working memory, it helps to know what it isn't. People often confuse working memory with short-term memory or long-term memory, so let's break it down.

> **You know that feeling when you walk into a room and immediately forget why you're there? That's probably not just age, distraction or bad luck. That's a lack of working memory, the brain's mental Post-it Note.**

Short-term memory holds a small bit of information, like a phone number or a name you just heard, for a few seconds. But unless you do something with that info, it disappears. You blink, and it's gone.

Working memory, on the other hand, **is mentally juggling small bits of information while you are doing or thinking about something else. It's not just about holding information, it's about actually using it.** Working memory lets you keep stuff in mind and manipulate it to do something useful: like doing mental maths, following multi-step instructions, or remembering the start of your sentence while finishing it.

Long-term memory is your brain's storage vault. Once something makes it in there (and it sticks), **it can last for days, months or even years**, like your old passwords, your favourite childhood snack or how to ride a bike.

So, if you regularly lose your train of thought mid-sentence or forget what you're doing halfway through a task, that's because your working memory isn't playing ball.

How working memory actually works

Working memory is more than just a mental storage box. **It's an active mental workspace that allows you to hold, manipulate and update information while you use it to accomplish something else.**

> **The key thing is that working memory is *active*. It's part memory, part attention and part problem-solving. That's why it's classed as an executive function. And it's also why it's such a common struggle for people with ADHD.**

Working memory is limited, typically, to only four to seven pieces of information at a time and is highly sensitive to distraction. And unlike long-term memory, which archives facts for years, **working memory is a fleeting, fragile thing. Lose focus, and the whole thing falls apart.**

The most widely accepted theory[1] says working memory has four main parts:

- **The 'ponological loop':** This keeps sounds and words on mental repeat (like remembering a phone number by repeating it in your head).
- **The 'visuospatial sketchpad':** This holds visual and spatial information (like remembering where the ketchup lives in the fridge).
- **The 'episodic buffer':** This links new information with what you already know.
- **The 'central executive':** This is the boss. Directs attention, switches tasks and decides what to hold on to and what to drop.

From a neuroscience point of view, **working memory activates a whole network of brain areas**, especially in the front and sides of the brain, places like the **prefrontal cortex, cingulate cortex and parietal lobes**. These regions act a bit like your brain's air traffic control, juggling incoming information and deciding what to hang on to and what can go. **The prefrontal cortex is especially important here**; it's the part of the brain that keeps things 'online' while you're using them, such as a goal, a rule or a plan.

Interestingly, **the prefrontal cortex doesn't just hold on to raw sensory details** (like 'the dog is brown'), **it deals in bigger-picture concepts**, like 'Don't let the dog out before checking the gate's closed'. The further forward you go in the prefrontal cortex, the more abstract the information it handles, like a mental manager moving from handling groceries to managing the whole shop.

But working memory isn't just a front-of-brain job. Other areas, like the striatum and basal ganglia, help decide what information is important enough to keep in mind, almost like a librarian at the door of your brain. The cerebellum and midbrain chip in too, along with sensory brain regions like the visual cortex, which holds on to details from the outside world, like what someone's face looked like a moment ago.

Rather than being one single 'working memory centre', the brain relies on a dynamic team of regions, working together across long-distance neural connections. These areas sync up using brainwaves (patterns of electrical activity). Think of it like a group chat between brain areas, where staying in rhythm matters. **The stronger the sync, the better your working memory tends to be.**

Working memory relies on effective neural connections. And the two most important chemical messengers involved? **Dopamine and noradrenaline** – key players, as you will know by now, in ADHD.

Are you going to keep banging on about dopamine?

Yes. Yes, we are.

For a long time, scientists treated **dopamine and noradrenaline** as separate systems, but we now know they often work together. They're made through similar biological pathways, can be released from the same brain structures (like the impossible to pronounce locus coeruleus: go on, try it) and even **target many of the same brain areas, including the prefrontal cortex and the hippocampus, two key players in memory and attention.**

Because of this, researchers believe **dopamine and noradrenaline** don't just work in parallel; they **may help the brain shift into the right state for learning and remembering.** Together, they support the transitions between brain modes, such as 'resting', 'focused', or 'ready for action', all of which affect how well working memory functions.

Even though they often team up, dopamine and noradrenaline have distinct roles in shaping memory:

- **Dopamine helps you focus on what matters.** It's the chemical highlighter for your brain, boosting the chances that relevant or rewarding information is remembered, and filtering out distractions. When dopamine activity is disrupted, that selectivity gets fuzzy, and you might store irrelevant details or miss the important ones.

- **Noradrenaline boosts memory when you're emotionally switched on.** It's closely tied to arousal, not the sexy kind of arousal, but the 'This is important, pay attention!' kind. Think of a time when you remembered every detail of a stressful or exciting event. That's noradrenaline at work.

Both chemicals also influence something called 'neural gain', which is a fancy way of describing how clearly the brain amplifies the 'important' signals while reducing background noise. **When this mechanism works well, you can hold and manipulate the right bits of information in your mind, even in busy or distracting environments.**

Why working memory matters for productivity

In the fast-paced and information-rich landscape of the modern workplace, working memory stands out as a fundamental driver of productivity. A growing body of evidence from cognitive psychology and neuroscience underscores the key role of working memory in professional success, with limitations in this area directly linked to decreased output and increased errors. The integrity of our working memory is directly proportional to our professional output. Maybe read that sentence again. Effective working memory is essential for a multitude of workplace demands, including:

- **Task management and planning:** Juggling multiple projects, prioritizing tasks and breaking down complex goals into manageable steps all rely heavily on the ability to hold and manipulate information in working memory.
- **Problem-solving and decision-making:** When faced with a challenge, working memory allows us to hold the various elements of

the problem in mind, retrieve relevant knowledge from long-term memory and mentally simulate potential solutions.

- **Focus and attention:** A strong working memory is crucial for maintaining concentration on a task, resisting distractions, and staying on track despite interruptions.
- **Learning and skill acquisition:** Acquiring new skills and knowledge requires the ability to hold new information in mind while connecting it to existing understanding.

When working memory is compromised, even simple tasks become more challenging. You may:

- forget what you were doing mid-task
- lose track of conversations
- keep making avoidable mistakes because you can't hold all the info you need in mind
- feel overwhelmed trying to juggle more than one thing at a time.

It's effectively a cognitive bottleneck.

Working memory in ADHD: what goes wrong

People with ADHD don't just have 'a bit of forgetfulness'. The science **shows working memory impairment is one of the most consistent and severe cognitive deficits in ADHD**, particularly affecting the central executive part that deals with manipulating information and holding attention steady.

About 75–81 per cent of children with ADHD have significant working memory deficits, particularly with tasks that require effortful control[2] – that is, not just remembering facts but updating and acting on them. And we know that this persists into adulthood.[3]

Importantly, research has shown that, while visuospatial short-term memory may be mildly impaired, and your phonological short-term memory (remembering sounds or words) is usually better, your **central executive working memory** (managing, manipulating and updating information) **is where things really fall apart. This is the part most linked to everyday ADHD symptoms.**

These deficits are rooted in the usual brain differences in ADHD: reduced dopamine and noradrenaline in key brain regions, structural differences in the key brain areas and weaker connectivity between the brain regions involved in attention and memory.

In other words, working memory is not about 'not trying hard enough'. **It's a brain-level issue, affecting how information is processed, remembered and acted upon.**

Daily life with poor working memory

Working memory deficits in ADHD are more than just frustrating; they can be functionally disabling in everyday life. Because working memory is the cognitive glue that holds plans, tasks and intentions together, when it falters, so does everything else.

Let's break down how this can show up, particularly in the context of productivity.

In work or study:

- Following multi-step instructions can become nearly impossible. ('Wait, what was step three again?')
- Losing your place mid-way through tasks, emails, or documents.

- Making careless errors, not because you don't know better, but because your brain dropped part of the process.
- Repeatedly rereading or rewriting because your mind blanks halfway through.
- Trouble juggling competing priorities, deadlines, or inputs – you can't hold it all in your head.
- Interruptions cause derailment – one distraction and the whole mental plan vanishes.
- Finishing what you start is hard because you forget the reason you started it.

These issues don't just slow you down; they can mess with your confidence and increase your stress levels.

Outside the workplace, in everyday tasks that influence productivity, we can see the following:

- Forgetting what you were doing while doing it (*Why am I in the kitchen?*).
- Struggling to recall verbal instructions (*Did they say 11am or 1pm?*).
- Losing track of what you've already done (*Did I take my meds? Did I send that email?*)
- Misplacing items, especially when routines aren't firmly established.
- Difficulty meal-planning, budgeting, or packing – any task that requires juggling multiple bits of info.

This cascade of errors, embarrassment and mental fatigue can lead to what many describe as a persistent sense of failure, even when you're working twice as hard as others.

Strategies for supporting working memory

Strategy 1: Develop a working memory toolkit

Below is a table of five strategies that in combination (the right combination for you), can help make up for working memory issues.

Strategy	What it is	How it works
Chunking	Breaking big tasks or information into smaller, more manageable pieces.	Reduces overload on working memory by limiting how much you have to hold in mind at once.
Visualization	Creating mental images or diagrams of the information.	Engages the visuospatial part of working memory, helping abstract or verbal information stick more easily.
Minimize distractions	Reducing external and internal interruptions (like noise or racing thoughts).	Frees up cognitive resources so your brain can focus on the task instead of constant reorienting.
Strategic use of external aids	Using calendars, timers, notes, reminders or apps to support memory.	Offloads the storage function of working memory so you can focus on thinking, not just remembering.
Healthy lifestyle	Getting enough sleep, regular movement and balanced meals.	Supports brain function, emotional regulation and memory by keeping your whole system running better.

Putting these strategies together doesn't mean reinventing your entire routine, it's about layering in small supports that work with your brain instead of against it. Let's say you've got a report to write. You might start by chunking it into mini-tasks (outline, section one, section two...), then set up a visual timer so you can see time passing as you work. Before you begin, stick a note on your monitor with the three main points you need to remember, and set your phone to 'Do Not Disturb'. You could also decide in advance that after finishing each chunk, you'll give yourself a reward, maybe a coffee or ten minutes of something fun.

AI can also be your friend here:

- **Chunking:** Task-management AI (like Goblin Tools or Notion AI) can automatically break big projects into smaller, actionable tasks based on a simple prompt ('Break this research report into steps'). This saves you the mental effort of deciding where to start and ensures no steps are forgotten.
- **Visualization:** Tools like Miro AI or FigJam AI can convert bullet lists or meeting notes into visual maps or diagrams. This engages the visuospatial part of working memory without needing you to manually build the diagrams.
- **Minimize distractions:** Focus apps with AI-driven blockers (e.g. Freedom or Motion) can predictively block distracting sites or apps based on your schedule or behaviour ('You usually get distracted here, should I block social media for 30 minutes?'). This reduces the cognitive cost of self-monitoring distractions.

- **Strategic use of external aids:** AI-powered reminders (Google Assistant, Siri Shortcuts with AI integrations) that detect delays ('You haven't opened your task app yet. Want me to read today's list aloud?'), smart summarization (e.g. using Google NotebookLM) can condense long notes into bullet points you can quickly revisit. This offloads some of the demands on your mental storage and lets you focus on the task rather than recalling details.
- **Healthy lifestyle:** Wearables with AI coaching (like WHOOP or Oura integrations) can detect patterns (e.g. poor sleep or low activity) and nudge you with specific, achievable actions ('Your sleep dropped 20 per cent, a 15-minute walk may help concentration today'). This can help to keep the body-brain system primed for memory without extra tracking work.

None of these tools are magic on their own, but together, they create the scaffolding that working memory often needs when ADHD is in the mix.

Strategy 2: Ask for organizational support

Let's face it, working memory issues often show up most when they come up against the demands of the processes, policies and people we work with. The table below provides some approaches for seeking support that is neuroinclusive. **These approaches are what we would call 'reasonable adjustments' at work.**

Support	What it is	Why it might help
Clear and concise communication	Sharing information in straightforward, structured formats (e.g. bullet points, check lists).	Reduces the load on working memory by making it easier to follow, process and recall key details.
Structured workflows	Established step-by-step procedures for common tasks.	Minimizes the need to hold instructions in mind by externalizing task sequences.
Promoting single-tasking	Encouraging staff to focus on one task at a time rather than multitasking.	Prevents working memory overload and supports deeper concentration and task completion.
Providing quiet spaces	Designated low-stimulation work areas for focused tasks.	Reduces environmental distractions, freeing up cognitive capacity for demanding work.

These supports are most effective when used in combination, not as a one-off initiative, but as part of a thoughtful workplace culture.

Imagine an employee who struggles to keep track of verbal instructions and loses momentum when switching between tasks. Their manager starts by sending follow-up emails with clear bullet points after meetings, making expectations easier to fulfil. They also map out a standard workflow for common tasks, so the employee doesn't have to start from scratch every time. The employee is encouraged to block off quiet time for focused work, without interruptions or meeting requests, and the team agrees to try a 'one tab open at a time' policy during key working hours. **Over time, these adjustments might not only reduce the cognitive pressure on an employee's working memory, but they could also signal that their needs are valid and that support is a shared responsibility, not a personal failing.**

Again, AI (especially if your employer pays for access to it) can be your friend:

- **Clear and concise communication:** AI summarization (ChatGPT, Google NotebookLM, or Teams Copilot) can auto-generate post-meeting bullet points and action items. This means you don't have to rely on memory for long discussions.
- **Structured workflows:** AI-driven workflow tools (like Asana's AI assistant) can create templates or next-step prompts based on your previous tasks ('Want me to set this as a recurring check list for future reports?'). This reduces reliance on remembering processes and allows for consistency.
- **Promoting single-tasking:** Apps like Sunsama or Sorted[3] (with AI) can show one priority at a time and reorder your day based on time left, energy level or meeting changes. This stops working memory from being pulled in five directions at once.
- **Providing quiet spaces:** Noise-cancelling AI can filter sound during virtual meetings or coworking. AI scheduling tools (Reclaim.ai) can auto-block 'focus time' into calendars by spotting gaps. This can help to automate environmental control so your memory isn't taxed by juggling interruptions.

Strategy 3: Use routines, automations and anchors

Routines, automations and anchors are so important they have a chapter of their own (Chapter 4), but their value to working memory in particular makes them worth revisiting here. Used together these strategies can create scaffolding for a forgetful brain.

- **Routines reduce the memory burden.** A well-worn routine can be like muscle memory for your day. Theoretically, once it's in place, you don't have to think about what to do next; your brain should know the next step. This can massively reduce the strain on working memory, because decisions are already made. Even something as simple as a set morning routine (tea, meds, stretch, check calendar) can prevent early-day derailment.

  The ADHD twist: **although we need routines, they can get boring fast, so it helps to rotate elements** (Monday = loud playlist, Tuesday = slower start), **or pair them with a bit of novelty to keep engagement alive.** You may also forget routines that you have put into place, so alarms to remind you to start your new routine and reminders or lists that tell you what the new routine is can be useful.

- **Anchors – attaching tasks to existing habits – can help to create consistency without relying on willpower.** Anchors work by tieing new behaviours to something you already do, sort of like 'habit piggybacking'. For example:

  - After I make my morning tea, I check my calendar.
  - When I brush my teeth, I lay out tomorrow's clothes.
  - As I shut my laptop, I update tomorrow's to-do list.

  These mini-pairings can help to turn chaotic, floating tasks into fixed rituals. The cue reminds your brain what to do next (no white-board required, as long as you remember the new behaviour you wanted to tie to your anchor!).

- **Automations let the tech do the thinking for you.** Technology can be brilliant for supporting working memory if you use it before your brain forgets what you needed it for. Think: reminders that go off before your deadline, calendar events that repeat weekly, smart speakers that announce when it's time to take a break or switch tasks. Even simple tools like:

- recurring alarms (e.g. 'Check to-do list at 2pm')
- IFTTT or Google Calendar auto-reminders
- to-do apps that show one task at a time (like Goblin Tools or Sorted[3])

...can act as external memory supports, freeing up your limited cognitive bandwidth for the actual doing part.

Combining all three sets of scaffolding might work best. Here's a real-life scenario as an example:

Meet Ben. Mornings used to be total chaos: forgotten meds, missed meetings and a lot of staring at the kettle, wondering what they were meant to be doing. So, Ben builds a working memory support system using routines, automations and anchors:

Routine: Ben sets a fixed order to the morning: wake up, shower, coffee, meds, check calendar. It's the same flow every weekday, so it will hopefully eventually become automatic (and less panic-inducing).

Automation: A smart speaker announces 'Take your meds and check your calendar' at 7:15am. There's also a repeating reminder in their phone that pops up with a check list if they haven't marked it done by 8:30am.

Anchor: They link the habit of taking medication to their morning coffee: 'When the coffee brews, I take my meds.' The coffee smell becomes the cue.

> Now, instead of juggling 12 things in their head before 9am, Ben relies on external structure to do the remembering for them. The routine sets the flow, the tech prompts the actions and the anchor keeps it all grounded in something that's already happening.

Finally, **here is how AI can support your use of routines:**

Routines: Tools like Notion AI, ChatGPT or Google Gemini can generate daily check lists that adapt based on your calendar ('Want me to create your morning routine list with today's priorities already added?'). This keeps routines consistent and dynamically updated without needing to remember adjustments.

Anchors: AI-powered smart speakers (Alexa, Google Nest) can use routines ('When you make coffee, announce "Take your meds and check your to-do list"'). This turns everyday actions into reliable prompts, no working memory needed.

Automations: Tools like Make or Zapier can build chains: 'When I finish a meeting, summarize notes with NotebookLM, send me a Slack ping to review, and schedule next steps.' And AI scheduling assistants (like Reclaim.ai or Motion) can dynamically re-plan your day when you miss something. This helps to 'offload' the entire 'remembering and rearranging' process, so you can follow the prompts.

And if any one of these tools breaks down? Try another or try again. **Trying again isn't a failure. It's how you build a brain-friendly system that actually works for you.**

Chapter summary

This chapter covered why:

- Working memory isn't just about remembering things. It's about using information in real time. It's the function that lets you juggle, update and hold information in your head while you apply it.
- It's one of the most consistently impaired functions in ADHD.
- Dopamine and noradrenaline play a big role. These neurochemicals help prioritize what to focus on, filter out distractions and keep the brain's network of memory regions in sync.
- When working memory falters, it messes with everything: task management, attention, problem-solving, learning – and your confidence.

The good news is, you can use tools to support your brain rather than blame it:

- Chunking, visualization and distraction management to reduce overload.
- External aids (timers, notes, reminders) to take the pressure off your brain's 'mental Post-it'.
- Routines, anchors and automations to build memory into your environment – not just your head.
- Organizational supports like clear communication, quiet spaces and single-tasking aren't just nice extras – they're workplace access tools.

And remember: it's not that you're careless or lazy. You're running a complex task list on a whiteboard that wipes itself every time someone talks to you.

Chapter 12

PROGRESS, NOT PERFECTION

(Especially when perfect never happens)

Perfectionism is something that Sam struggles with constantly. It eats up their time and stops them from doing so many things! It is the reason that they can spend over an hour responding to an email – because they want to make sure that they are not just understood but that whatever they have to say is received in the right way. So, it has to be perfect, this phantom standard that they are always reaching for. And yet, despite having never achieved it, they still aim for it and end up crestfallen and full of self-loathing when yet again, they miss the mark. Even if they do manage to do something really well, they will always minimize their contribution or success. They are the poster girl for maladaptive perfectionism.

They have been trying and failing to write an episode for the podcast for over a year because they want it to be perfect, but as they don't know what a perfect episode would look like, all their efforts are futile. The same goes for the podcast of their own they've been wanting to start for over two years now. They have a plan, they have a name, they have a rough outline for the first three episodes, but the fear of it not being perfect is stopping them from actually getting started, even though the people that would listen to this podcast would not expect perfection. In fact, they'd probably be disappointed if Sam did produce a polished and professional podcast because that would not be authentic!

What's wrong with perfect?

Perfectionism might sound like a harmless or even admirable trait (who doesn't want to do things well?), but psychologists define it quite differently. At its core, perfectionism is about much more than simply aiming high. It's **the relentless drive to meet impossibly high standards, often fuelled by the belief that anything less than flawless equals failure.** It's less about excellence and more about fear: fear of criticism, of letting people down, of not being 'good enough'.

According to the American Psychological Association, perfectionism is 'the tendency to demand of others or oneself an extremely high or even flawless level of performance, in excess of what is required by the situation'. It's strongly linked to anxiety, depression, eating disorders and burnout. In other words, **perfectionism doesn't just make things harder, it can make life feel unbearable.**

Perfectionism can be **'self-oriented'** (I have to be perfect), **'other-oriented'** (you have to be perfect) or **'socially prescribed'** (everyone expects me to be perfect).

Healthy vs harmful perfectionism

In the 1960s and 1970s, perfectionism was viewed as a purely negative trait, a sign of neurosis or deep insecurity. Researchers described it as 'a rigid, obsessive need to achieve, tied to a fragile sense of self-worth'. This version of perfectionism believed that if you weren't perfect, you were nothing. Unsurprisingly, **this version of perfectionism was linked to procrastination, chronic stress and self-sabotage.**

But starting in the 1990s, the understanding of perfectionism became more nuanced. Psychologists began to recognize that perfectionism isn't one-size-fits-all. **Some people strive for excellence in healthy ways**, setting high yet realistic standards, taking pride in their progress, and bouncing back from failure. **Others, though, get stuck in a toxic loop of self-criticism and avoidance.** These different styles became known as **adaptive** and **maladaptive perfectionism.**

This shift matters. Because it helps us to see that wanting to do well isn't the problem. It's the cost of that drive – how much it hurts us, how much it gets in the way – that tells us whether perfectionism is helping or harming us.

Adaptive perfectionism: when striving is supportive

This is the 'healthier' side of perfectionism, sometimes called 'perfectionistic strivings'. **People high in adaptive perfectionism aim high and care deeply about doing well.** They're often organized, hardworking and persistent. **But crucially, they know when to stop. They can accept that a piece of work is 'good enough' even if it's not**

flawless. Mistakes don't shatter their sense of self; they're seen as part of the process.

This type of perfectionism is linked with:

- higher self-esteem
- greater life satisfaction
- increased resilience
- less engagement in risky health behaviours.

In short, this kind of striving can be energizing, rather than exhausting.

Maladaptive perfectionism: when 'good enough' feels like failure

Then there's the darker twin: 'perfectionistic concerns'.

Maladaptive perfectionism is driven by fear rather than passion. People in this category often **set impossible standards and then punish themselves for not meeting them.** Even successes can feel hollow because they're quickly dismissed. If you've ever said, 'I only did well because I got lucky', or 'That wasn't real success', then this may resonate with you. (This feels like an unnecessary personal attack on Sam because all of this describes them a little *too* well!)

People with maladaptive perfectionism tend to:

- ruminate on flaws, no matter how small
- struggle to start tasks for fear they won't do them perfectly
- feel their self-worth is entirely tied to performance
- view anything less than perfect as a failure.

This kind of perfectionism is strongly linked to anxiety, depression, burnout, eating disorders and even suicidal thoughts. It's not just stressful, it's unhealthy and unsustainable.

The table below compares these two forms of perfectionism.

Characteristic	Adaptive perfectionism (perfectionistic strivings)	Maladaptive perfectionism (perfectionistic concerns)
Core mindset	Striving for excellence and personal growth	Fear of failure and avoidance of mistakes
Goal setting	Sets high but realistic and achievable standards based on personal strengths	Sets excessively high, rigid and often unattainable standards
Reaction to mistakes	Tolerates imperfections; views mistakes as learning opportunities without harsh self-criticism	Feels intense shame, guilt and self-criticism; views mistakes as proof of personal failure
Emotional experience	Derives pleasure, satisfaction and pride from effort and accomplishment	Experiences chronic anxiety, stress, dissatisfaction and relief rather than satisfaction upon completion
Focus of attention	Focuses on doing things right and achieving positive outcomes	Focuses on avoiding errors and negative consequences
Associated outcomes	Higher self-esteem, conscientiousness, motivation, life satisfaction and positive affect	Higher rates of depression, anxiety, burnout, eating disorders and suicidal ideation

The spectrum: an overlooked third group

Research now recognizes that perfectionism isn't a binary, it's more like a spectrum with **a third, slightly unimaginatively titled group: non-perfectionists**, AKA, James. (If you have ever received an email from James, you'll very quickly see perfectionism isn't on his radar.)

So, the three groups are:

1. **Healthy perfectionists:** High in striving, low in self-critical fear. They aim high but aren't crushed by imperfection.
2. **Unhealthy perfectionists:** High in both striving and fear. They push themselves hard but never feel good enough.
3. **Non-perfectionists:** Low on both fronts. These folks may not set intense personal standards and are less affected by mistakes.

What does perfectionism look like?

Interestingly, it's not always obvious! One model of perfectionism identifies overt and covert perfectionists.

Overt perfectionists are openly critical of themselves and others. You can usually spot their high standards and frustration. **Covert perfectionists, on the other hand, look calm on the outside but are quietly battling intense self-criticism and anxiety.** This hidden pressure can be just as harmful, if not more so.

Psychologists have built various models of how perfectionism shows up in our thoughts and behaviours. They break down into six key components:

- **Concern over mistakes:** Seeing mistakes as disasters rather than learning opportunities. A core feature of unhealthy perfectionism.
- **Doubts about actions:** Second-guessing yourself constantly, never quite sure if you did something right.
- **Personal standards:** Setting high goals for yourself. On its own, this can be healthy striving, but paired with fear or shame, it can become a trap.
- **Parental expectations and parental criticism:** Feeling like your worth depends on meeting high (or impossible) standards set by caregivers. These beliefs often stick around well into adulthood.
- **Organization:** Liking things neat, tidy and planned. Nothing wrong with that, unless your need for control starts making life harder instead of easier.

This model helps us to see that **perfectionism isn't just one thing, it's a pattern of thoughts and habits that can build up over time, especially if we were raised to fear failure more than we were taught to embrace growth.**

How does this impact productivity?

Perfectionism often gets mistaken for a badge of honour in school or at work, something that signals dedication, high standards and future success. But the research tells a different story.

A study published in 2018[1] examined decades of data and found that **perfectionism has a minimal, if any, meaningful link to job performance.** Regardless of whether someone was a so-called 'healthy' perfectionist (chasing excellence) or an 'unhealthy' one (terrified of failure), the impact on actual performance was...almost zero.

So, what's going on?

It turns out that **the benefits of 'healthy' perfectionism, like conscientiousness and motivation, are often cancelled out by the costs: stress, burnout, decision paralysis and self-doubt.** You might push yourself to do something brilliantly, but waste hours tweaking tiny details, second-guessing your decisions or avoiding the task altogether.

And ironically, trying to get one thing 'just right' can mean missing deadlines, neglecting other tasks or never finishing anything at all.

When perfect becomes paralysis

For many people, especially those with maladaptive perfectionism, it doesn't lead to action. It leads to inaction.

Maladaptive perfectionism is one of the strongest psychological predictors of chronic procrastination (covered in Chapter 7). When the bar is set impossibly high, the stakes of falling short feel terrifying. The thought of not doing something perfectly creates so much anxiety that it feels safer not to start at all. **Procrastination can become a coping mechanism, a temporary way to escape shame, self-criticism or imagined judgment.** But of course, it only makes things worse in the long run.

Another common trap is waiting for the 'perfect moment' to begin, when your mood is right, your to-do list is clear and your energy is high. That moment rarely comes. And so, the task stays undone, feeding guilt and reinforcing the perfectionist loop.

People with 'socially prescribed' perfectionism often fear letting others down. If you're convinced that your boss, partner or peers expect perfection, even starting a task can feel like walking into a trap. It's easier to delay and blame time than to risk feeling judged or exposed.

Perfectionism can also show up as analysis paralysis, getting stuck in an endless loop of overthinking, second-guessing and avoiding decisions altogether.

The core belief? That there's one 'right' answer and choosing anything less means failure.

Underneath all this is often a deep fear of regret, of making the 'wrong' decision and feeling the emotional fallout. So, rather than risk that, perfectionists often choose inaction. But indecision is a decision in itself – one that drains time, energy and momentum.

The burnout spiral

Finally, perfectionism doesn't just slow you down. Over time, it wears you out.

Maladaptive perfectionism is strongly linked to burnout (covered in Chapter 2), especially in high-pressure environments like academia, healthcare or corporate jobs. It's one of the most reliable predictors of exhaustion, becoming emotionally detached or disillusioned with your work, and feeling like you're not good enough, no matter how hard you try.

This pattern is often fuelled by relentless worry, ruminating on mistakes, doubting yourself and mentally rehearsing worst-case scenarios. And the cost of that constant pressure? Burnout.

Even the more 'adaptive' form of perfectionism, setting ambitious goals and pushing yourself, can lead to burnout if it isn't balanced with rest, compassion and a realistic view of what's sustainable.

ADHD and the pressure to be perfect

If you live with ADHD and also struggle with perfectionism, you're not alone, and you're not imagining the connection. **For many of us, perfectionism isn't about wanting gold stars or being the best. It's about fear. Shame. Exhaustion. And the desperate hope that if we just get things 'right', maybe we won't get it wrong again.**

Perfectionism isn't officially a part of ADHD. However, it often appears as a survival strategy.

Growing up with ADHD often means hearing things like 'you're not working hard enough', 'you're careless', or 'why can't you just focus?' These messages stick. Over time, they can harden into a belief that *you* are the problem, and that maybe, just maybe, if you never mess up again, people will stop being disappointed in you.

This is where perfectionism kicks in, not as ambition, but as armour.

Why ADHD makes perfectionism harder (and harsher)

The ADHD brain struggles with executive function (we covered this in Chapter 1). Striving for perfection, on the other hand, demands structure, control and flawlessness. It's a mismatch made in hell.

Executive dysfunction means we often can't start unless the conditions feel 'just right', or we can over-plan or over-prepare to feel in control and end up creating elaborate systems we can't keep up with.

When we add RSD (rejection sensitive dysphoria) and emotional dysregulation into the mix (covered in Chapter 10), arguably the biggest drivers of perfectionism in ADHD, **we can try to be perfect, not to impress, but to avoid the hurt.**

If you've ever felt like 'If I don't get this exactly right, I'll feel destroyed', you're not being dramatic. **For people with ADHD and RSD, the emotional fallout of failure or judgment can be genuinely overwhelming.**

The ADHD-perfectionism cycle: a trap with no exit

Perfectionism in ADHD isn't just a bad habit; it's a cycle. Let's put this cycle into a real-world scenario.

> Meet Priya. Let's say Priya has ADHD and works in a fast-paced job where she's expected to juggle multiple projects. One Monday morning, she forgets to submit a monthly report, again. It's the third time this quarter. Here is how the cycle can go:

1. **She misses the deadline:** She started it, but got distracted by an 'urgent' email, then hyperfocused on fixing a formatting issue in another document, then ran out of time. Classic ADHD time blindness.
2. **She feels awful:** As soon as she realizes, shame hits like a freight train. Her stomach drops. Her manager's going to be disappointed (again). She starts spiralling: 'Why can't I just get it together?'
3. **She makes a new rule:** 'I have to be more organized'. She creates

a colour-coded, hyper-detailed task system, schedules multiple check-ins and tells herself, 'This time, I'll stay on top of everything. No mistakes.' (This paragraph feels so on the nose, it may as well be a diagnostic symptom of ADHD).

4. **Then she freezes:** The new system is so complex it's overwhelming. She spends more time tweaking the structure than doing the work. Her brain avoids even opening the file because it feels too heavy to face.
5. **Another ball drops:** She misses a follow-up meeting because she forgot to check the new reminder system. Cue more shame, more self-criticism. 'I knew I'd mess it up.'
6. **She doubles down:** In response, she adds more structure. More alarms, more folders, more guilt. The cycle resets, only now it's even harder to break.

Perfectionism, especially with ADHD, is about fear, overwhelm and trying to outrun a lifetime of 'not good enough'. And round it goes, eating away at confidence, energy and mental health.

The good news is that there are strategies for trying to take the sting out of perfectionism, and we'll cover those next.

Strategies for working on perfectionism

If perfectionism has been running you into the ground, this section is your toolkit for changing that. Whether your perfectionism shows up as procrastination, paralysis, or endless tweaking, these evidence-based strategies can help you do the thing, even if it's messy.

Strategy 1: Behavioural strategies that break the cycle

- **Focus on the process, not the outcome:** Instead of 'Finish this perfectly,' try 'Work on this for 25 minutes.'
- **Behavioural activation:** Action creates motivation; it's not always the other way around. Start ridiculously small (e.g. 'Open the document' or 'Write one sentence') and completing that small, achievable task can get the dopamine flowing.
- **Test the rejection fear:** Exposing yourself to how people respond to 'good enough' often helps to take the fangs off perfectionism. To make this slightly less painful, share a draft with someone you trust. See what happens (spoiler: it's rarely catastrophic).

Strategy 2: Practising self-compassion to challenge self-criticism

Perfectionism thrives on self-criticism: that inner voice telling you you're lazy, useless or 'should have done better'. The research is clear on this; beating ourselves up doesn't improve performance. It just adds shame on top of struggle. Self-compassion, on the other hand, has been shown to reduce perfectionism, anxiety and burnout. Showing yourself compassion, as challenging as it can be, is a practical tool for getting unstuck.

Here are a few ADHD-friendly ways to start:

- **Talk to yourself like a friend.** If your best mate made a mistake, you wouldn't call them a failure. You'd probably say something like, 'That was rough, but you'll figure it out.' Try offering yourself the same words. Out loud, if possible (it lands differently if spoken and has more psychological power).

- **Name what's hard.** Instead of 'I'm rubbish at deadlines,' try 'Deadlines are genuinely tough for my ADHD brain.' This reframes the problem without blaming yourself.
- **Try a micro-pause.** When the self-criticism spiral kicks in, take a breath and say, 'This is hard. I'm allowed to find this hard.' Then do the smallest next step you can.
- **Keep a kindness note.** Write down one supportive phrase (e.g. 'Good enough is good enough' or 'Progress, not perfection') and stick it somewhere you'll see it mid-task.
- **Write a compassionate letter to yourself.** Writing a letter to yourself from the perspective of someone who unconditionally loves you, in their compassionate voice, can 'self-soothe the self-critic' via writing. It doesn't have to be an essay, even spending five minutes writing a short compassionate letter to yourself about one mistake or challenge can sometimes help.

The point isn't to erase self-criticism altogether; that voice may always show up from time to time. The goal is to balance it with compassion, so you can move forward instead of freezing.

Strategy 3: Use the tools of therapy

Talking therapies, such as CBT or ACT, or coaching, can help some people with perfectionism. But, as many people can't access or afford these services, borrowing from them can help you to make a start.

For example, CBT can help you to spot and change the unhelpful thoughts and behaviours that feed perfectionism. So, **try challenging**

all-or-nothing thinking: Instead of 'If this isn't perfect, I'm a failure,' try 'Doing it imperfectly still moves me forward.' Say it out loud. Repeat it. Make challenging those thoughts a routine.

This next tool may feel terrifying, but taking an 'exposure therapy' approach can show that, by testing our fears in a safe way, we can take away their power. **Deliberately do small things imperfectly (send an email with a typo, leave a dish unwashed). Notice the world doesn't end.**

ACT teaches you how to unhook from perfectionistic thoughts instead of fighting them. So:

- **Name the thought:** 'I'm having the thought that I'm a failure' is different from 'I am a failure'.
- **Allow the feelings:** Fear, shame and anxiety can come along for the ride, but they don't get to drive.
- **Focus on values:** Ask yourself, 'What matters more than being perfect?' Then take one small action that moves you towards it.

Strategy 4: Can AI help?

Short answer? Yes – if you use it the right way.

For some people with ADHD, perfectionism can often lead to paralysis. You spend ages rewriting the same email, can't finish a task because it's 'not quite right', or avoid starting something because the bar you've set is impossibly high. **AI tools, like ChatGPT, Grammarly, or Notion AI, can help to break the cycle by reducing the pressure to get things perfect before you begin.**

But let's be clear: **AI is a support, not a solution.** It won't fix the fear of failure or magically rewire your self-worth. What it can do is act as an external brain that speeds up the messy parts: getting started, drafting and finishing. Sam can easily spend over an hour writing one email; when they remember that AI exists, they use it to give them a starting point that they can tweak.

Here's how AI might actually help:

- **Getting unstuck:** Staring at a blank page? Ask an AI to draft an outline, generate ideas or write a first version. Having something, anything, on the page can stop the perfectionist spiral before it starts.
- **Quicker editing:** If you rewrite sentences over and over, let AI suggest edits. Tools like Grammarly or ChatGPT can smooth out grammar or tone, giving you a version to accept, reject or adapt instead of chasing the mythical 'perfect sentence', e.g. 'Write a rough first draft of a cover letter for a graphic design job. Keep it short, friendly and confident.'
- **Reality checks:** Perfectionism can distort what's good enough. AI can offer a second opinion or provide examples of what a 'standard' answer, bio, or message looks like. This can help to recalibrate your expectations so that you can stop overdelivering on everything.
- **Reducing overwhelm:** When everything feels huge and complicated, you can use AI to break things down into steps. It's like having a calm co-pilot to help you chunk big tasks into something more doable. Example: 'Break down writing a report into five simple steps I can follow.'

Chapter summary

Perfectionism is often misunderstood as a sign of high standards or strong motivation, but for many of us, especially those with ADHD, it's something else entirely: a defence mechanism. It's about fear more than it is excellence.

For ADHDers, perfectionism often grows out of a lifetime of being told we're lazy, careless, or not trying hard enough. It becomes a shield, an exhausting attempt to avoid criticism or rejection by doing things flawlessly. But that shield is heavy. And it doesn't work.

The research is clear: perfectionism doesn't improve performance. In fact, it's strongly linked to procrastination, decision paralysis, burnout, anxiety and shame. When your standards are impossibly high, just starting a task can feel terrifying. When your self-worth is tied to getting everything right, even success feels hollow.

This chapter offered practical, evidence-based tools for managing perfectionism in a neurodivergent-friendly way. These include the above, plus:

- Reframing your goals from outcomes to process
- Using tiny, achievable actions to create momentum (not wait for it)
- Testing your fear of 'not being good enough' in low-risk ways
- Practising self-compassion as a counterweight to self-criticism

- Adapting therapy tools like CBT and ACT to work with your brain, not against it.

You don't need to aim lower; you need to aim differently. 'Good enough' is not a failure; it's the foundation of sustainable progress. And the bravest thing you can do isn't getting it perfect. It's getting it done.

Chapter 13

WHEN ADHD MEETS AUTISM

AuDHD and doing things differently

Sam has always loved working and is usually consistently productive. Their special interests change frequently, often coinciding with their current job, and they frequently change jobs. They absorb themselves in their new chosen career. It's all they want to do all the time, and they will often neglect everything else in their life in favour of work. Their job becomes their everything, and they are happy and productive...until their brain suddenly loses interest, leaving them feeling lost and empty. Suddenly, they are unmotivated, their brain refuses to engage with work, and emotional dysregulation, lack of energy and multiple sensory issues leave them overwhelmed. Before they knew that they were AuDHD, they would be signed off work with depression. They would rest and then, after a while, they'd find a new career and start the cycle again.

When engaging in work tasks, their 'autistic brain' wants them to do ALL the preparation before they can even start, but this can lead to their 'ADHD brain' getting bored before the task has even begun. It will often block them from even opening documents they've already started, so they have to restart them. They aim to be organized and will plan out a detailed schedule of what they'll do when, but the minute they fail to stick to that schedule, their 'autistic brain' will refuse to engage because they haven't stuck to the plan. So, they'll make a new plan. This usually continues until the point of the deadline, when they enter crisis mode, a magical state that suddenly enables them to accomplish so much. It can often allow them to suddenly be able to hyperfocus for however long it takes to get the task done. But that means they won't eat, they won't drink, they won't go to the toilet, they won't notice their exhaustion or the fact that they've started menstruating and are in severe pain...until they finish. Then everything hits at once, and James will usually find them hysterical or in shutdown. They'll get some rest, and then the next big task will come in, and they'll start the cycle yet again.

Sam loves being in crisis mode and loves hyperfocusing. It makes them feel superhuman! It doesn't always work out, though. They've never been able to choose what they hyperfocus on (very few people can), so they have been known to completely miss deadlines because they've spent an entire day focusing on one tiny detail of a project, leaving the majority of the work incomplete. Or they might hyperfocus on something utterly unrelated to the project, because their brain has led them down that path. When it does work out though, it feels incredible, until they inevitably crash. And the older they get, the longer it takes them to recover and the more frequently they burn themselves out.

All of this can be exhausting and dysregulating emotionally, but knowing that they are AuDHD (thanks initially to some podcast listeners who wrote to the show insisting that Sam was AuDHD just like them), and learning about the way their brain works, has really helped Sam to finally start to manage their energy levels, overwhelm and over-reliance on crisis mode to get shit done. It's not easy, and they often slip up and have to trick their brain and rely on external accountability to help get them back on track, but they feel much more aware and in control than ever before.

What is AuDHD?

If you've ever wondered why traditional ADHD strategies don't quite work for you, or why you find yourself caught between wanting rigid structure and constant novelty, there's a good chance you're part of a growing group realizing they are what's become known as **AuDHD: autism and ADHD, together in one brain.**

As much as it *obviously* should be, **AuDHD** (pronounced awe-dee-aich-dee) isn't an official diagnosis. **It's a community-coined term that describes having both autism and ADHD, not as two separate conditions, but as a single, intertwined neurotype with its own challenges, contradictions and strengths.**

Clinically, you'd be diagnosed with both Autism Spectrum Disorder and Attention-Deficit/Hyperactivity Disorder. But that really doesn't capture the experience of being AuDHD – the way traits from both conditions interact, amplify, or conflict with each other in daily life. It's not ADHD plus autism. **It's something uniquely different.**

For years, autism and ADHD were thought to be mutually exclusive. In fact, until 2013, the diagnostic manual (DSM-4, at the time) only allowed clinicians to diagnose one or the other, not both, even though the overlap was staring us all in the face.

When that changed with the DSM-5, suddenly the data confirmed what many people already knew: these conditions co-occur a lot. **Around 40–70 per cent of autistic people meet the criteria for ADHD,[1] and approximately 20 per cent of people with ADHD also show strong signs of autism.[2]** But diagnosis is still tricky, especially since many traits look similar on the surface but come from different roots. For example, someone who seems unable to keep still could be hyperactive (more commonly associated with ADHD) or be stimming (more commonly associated with autism), or both. **Lots of people with ADHD may also have some autistic traits but may not meet the diagnostic criteria for autism and vice versa**, further complicating matters.

Also, autism and ADHD are commonly diagnosed using two separate assessments. This can be tricky if the diagnosing psychiatrist is not aware of how the combination of both conditions may present together in one person. Add to this the survival instinct that causes many to mask their symptoms, the frequent misdiagnoses, the long waiting lists or lack of available assessments in some areas, the fact that **the diagnostic tests for both autism and ADHD were developed using young, cis-gendered, straight, white boys who present in a stereotypical way**, and it's not difficult to understand why so many people are unaware that they could potentially be AuDHD or are perfectly aware but are unable to get a diagnosis.[3]

Why does this matter?

Understanding AuDHD as **a distinct neurotype** helps to explain some of the more confusing, contradictory and frustrating aspects of life with overlapping traits. Sam often refers to their 'ADHD brain' and their 'autistic brain' as if they are two separate entities, even though they are both the same brain. This is because **they can often feel like they are battling one another.** For example:

- Your 'autistic brain' might have an extreme need for structure, organization and predictability...but your 'ADHD brain' craves novelty and might struggle to stick to a routine or even remember what the routine was.
- Your 'autistic brain' may get lost in a task's tiny details and want to work slowly to avoid making mistakes...but your 'ADHD brain' can hate the tiny details, loathe working slowly and may not spot mistakes...It may completely refuse to look at the tiny details at all!
- Your 'autistic brain' might enjoy boring, monotonous tasks that involve repetition because this can be soothing and rewarding... but your 'ADHD brain' may refuse to let you engage with tasks like this because it prefers novelty and *hates* boring, repetitive tasks.
- Your 'ADHD brain' might crave novelty and want to experience new things and feel a need to change things often...but your 'autistic brain' might feel overwhelmed by that novelty, change or experience.
- Your 'ADHD brain' may crave stimulation, like bright lights, music and crowds of people... but your 'autistic brain' may become quickly overstimulated and overwhelmed.
- Your 'autistic brain' may feel safer and more able to cope with one friend at a time...but your ADHD brain may tire quickly of people and want you to seek out more people and more relationships, which your 'autistic brain' may not be able to cope with.

- Your 'autistic brain' might want to make perfectly detailed plans... but your ADHD brain may find it incredibly difficult to actually start the thing.

You may feel like a walking contradiction...because you are – your brain is managing competing needs.

Being AuDHD isn't just ADHD plus autism; it's a unique condition that sits on the same 'spectrum' as ADHD and autism.

The biology of AuDHD: same genes, different directions

Understanding why life with AuDHD feels so paradoxical starts with the brain itself. While ADHD and autism are often talked about separately, **modern neuroscience shows they're closely related at a biological level** and, crucially, **have unique patterns that only appear when the two conditions co-occur.**

Autism and ADHD are **both highly heritable neurodevelopmental conditions**, meaning that they're strongly influenced by genetics. Genetic studies reveal that the **same clusters of genes are involved in both conditions**, particularly those linked to brain development, dopamine signalling and neural signalling. But...here is where it gets complicated.

One of the most interesting findings from research into AuDHD is a concept called 'discordant pleiotropy' (try saying that six times quickly!). Discordant pleiotropy describes a situation where a single genetic difference has effects on multiple traits, but those effects go in opposite directions: **beneficial for one trait and harmful for**

another. For example, some genes might reduce the risk of heart disease but increase the risk of diabetes.

In the case of neurodivergence, for example, research has shown that the same **genetic markers that in autism are associated with higher academic achievement are linked to lower achievement in ADHD**. In other words, when combined in AuDHD, these genes don't add to each other; they are in conflict.

Understanding the brain helps us understand AuDHD

Imaging studies show how autism and ADHD leave both distinct and overlapping marks on the brain. This mix of divergent (splitting off) and convergent (merging) brain differences points to a unique AuDHD brain, rather than a simple 'ADHD + autism' brain.

For example:

Divergent brain features	Convergent brain features
Brain size: Autism is often linked to early brain overgrowth, while ADHD is more often tied to smaller brain volume and delayed development.	**The cerebellum:** Both conditions show reduced volume in the cerebellum, important not just for movement but also for thinking and emotional regulation.
The amygdala: In autism, the amygdala, key for fear and social processing, can be enlarged, which may connect to anxiety and social differences. In ADHD, amygdala size tends to look more typical.	**The fronto-striatal circuits:** In both autism and ADHD, the neural loops linking the prefrontal cortex and basal ganglia, crucial for executive functions like planning and inhibition, are commonly atypical.

What the above table tells us is that the AuDHD brain isn't simply bigger or smaller in childhood (for example), but instead shows a mosaic of structural differences, causing brain networks to sometimes pull in opposite directions. While autism may bring features like an enlarged amygdala, and ADHD a smaller prefrontal cortex, **both conditions are similar in how their networks misfire**. So, in AuDHD, these opposing structures and fragile connections collide, creating **a system that is less stable and potentially more disrupted** than either condition alone.

The AuDHD tug-of-war

In the 'AuDHD brain', these networks collide minute by minute, as if there is a constant tug of war. **This internal, neurological tussle brings with it unique strengths, but equally unique challenges.**

For example, **ADHD is a 'novelty-seeking' condition.** The brain is constantly scanning for stimulation and reward. Routine is boring, familiarity is dull. You thrive on newness and urgency. But **autism is a 'sameness-seeking' condition.** Predictability feels safe. Routine helps reduce chaos. Sudden change is often stressful or disorienting.

Brain scans show that **people with AuDHD have distinct patterns of neural activity that don't match either autism or ADHD alone.** Autistic traits in AuDHD often show up in similar brain dynamics to autism-only individuals, but ADHD traits in AuDHD show up differently than in 'pure' ADHD; meaning the cause of distractibility or inattention may not be the same.

The unique productivity challenges of AuDHD

It's fair to say that, as challenging as ADHD is in terms of productivity, AuDHD, depending on the individual and their circumstances, can be more challenging still.

Typical productivity advice tends to assume a consistent brain; one that responds predictably to systems, rewards and willpower. **But the AuDHD brain doesn't run on consistency. It runs on conflict, cycles and context.**

Living with AuDHD means your internal experience is constantly being tugged in opposite directions: structure and routine vs spontaneity, overstimulation vs sensory seeking, deep focus vs distraction. And that **internal tension makes productivity feel not just difficult, but often impossible to sustain.**

Here's how it can show up.

Executive function in conflict with itself

Both autism and ADHD involve executive dysfunction, but not always in the same way.

Studies suggest AuDHD combines the central deficits from both conditions: **poor cognitive flexibility and planning** and **poor impulse control.** This creates a particularly tough mix. For example, someone may build a rigid, detailed plan (autism side) but constantly derail it through impulsive detours (ADHD side). When the plan collapses, inflexibility makes it hard to adapt, fuelling anxiety and a cycle of frustration.

AuDHD's executive function profile appears cumulative, layering the hallmark difficulties of autism and ADHD on top of each other. But, in reality, these deficits interact in ways that amplify or oppose each other, making everyday life especially challenging. **You don't just get more dysfunction; you get contradictory dysfunction.**

This highlights **key productivity challenges for AuDHDers:**

- You want to plan everything in perfect detail (autism)... but struggle to stick to the plan or remember where you put the list (ADHD).
- You need a structured routine (autism)...but also find it crushingly boring and impossible to follow (ADHD).
- You desperately want to start something important...but your brain won't give you the green light until every condition is perfect, which it never is.

This is the AuDHD executive function experience: **stuck between a perfectionist and a procrastinator** in a very small room.

Routine vs novelty

Routine is calming. Familiarity is safe. You might create a beautiful schedule, complete with colour-coded blocks, visual timers and structured breaks. But then the ADHD part of your brain wakes up and goes: 'Cool, but let's abandon that and learn everything about Icelandic horses instead.'

But if you give in to the novelty, the autistic side might panic: 'What happened to our routine? I don't feel safe! This is chaos!' The result? **You bounce between rigid structure and total rejection of it (often within the same day).**

This routine–novelty conflict makes most traditional productivity systems feel either too loose or too tight. You may either feel trapped or completely unanchored.

Why can't I just pick one task?!

It's not just doing the tasks that's hard, it's picking which one to start with. Your autistic traits are looking at your list and thinking: 'Which task should take priority, logically?', 'Which one fits the schedule I made?', 'Which one will bring the most long-term benefit?', and 'Am I in the right headspace to do it to my standards?'

Meanwhile, your ADHD traits are shouting: 'Which one is shiny?', 'Which one feels fun?', 'Which one will give me a dopamine hit right now?' Or, failing that... 'What's due in the next 11 minutes that might set my arse on fire if I ignore it?'

This internal push and pull can create a kind of cognitive traffic jam; both 'sets of traits' have very strong opinions, but neither is driving.

Often, paralysis wins. You either do something completely unrelated (alphabetize your Spotify playlists), or you pick the lowest-effort task and resent it the whole time. And the worst part? Even when you do start something, there's a nagging voice whispering, 'Shouldn't you be doing something else?'

The attention paradox

Attention in AuDHD is a cruel paradox. It is easy to either hyperfocus on one topic for 14 hours with no food or toilet breaks (you usually can't choose the topic, so this isn't always useful and can often be detrimental), or struggle to finish a two-minute email because your brain won't hold the thread long enough.

To complicate the attentional issues in AuDHD, we have **the clash between monotropism and hyperfocus.**

Monotropism + hyperfocus = productivity chaos

One of the most unique features of AuDHD is the way attention works. **Autistic monotropism refers to the tendency of autistic brains to focus attention in a narrow but incredibly deep way.** Rather than spreading attention thinly across multiple topics, **the brain locks into one or two areas of interest, exploring them with *intense* curiosity, emotional connection and long-term commitment.** This isn't just 'liking something a lot', it's a cognitive style where a few selected topics become central to thinking, learning and even identity. The rest of the world can fade into the background when attention is locked in, and switching focus away from that area can feel *very* distressing. Monotropism can lead to extraordinary depth of knowledge, but also to difficulties with task switching, multitasking and adapting to sudden change.

The 'ADHD version' of this is hyperfocus. **ADHD hyperfocus is a state of intense, immersive concentration** that kicks in when something is novel, urgent or highly rewarding. **Unlike monotropism, which is steady and enduring, hyperfocus tends to be more short-lived and unpredictable.** You might suddenly find yourself glued to a task or hobby for hours, skipping meals, forgetting the time and blocking out the world, but only if it captures your interest. The catch? **You usually can't choose when it happens or what you hyperfocus on.** It's driven by the brain's reward system and is often triggered by stimulation or pressure. Hyperfocus can drive incredible productivity *when it shows up*, but because it's inconsistent and aimed where the brain wants, it often leads to frustration, burnout and an ever-growing pile of half-finished projects.

Monotropism provides the *target* (the deep interest) and **hyperfocus** provides the *fuel* (the intense burst of energy). But here's the rub: **an AuDHD brain may experience both. At the same time.**

This often leads to a strange pattern:

- **Falling into a deep focus hole on one topic:** having one (or more) deep interest that feels meaningful and completely absorbing over a period of months or years and frequently within that time disappearing into research, writing or creating for hours on the same subject with incredible intensity.
- **Abandoning it suddenly:** not because you've lost interest – you loved this subject, it was everything to you – but your brain no longer finds it rewarding, often because something newer or more stimulating has hijacked your attention.
- **Feeling ashamed or grieving:** not finishing what felt important or meaningful hurts, so you try to fix that feeling by diving into *another* project...and repeat the cycle all over again.

When they align, it's magic. When they clash, it's hell.

The routine trap

As we've already covered, routines can be the holy grail of productivity. For AuDHD brains? Not so much.

On one side, **the 'autistic brain' craves routine, not for productivity, but as a survival tool.** Predictability reduces sensory and cognitive overload. Knowing what's coming means less decision-making, less stress and a stronger sense of safety in a world that often feels chaotic or overwhelming. For many autistic/AuDHD people, routines aren't just nice to have, **they're essential for regulating energy and emotions.** And when that structure is disrupted, the fallout can be instant: anxiety, shutdown, meltdown, or just feeling totally untethered.

But on the other side, **the 'ADHD brain' can rapidly rebel against routine.** Repetition can quickly become boring. Structure can feel like a cage. The same breakfast three days in a row? Forget it. A calendar that tells you what to do every hour? Ignore. **The ADHD nervous system runs on novelty and interest; it needs variety to stay engaged.** Too much sameness and your brain can check out, go rogue, or start ANYTHING instead of doing the thing intended.

So, what happens when you have both needs in one brain?

Welcome to the routine trap: where you build a carefully crafted daily plan to feel safe and in control and tear it up by Tuesday because it's suffocatingly dull.

This is why **rigid productivity systems tend to break down quickly for individuals with AuDHD.**

The AuDHD productivity cycle: sprints and slumps

Recognising AuDHD as a distinct neurotype helps shift the narrative from 'What's wrong with me?' to 'What works for me?' It can also help to reduce the shame at advice or strategies tailored for either ADHD or autism not quite fitting – they weren't developed for AuDHD!

Most productivity advice assumes that people are relatively consistent. You plan the work, work the plan, and your output chugs along in a predictable way.

That is... not how AuDHD works.

For people with both autism and ADHD, productivity doesn't follow a smooth curve; it comes in sprints and slumps. Periods of intense focus, creativity, or output are followed (often abruptly) by burnout, shutdown or total inertia. This cycle is a pattern rooted in how your brain functions, and it requires an entirely different set of tools.

1. The sprint

The sprint is when everything finally clicks:

- You're in flow or even hyperfocused, motivated and possibly even having fun.
- You achieve more in three hours than you did in the previous two weeks.
- You might forget to eat, miss appointments, or work through the night, but it feels worth it because something inside has finally switched on.

For AuDHDers, sprints can come from:

- an exciting new interest or idea
- a high-stakes external deadline
- a sudden emotional surge (panic, injustice, fear, curiosity)
- the rare and magical alignment of energy, clarity and the right environment.

But **while sprints feel amazing, even addictive, they come at a cost. That cost is the slump.**

2. The slump

The slump is what follows. The reward has gone. The task is now old or overwhelming. Your brain feels foggy, your body feels heavy and no amount of lists or moral pep talks seem to help.

You might:

- abandon half-done projects you were once obsessed with
- struggle to start any task, even easy ones
- enter a shame spiral about how you wasted your sprint.

This is a form of neurological exhaustion. AuDHD brains can run hot, especially during a sprint, and the slump is your system force-quitting all open tabs.

Over time, many AuDHDers can develop a pattern of:

1. **Frantic productivity > sprint**
2. **Collapse or avoidance > slump**
3. **Guilt and shame > paralysis**
4. **New idea or deadline > repeat**

It can feel like living life in bursts; constantly catching up, burning out or starting again.

As traditional productivity advice can often fail people with AuDHD, what often works, depending on the individual, tends to be dynamic, forgiving strategies that are designed to flex with the sprint–slump cycle.

Think:

- systems that **support you even when you're not functioning well**
- strategies that **don't punish inconsistency, but plan for it**
- tools that **combine structure** (to soothe your autistic brain) **with flexibility and novelty** (to feed your ADHD brain).

Strategies that can help AuDHD brains

As we've said many times before in this book (and will say again) we are all completely unique individuals who have brains that love something one moment and completely refuse to engage with it the next. **ADHD brains are unpredictable and AuDHD brains even more so.** Here are lots of practical strategies and tools for you to choose from so that you can try the ones your brain will let you try now and save the others for when your brain gets bored.

Burnout can occur often when you are AuDHD. We want these strategies to take that into account so that you can learn to be productive in a way that doesn't constantly deplete you.

We've tried to split these tools, strategies and exercises into categories so that you can skip to the things you're struggling with/want to work on.

Strategy 1: Energy management

Many AuDHDers can do the task, but the sensory/social/emotional load can make it exhausting. Learning what sorts of tasks exhaust you and which activities can help to replenish energy can be instrumental if you want to build a pacing system to help you to avoid burnout.

- **Do an energy audit**

Before you can manage your energy well, you need to pay attention to which tasks drain you, which don't affect you much, and which ones boost your energy, lift your mood, calm you, or simply feel like a real break.

An 'energy audit' simply means noticing:

- **what drains you**
- **what restores you**
- **what feels neutral.**

Even brief check-ins can reveal patterns you might otherwise miss.

You don't need anything fancy, just jot a note in your phone, mark it on a planner, or even use stickers or emojis. After tasks, ask yourself simple questions: *Do I feel more or less tired? Has my mood shifted? Do I want company or solitude? Am I tense, restless or calm?* These small reflections build a clearer picture of your personal energy landscape.

Once you start to understand the reasons that particular tasks/activities impact you negatively, you can begin to address those reasons and start to work on things that might help, such as building routines (see Chapter 4), time management (see Chapter 9), working with perfectionist tendencies (see Chapter 12) and helping with transitions (see Chapter 15).

You'll find exercises you can use to do your own energy audit in our online resources (see p.343).

- **The Red/Yellow/Green day plan**

Not every day brings the same challenges. Scanning the day ahead can help you to structure your day to use energy wisely. Here is a simple approach:

- List today's tasks and colour code: Red (draining), Yellow (neutral), Green (fun/easy/energy /or mood boosting).
- Build the day as Green > Red > Green, never two Reds back-to-back.
- Put a five to ten-minute decompression buffer after each Red (quiet, stim, walk, weighted blanket).
- If you get to your Red task and can't do it, replace it with two Greens and move the Red to a better energy window. When do you usually have more energy/capacity? First thing in the morning? Move it to then.
- If you're having a low energy/mood day, only plan to do one Red task.

- **Weekly energy review**

Weekly reflection can also be useful in informing how we approach things. Here is a simple approach to a weekly energy review:

- Mentally skim over last week. Which two to three things drained your energy the most? Which two to three helped?
- Pick one drain to shrink this week – delegate it to someone else, automate it or use a template to help (see below) or move it to another time.
- Write a one-sentence boundary you'll *actually* use:
  - *I'm at capacity this week. Can we revisit this on Tuesday?*
  - *I can do X or Y by Friday, but I don't have the capacity to do both. Which is more useful?*

Strategy 2: Externalize memory and decisions

When we're under stress because we have so many things that need doing, it can be difficult to know where to start. Decision-making can take some of us a long time. And because we don't like making decisions, we can very easily fall into the trap of procrastinating to avoid them, which can then result in lots of negative self-talk. Here's a few things that can help with this.

- **Build your 'external hard drive'**

Having somewhere to dump all the information needed for tasks, including your master task list (see Chapter 3), can help to free your brain up to help reduce overwhelm/stress. Making this system fit how your brain works is important, so here are some approaches you can adopt:

  - Use whatever system works for you and remember you may need to change it when your brain gets bored. Options include visual task boards (Trello, Notion, a whiteboard, or sticky notes), physical planners or notebooks, digital notes or reminder apps

(Apple Notes, OneNote, Google Tasks), or automated reminders (e.g. Todoist).

- Capture tasks in the way your brain works best: record voice notes, use paper, or an app you can access from any device. Pick something you can update whenever a thought pops up, an email arrives, or you're in a meeting.
- If you're also doing an energy audit, you can keep more than one master list and separate tasks into categories. Sam does this in OneNote with different tabs, but you could also colour-code tasks. Organize it however works best for you.

- **Pick your prioritization tool**

Once you've got your 'external hard drive' and 'master task list' set up, the next step is choosing what to tackle first. You can decide day by day, especially helpful if your energy levels fluctuate, or plan a week (or even a month) ahead if you prefer more structure. Having a system can make it easier to decide what to do first/next.

There are also tools to help with this in Chapter 6.

If planning in advance feels boring, triggers demand avoidance, or just isn't working that day, try a more flexible approach.

- **Introduce 'helpful flexibility'**

Making sure that your system has room for flexibility when needed can help you to engage on days when your brain is being difficult.

- **Choosing tasks at random** can help when your brain refuses to stick to a system. Sam gamifies this by picking six tasks from the master list and six fun 'side quests', numbering each 1–6. They roll a die to decide which list to start with and which task to do. To add extra gamification, they roll their gravity timer to see how long they'll do it – maybe crocheting for an hour or tackling admin for five minutes. Whatever the die and timer decide, they stick with it.

- There are also websites and apps that pick tasks at random (search 'random task generator'), or you can even ask AI. The paid app Amazing Marvin includes a random task generator, prioritization tools and further ways to gamify tasks.

If you're struggling, pause and ask yourself: 'Which task can I face right now, or which would feel good to at least start? Sam often begins with a quick, enjoyable task to get moving and earn a little dopamine boost – both from doing something fun and ticking it off the side quest list.

- **Use ready-made templates**

If there are tasks/activities that you do regularly, you might, when you have the capacity, try making some templates to help make them easier to do. You can make templates for anything – Sam even has a step-by-step list on the bathroom wall to avoid getting paralysed by whether they should brush their teeth, take medication or shower first.

- Templates take a bit of time upfront but save effort later by reminding you exactly what needs doing. You can create new ones for any tasks you learn going forward.
- The easiest way is to build the template while doing the task. Break it into the tiniest steps. If you ever delegate, the template will also give someone else clear instructions.
- If it's something you usually do for others, but they could handle,

send them the instructions so they can do it themselves next time.
  - Breaking tasks into tiny steps also helps you to spot parts that could be automated (see Strategy 7 below).
  - If you answer similar emails often, create templates you can tweak instead of rewriting each one.

Strategy 3: Body doubling

Body doubling is covered in more detail in Chapter 5. Not only can it help with procrastination, motivation and task initiation by providing external accountability, it can also help to alleviate feelings of isolation if you often work alone. Depending on the format and people involved, it could possibly help by co-regulation (helping each other to regulate emotions).

Strategy 4: Minimizing distractions/overwhelm/sensory stress

Many of us are heavily affected by sensory input. Unlike non-neurodivergent people who can filter it out, we often have more to process. This drains energy, distracts us and, on bad days, can feel overwhelming.

For sensory safety, manage your sensory input and transitions:

- **Minimize stressors:** Create a workspace that feels safe and predictable to reduce the effort of filtering sensory input and make focusing easier.
- **Create a sensory space:** Set aside a spot where you can

self-regulate, whether in the morning, between tasks, or at the end of the day to decompress. Some people even use sensory tents.

- **Support transitions:** Since these can be especially tough with AuDHD, include things that regulate, soothe or delight you to ease the shift between tasks.
- **Make it portable:** If you can't set up a space, put together a sensory 'kit' you can use to ground you wherever you are.

You'll find a sensory safety exercise in our online resources (see p.343).

Strategy 5: Chunking and micro-tasks for reduced capacity days

Chunking means breaking down big tasks into smaller, more manageable steps. This is really useful on days when you have reduced capacity. If you've already made a template for a task (see Strategy 2 above) that tells you step-by-step what you need to do, then this will be useful here!

Breaking it down:

- Break tasks into very tiny, concrete steps (e.g. 'Open the document' is a valid step).
- Use the first tiny step to help overcome inertia but stop if your energy is fading.
- Pair this with a **compassionate stop rule**, e.g. 'It's OK to pause or stop when you feel overstimulated or tired,' or 'Stopping is a skill, not a failure.'
- Do one tiny step at a time, if possible, ticking them off as you go.

- Evaluate how you are feeling after each tiny step. If you can continue, move to the next tiny step. If you can't, then pause or stop altogether.

Remember your compassionate stop rule and remind yourself to use it.

Strategy 6: Flexible routines and pacing

Strict schedules can often collapse under the combination of ADHD impulsivity and autistic rigidity. Instead, try rhythms or time anchors and gentle patterns rather than rigid times (e.g. 'After breakfast I check emails' rather than '8am: check emails'; or 'Before bed I set clothes out'). Pacing can help to manage energy levels by alternating blocks of activity with blocks of restful or energy boosting activities.

You'll find an exercise that can help with pacing in our online resources (see p.343).

Strategy 7: Delegation and automation

If you have more work than you can handle, then working out what you can delegate to others or automate could really help.

- **Positive delegating**

Lots of us can struggle with delegation. It can feel like a loss of control or a personal failure. James helped Sam reframe delegation, to be more positive by simply asking Sam how they felt when helping someone else out. They loved it! 'Well then, why would you deny someone else that feeling?' James asked. Rather than helping their work colleague, what they'd been doing was acting as a barrier to their development.

Delegating tips

- **Start with a conversation:** If you can delegate, talk to the person first about how they'd feel about taking it on.
- **Be open about struggles:** In a supportive workplace or family, sharing what you find difficult and problem-solving together can ease pressure.
- **Remember the bigger picture:** Delegation can prevent burnout and can be the difference between months off and being able to keep going.

If support is lacking: Seek help to access reasonable adjustments, find a mediator or, if needed, make a plan to move away from the situation.

- **Automating tasks**

If you've already written clear step-by-step instructions for any task you repeat, that's essentially the blueprint for automation.

- There are automation platforms that don't require any coding, like Zapier, Make, Kissflow and IFTTT which connect apps together. For example: when a form is submitted, create a Google Doc and email it to someone.
- If you're open to light coding, JavaScript or Python scripts can replicate instructions exactly.

- You can use AI to help with this. Just upload your step-by-step instructions and ask it to tell you how to automate them.

Strategy 8: Don't beat yourself up

Lastly, sometimes **the most effective tools you can use are self-acceptance and self-compassion.** They can be really difficult for a lot of us to practise, so we would recommend taking tiny steps towards them. Sam's first tiny step was to challenge negative self-talk by saying 'that's not helpful!' out loud. This can help them to stop the shame and self-hatred cycle. Think about what your first tiny step could be...

Chapter summary

This chapter covered how AuDHD isn't just autism and ADHD combined but a completely distinct neurotype that presents its own unique and often conflicting, challenges. It can make you feel like your brain is at war – with itself.

We looked at how the brain structure in AuDHD can differ from autistic and ADHD brain structure and the specific productivity challenges of AuDHD, including:

- Monotropism (steady and enduring narrow focus) vs hyper-focus (intense, immersive concentration) and how AuDHDers can experience both at the same time.
- The conflicting needs for routine *and* novelty.

We looked at how this leads to productivity often occurring in sprints (periods of intense focus/creativity/output) and slumps (burnout/shutdown/total inertia) in AuDHD, a cycle that can be completely overwhelming and debilitating.

Lastly, we looked at practical strategies that can help:

- Managing energy levels
- Externalizing memory and decision-making
- Body doubling
- Minimizing distractions/overwhelm/sensory stress
- Breaking tasks down into micro-steps
- Flexible routines and pacing
- Delegating and automating tasks

Finally, we asked what your tiny first step towards self-acceptance and self-compassion could be. Because you didn't ask for a brain that's constantly battling itself, and it's f*cking hard work coping with this, so you deserve to cut yourself some slack.

Chapter 14

LEARNING TO SAY NO

Self-care, boundaries and people-pleasing

It's not that James never wanted to set boundaries; he just never quite knew where the edges were supposed to go. Towards the end of his academic career, this lack of boundaries reached Olympic levels of absurdity. At one point, he simultaneously held five roles: he was a lecturer, a researcher, the departmental admissions tutor, the College Associate Dean for Public Engagement and the Director of the Aston Research Centre for Healthy Ageing (ironic, given all these roles aged him rapidly).

That should have been a red flag. Instead, it felt like a badge of honour. A sign he was doing all the right things. Until it wasn't.

Very soon after came the pandemic. Like many, James shifted to working from home. But without the physical separation of leaving campus, the blur between work time and home time became complete. Emails at 5:30am? Of course. Record online lectures during dinner? Why not. Editing papers in bed at midnight? Sure, just until his eyes gave up. It didn't matter that no one had asked him to do any of this; his internal boundaries were as absent as his work-life balance.

The result wasn't pretty, let alone productive. The result was burnout. The type of burnout that creeps up wearing productivity's face, whispering, 'Just one more task,' before kicking you in the balls the very second work stops at the end of the term, forcing you to your knees. His brain shut down in protest. He initially withdrew from work before completely dropping off the map and spiralling into a mental health crisis.

The guilt of saying no had always felt worse than the cost of saying yes. But eventually, that cost became undeniable. What looked like commitment from the outside was actually a complete erosion of self-protection.

Learning to set boundaries, real ones, with actual consequences, didn't come easily. It still doesn't. But it began with an uncomfortable truth: James wasn't indispensable. No one would spontaneously combust if he declined a meeting. And working until you break doesn't make you dedicated; it makes you broken.

Now, James still over-commits, still wrestles with the fear of letting people down, but he's learning. Learning to protect his time like it matters. Learning to say no before his brain and body (or Sam) scream it for him. Learning that **boundaries aren't barriers to productivity; they're the scaffolding that keeps it from collapsing.**

And that, for someone with ADHD, might be one of the most radical acts of self-care there is.

Boundaries: not barriers, but bridges

Having boundaries doesn't make you selfish, difficult or dramatic. In fact, the opposite is true. Boundaries are the invisible scaffolding that help us stay upright – emotionally, physically and mentally – especially when life feels like a series of back-to-back overwhelm events.

If you've got ADHD, chances are you've spent years saying 'yes' when you really meant 'I can't' or 'not now' or 'absolutely not, are you kidding?'. Whether it's people-pleasing, time blindness, guilt or fear of confrontation, setting boundaries can feel like an impossible task, or worse, like letting people down.

But **boundaries aren't about controlling or rejecting others. They're about respecting yourself.** They tell the world: 'This is what I need to feel safe and function well.' And when you put them in place, you're not being unkind; you're giving people a way to relate to you that actually works.

What are boundaries, really?

Think of boundaries as the rules of engagement for being around you: the dos and don'ts that help you feel comfortable, respected and in control. They help you figure out where you end and other people begin. And they can cover everything from how you want to be spoken to, to how often you check your work emails, to whether you're OK with hugging your colleague who smells faintly of soup.

Crucially, boundaries are *not*:

- punishments
- threats
- a way to avoid intimacy
- a selfish luxury you haven't earned.

Boundaries *are*:

- a form of self-care
- a communication tool
- a way to make relationships healthier, not colder
- a necessity for anyone trying to get things done without collapsing.

And if that still feels hard to accept, here's something worth remembering: you can't be truly generous if you're running on empty. **Boundaries help make your energy sustainable, your time manageable and your relationships less like emotional roller coasters and more like something vaguely stable.**

Sam had no boundaries for most of their life. They felt like too many people were relying on them to enable them to say no to anything. Plus, cripplingly low self-esteem. Then, fairly recently, as they sped towards the brick wall of complete and utter burnout (speeding up so that they could get more done before they hit the brick wall), they also got Covid, which became long Covid, and suddenly they couldn't do anything, for anyone, not even themselves, for seven months. During that time, Sam learned that they are not essential. The world still kept on turning. They also learned that putting boundaries in place was essential to helping them recover so that they could once again support all the people who relied on them.

If you love helping others or other people rely on you, then boundaries are important because if you don't protect yourself from burnout, you won't be able to help anyone else. If you can't set boundaries for yourself, do it for the people you care about.

The different types of boundaries (and where they might be leaking)

There isn't just one kind of boundary. In fact, understanding the different types might help you notice where you're regularly over-extending, or if you're ending the day feeling drained but confused about why.

Here's a breakdown:

- **Physical boundaries:** Your personal space and body. Do you hate hugs from acquaintances? Need people to knock before entering your room? This is your domain.
- **Emotional boundaries:** Knowing that you're not responsible for fixing other people's feelings. It's OK to care without carrying.
- **Time boundaries:** Letting people book your calendar into oblivion doesn't help. Decide how long you'll spend on a task, or a person, and protect that time like it's your last remaining chocolate bar (insert other desirable snack here).
- **Mental/intellectual boundaries:** Everyone's entitled to their own thoughts, beliefs and opinions, including you. You don't need to argue with someone just because they want you to.
- **Material boundaries:** Your stuff is your stuff. Whether it's money, your favourite mug or the charger you always lose. It's OK to say no to lending or sharing if it leaves you feeling resentful.

- **Conversational boundaries:** You don't owe anyone an explanation for not wanting to talk about your dating life, your diagnosis, or what your aunt said to you in 1993. 'I'm not comfortable discussing that' is a full sentence.

Why boundaries matter for productivity (whether or not you have ADHD)

Let's zoom out for a minute.

Boundaries support three crucial productivity foundations:

1. **Focus:** Boundaries reduce distraction; not just digital or environmental, but interpersonal. Every time you're interrupted by a 'quick question' at work, or pulled into someone else's drama, that's a cognitive detour. **Clear expectations about when and how you're available can help protect deep focus time**, which, let's face it, is in short supply for many of us.
2. **Energy:** Helping others, navigating awkward conversations and pretending to be happy with something you're not are all emotionally expensive. **Without boundaries, your energy leaks out all day, and by the time you get to your own priorities, there's nothing left.** Boundaries help you spend energy on purpose rather than constantly recovering from being overstretched.
3. **Time:** Most people think of time management as planners and calendars, but it's just as much about boundaries. That means:
    - Saying no to requests that don't align with your capacity.
    - Protecting time for breaks, rest or creative work.
    - Not answering messages at 11:45pm because someone else is in panic mode.

Setting these limits isn't selfish. It's how you make sure your time actually serves your values and goals, not just everyone else's agenda.

Weak or inconsistent boundaries are one of the biggest silent saboteurs of productivity. They are rarely the issue people list when asked what's stopping them from getting stuff done, but they show up everywhere:

- saying yes to things you don't have time for
- feeling resentful after helping someone (again)
- working late because you didn't protect your start-of-the-day focus
- taking on responsibility for problems that aren't yours to fix
- avoiding conflict and ending up overloaded.

These all come down to boundaries, or rather, the absence of them.

The psychological pay-off: less stress, more control

Psychologists often describe boundaries as a core skill of emotional regulation and healthy functioning. Clear boundaries create a sense of internal safety: I know what I'm responsible for and I know what I'm not.

Research consistently shows that people with healthy boundaries experience lower rates of stress and burnout, better work-life balance, greater self-esteem and higher life satisfaction, and improved communication and fewer conflicts.

That's because **boundaries** act like internal guard rails. They **reduce ambiguity, give you tools to navigate tricky situations and help you feel in control of your time, energy and choices.**

This is especially important if you struggle with perfectionism, people-pleasing, or fear of disappointing others, because those tendencies often mean you're ignoring your own needs in favour of keeping the peace. But **long-term peace requires mutual respect, and boundaries are how you teach people to respect you and how you respect yourself.**

Without clear limits, you may find yourself constantly overwhelmed and behind schedule, resenting people you care about, feeling guilty all the time (because you're always letting someone down), or losing track of what you want or need.

And when that becomes your norm, productivity stops being about thriving and turns into barely surviving.

Boundaries are a productivity tool (even if they don't look like one)

Here's the big reframe: **boundaries aren't just emotional self-care, they're structural**. They're the framework that shapes what work gets done, when it gets done and how you feel while doing it.

If your goal is to have a life where you can do meaningful work without collapsing at the end of every day, boundaries aren't optional. They're essential maintenance.

Take a moment to ask yourself, 'Where in my life do my boundaries feel leaky, missing or ignored?' or 'What would it feel like to reinforce just one of them?'

You don't need to fix everything overnight. Start with the place where your time, energy or peace feels most under siege and go from there.

The hidden cost of saying yes

For many of us with ADHD, saying yes feels like proof that we're a 'good person'. Every time we agree to help a colleague, volunteer for a project or say yes to that last-minute favour, we're confirming something about ourselves:

- I'm helpful.
- I'm kind.
- I'm dependable.

And those are important values! Many ADHDers deeply value connection, fairness and altruism. Helping others gives a burst of dopamine and social reward, which can feel motivating in the moment. It also protects us from the discomfort of rejection sensitivity, because if we say yes, we can't be accused of being selfish, lazy or unkind.

But...every yes is also a no to something else. Each time we agree to help, we're often sacrificing our own energy, focus or well-being. What looks like generosity on the outside can quietly erode us from the inside:

- burnout from over-committing
- resentment when our own needs get pushed aside
- less time for rest, creativity, or simply catching up with our own tasks.

It's not that saying yes is bad, it's that that automatic yes can come at our own cost. The challenge is to separate values-based giving (helping in a way that honours who we are) from self-sacrificing giving (helping in a way that slowly empties our tank). Boundaries don't mean abandoning your values; they mean protecting them so you can keep living them without collapsing under the weight.

Why saying no can make you better at your job

One of the biggest myths in the modern workplace is that being constantly available makes you more productive or valuable. In reality, the opposite is often true. **When you say no strategically, that protection of your time, energy and focus means you're more likely to deliver work that's not just done but done well.**

This is the great productivity paradox: **boundaries help you get more done, not less.**

Saying no is uncomfortable, especially if you're a people pleaser (hi, welcome), but **learning to set limits is one of the most powerful ways to improve your focus, reduce overwhelm and actually enjoy your job again.**

Here's how:

- **Boundaries help you focus on the right things**

If you try to do everything, you'll end up doing most of it badly. When you are clearer about what you can and can't take on, you create space to focus on the stuff that really matters: the tasks aligned with your role, your skills and your goals. That's where your energy is most valuable.

- **Boundaries make you look more professional**

Setting boundaries doesn't mean being difficult; it means being realistic.

Communicating what you can take on (and when) shows self-awareness, maturity and respect for your own limits. That's not weakness – it's professionalism. You can probably think of people you've worked with who have had healthy boundaries, and we're pretty sure you wouldn't have thought they were weak.

Saying something like 'I can start Project B, but only if we pause Project A. What would you like me to prioritize?' shifts the responsibility back to the system. You're not dropping the ball. You're flagging that too many balls are being thrown at once.

- **Boundaries increase job satisfaction**

There's nothing quite as demoralizing as feeling like you're drowning in work and still letting people down. **When you have clear boundaries, you can regain a sense of control.** You can start finishing things. You stop dreading your inbox. You can begin to feel competent again.

And when you feel like you're actually good at your job? Motivation and satisfaction may just follow. It's almost like a magic trick, but it's just sustainable workload management.

- **Boundaries are a kind of advocacy**

When someone says, 'I can't take that on right now,' they're not being flaky or disobedient. They're forcing the system to confront its own unrealistic expectations. **Boundaries challenge dysfunctional workplaces to get better.** They start a conversation about priorities, resourcing and fairness. And yes, sometimes they make you unpopular in the short term. But they also keep you from quietly burning out while everyone else benefits from your silence.

Why setting boundaries can feel so hard when you have ADHD

The chances are, if you struggle to hold boundaries, that saying no is an issue. ADHD and its collection of **executive dysfunction, time blindness and emotional challenges can make saying no feel almost impossible.** Let's look at all three of these barriers to saying no individually.

1. Executive function challenges

Even when you want to set a boundary, know you should set a boundary, and have even planned how to set the boundary, actually doing it in the moment can feel impossible. Often, this is due to executive dysfunction, which can appear like this:

- **Impulse control issues mean we often say yes before we've had a chance to think it through.** You might want to say, 'Let me check my schedule and get back to you,' but instead you blurt out 'Sure!' because it feels easier, faster or less awkward in the moment. This is the classic 'impulsive yes'; a reflex driven by our brain's difficulty with pausing between stimulus and response.
- **Working memory challenges mean we don't always have access to the reasons we intended to say no.** Boundary-setting often relies on recalling past experiences, like the fact that you burned

out last time you agreed to a similar thing, or that you told yourself to keep this week clear. But ADHD can make it hard to hold that information in mind when it matters most. So, you forget and say yes...and remember only once it's too late.

- **Difficulties with planning and prioritising make it harder to anticipate future overload. ADHD brains often struggle to zoom out, see the big picture and weigh up how a new task will impact your existing workload.** So, we agree, only to realize later that we've backed ourselves into another unsustainable corner.

The result can be a frustrating and demoralizing pattern: we make promises we can't keep, and we blame ourselves for being 'flaky' or bad at adulting. **Accepting that this is partly down to how your brain works differently can help start to lift the shame**, and instead of telling yourself to 'just be more disciplined', you can start using ADHD-friendly strategies to build boundaries that actually stick.

2. Time blindness: when the future feels too far away to matter

Another major ADHD trait that sabotages boundary-setting is time blindness, covered in Chapter 9. Time blindness is not just about running late (although, yes, that happens too). It's also about how the ADHD brain experiences time itself: not as a smooth, linear timeline as most people experience it, but as a fuzzy blur of now and not now.

This 'temporal fog' makes it hard to judge how long something will take, when you'll need to start it, or whether your future self will have the capacity to do it at all. Which leads to one very predictable pattern: when someone asks you to take on a task that's due in a few days or weeks, your brain doesn't sound the alarm that it should. Instead, it might register: 'Oh, that's future me's problem. Loads of time. Should be fine.'

> **You say yes to something next week, because next week feels miles away. Then next week becomes tomorrow. And suddenly, you're drowning. Again.**

So, you agree. You might even feel good about saying yes: generous, capable, maybe even a little productive. But the decision is based on a faulty mental map. **Your brain hasn't factored in everything else on your plate. It hasn't imagined the future stress, the late nights or the other commitments you've already made and forgotten about.**

This neurological distortion makes future costs feel emotionally weightless until they crash into the present.

Time blindness doesn't just affect your schedule; it can affect your relationships, too. Our time is finite, so time is a boundary. If we can't see that and agree to take on extra work that we have neither the time nor capacity to do, it can look like laziness or disrespect to others. People might assume you didn't care about letting them down, or you couldn't be bothered, when in reality, your brain just hasn't given you accurate time signals to work with. Or you may agree to take on extra work to please your boss, which then means you have less time to spend with loved ones, leaving them feeling neglected and less important than work.

And when this happens repeatedly, it chips away at your confidence in setting any boundaries. You start to feel like you're always letting people down. So, you say yes again, trying to make up for it, and the cycle repeats.

Emotions: the biggest barrier to having boundaries

Most advice about setting boundaries skips over the emotional part. It assumes you can just stay calm, assert your needs and move on.

But if you have ADHD, the problem isn't just knowing you need to say no, or knowing you have no capacity to take on more work, it's the tidal wave of feelings that crash in the second you try. **Emotional dysregulation and rejection sensitivity can make boundary-setting feel less like a rational decision and more like walking into a lion's den.**

Emotional dysregulation (covered in Chapter 10) is a good place to start when it comes to understanding emotional barriers to healthy boundaries. Experiencing emotions more intensely and struggling to manage or recover from them is like having an emotional volume knob that goes from zero to one hundred with very little warning.

So, imagine being asked to take on another task when your plate is already full. You may not even have to try to imagine; this may have happened this month (or even this week). Instead of calmly weighing the pros and cons, your brain might instantly serve up guilt ('They'll think I don't care'), anxiety ('They'll be upset with me'), and shame ('I should be able to cope like everyone else').

> ***Why is it so uncomfortable to say no?***
>
> **An emotional flood of guilt, anxiety and shame can be so uncomfortable that we'll agree to almost anything, just to make the feelings stop. While we see this as a boundary failure, it's really a protective mechanism. It's short-term emotional survival.**
>
> **Then we have the monster that is RSD, the intense, sometimes physically painful emotional response to perceived criticism, failure or disappointment. So, when someone asks you for help, and your no might cause them to frown, pause or say 'Oh OK then...' your brain registers that as danger. Emotional pain incoming.**
>
> **And so we say yes. Not because we want to. Not because we can. But because the alternative feels like getting hit by a truck made of shame, fear and self-loathing.**
>
> **This is the emotional root of people-pleasing in ADHD. Saying yes to protect yourself from pain now, even though it will deliver pain in the future.**

The final emotional aspect worth mentioning is how we view ourselves – our self-worth and self-esteem. Many adults with ADHD grow up being told they're lazy, selfish, unreliable or just not trying hard enough. And eventually you internalize it. You start to believe it. You start to feel that you have to over-deliver just to be 'enough'. That **your value comes from saying yes, being helpful, always being available, even at the expense of your own well-being.**

This creates what something called **'the overcompensation cycle'**:

1. You say yes to everything, trying to prove your worth.
2. You get overwhelmed, forget things or burn out.
3. You miss deadlines or let people down.
4. That 'failure' confirms your worst fear: 'I'm not good enough.'
5. You double down on proving yourself again...by saying yes to everything.

And round you go. In real life, this can look like the following scenario:

> Meet Laura. Laura has ADHD, a demanding job and a deep fear of letting people down. They're known as 'the helpful one', the person who always steps up, takes on extra projects and replies to emails at 10:47pm. But Laura is the proverbial swan that appears graceful and serene on the surface, but underneath, their webbed feet are paddling like crazy just to propel them forward.
>
> **Step 1: The yes that feels good (for 12 minutes)**
> Laura's manager casually asks, 'Can you take the lead on the client report next week?' Laura's brain screams, 'No, we're already drowning!'...but their mouth says, 'Of course!' before they even finish blinking. The hit of approval, of being seen as capable and helpful? That feels amazing. For now.
>
> **Step 2: The realization hits**
> Later that night, Laura sits down to plan their week and remembers:
>
> - the team meeting they're running
> - the unfinished slide deck from last week
> - the dentist appointment they definitely can't reschedule again.

Cue rising panic. They've overcommitted. Again.

Step 3: The crash

By Thursday, Laura is staying up until 2am trying to catch up. They've forgotten lunch twice. They miss a deadline for another project they agreed to help out with last week. Someone sends a slightly annoyed follow-up email. Laura reads it 12 times, convinced they're about to be fired.

Step 4: The shame spiral

Laura's inner critic kicks in hard: 'Why can't I get it together? Everyone else can cope. What's wrong with me?' They feel like a failure, a fraud and a flake, all the f's at once. The only way to shake off the shame? Try harder next time.

Step 5: The overcompensation

So, when a new request comes in the next day, guess what Laura says?

'Sure, I can do that.'

Not because they have the time or capacity. But because deep down, they still believe that saying yes = being worthy. And they're desperate to outrun the guilt of last week's slip-ups.

And so, the cycle continues. This cycle doesn't break with generic advice like 'just be assertive' or 'you have to put yourself first'. **It breaks when we recognize that saying no isn't selfish, it's a form of emotional self-protection. And that boundaries aren't walls, they're lifejackets.**

Now we have a clearer understanding of the challenges in building or maintaining boundaries for self-care, let's look at some strategies that can help keep those boundaries firm!

Strategies for building healthy boundaries

Our colleague and fellow ADHDer Dr Alex Conner lives by the saying: **'If it's now, it's no.'** This simple phrase highlights the importance of not saying yes without first checking if you have the spoons to take on a task or responsibility.

The first two strategies we'll cover here are about saying no and can help to reduce that ever-growing list of tasks that can build from an impulsive yes!

Strategy 1: The 'Positive No'

For many of us with ADHD, saying no feels like we're letting people down, risking conflict or missing out. We might say yes because we don't want to upset anyone, because we forget what we've already committed to, or because we genuinely believe we'll have the time/energy/motivation later. (Spoiler: we won't.)

But saying yes to everything is a fast track to burnout, overwhelm and doing a mediocre job at five things instead of a decent job at one.

That's where the **Positive No** comes in.

It's a way to protect your time, energy and capacity without damaging relationships, getting labelled difficult, or needing to over-explain yourself. It's built on three parts:

1. **Gratitude – thank the person**
2. **Honesty – explain briefly and tactfully**
3. **Helpfulness – offer an alternative, if possible.**

This approach can be especially useful for people with ADHD, because our energy levels fluctuate wildly, and our executive function can vanish mid-week. **Having a script or structure for saying no can reduce guilt and decision paralysis and help us avoid people-pleasing ourselves into a meltdown.**

Example 1: The overloaded teammate

Scenario: Your manager asks if you can take on another report due Friday. You're already behind on your own deadlines.

Positive No response: 'Thanks for thinking of me for this, I really appreciate your trust. I've got a couple of high-priority deadlines this week, so I wouldn't be able to give this the attention it deserves. I wonder if [Colleague X] might have the capacity?'

Why this can work: It shows you're thoughtful, aware of your limits and still collaborative. You don't make it their problem – you stay constructive, without automatically saying yes.

Example 2: The friendly favour spiral

Scenario: A friend asks you to volunteer at an event this weekend. You've already planned to rest and catch up on overdue tasks.

Positive No response: 'Thank you for thinking of me. I've had a hectic few weeks and promised myself this weekend would be proper recovery time, so I'll have to pass this time. I hope it goes brilliantly – send me a pic from the day!'

Why this can work: It communicates your needs clearly, without guilt-tripping or ghosting. And it gently reminds both of you that rest is valid. (You don't have to 'earn' it by being completely broken.)

Quick tips to practise a 'Positive No'

- **Write a script in advance** for common asks you find hard to refuse (e.g. *'Sorry, I don't take meetings after 4pm – can we do tomorrow morning instead?'*).
- **Use boundaries as defaults** – decide in advance what you will say yes to.

Remember: *No is a complete sentence*. But a Positive No softens the edges.

Saying no might feel hard at first – especially if you're used to being the dependable one, the helper, the yes person. But **every no you say is a yes to something else: your time, your values, your brain's actual limits.**

Strategy 2: Ask 'If I say yes to this, what am I saying no to?'

Many of us with ADHD have a love-hate relationship with saying yes. We want to be helpful. We want to say yes to exciting ideas, to people we care about, to random Tuesday enthusiasm. But thanks to time blindness, fluctuating energy and a sometimes shaky grip on our own limits, we often don't notice what we've signed up for, until it's too late.

That's where asking yourself this deceptively simple question comes in:

If I say yes to this, what am I saying no to?

It's not meant to guilt you out of helping or to squash spontaneity. It's a way of pausing long enough to reality-check your resources. Time blindness and people-pleasing mean that people with ADHD can struggle with future consequences – we're wired to respond to the now.

Asking this question taps into a few key productivity and self-awareness tools:

- **It externalizes priorities.** ADHD can make internal mental juggling hard. Making the trade-off visible helps you spot whether it's really worth it.
- **It builds in decision-making time.** We're more likely to make impulsive commitments under pressure. A pause protects us from overcommitting out of habit or guilt.
- **It reframes no as strategic.** You're not just refusing something for the sake of it – you're preserving time for what actually matters (even if what matters is a nap).

How to use this question:

- Say it out loud (or write it down) before responding to any new request, task, or event.
- Pair it with your actual calendar: what time or energy are you really spending?

- Be honest with yourself about what you're giving up; even if it's 'just' rest or a bit of peace.

Let's try it in practice:

Let's say you're asked to help review a colleague's presentation this evening.

- **If you say yes...** You might be saying no to cooking a real meal, decompressing after a full day, or finishing that task that's already overdue.
- **If you say no...** You might protect your evening energy and be more present and productive tomorrow.

Neither option is wrong. **The point is to choose consciously, not reflexively.**

You don't need to justify your no with a packed schedule. 'I've got too much on my plate already' is enough, even if what's on your plate is a quiet night and some leftovers.

If you find this doesn't work, you can try alternatives:

- *Will Future Me thank me for this?*
- *Do I actually have time/energy for this?*
- *If I say yes now, what am I dropping later without realizing?*

Strategy 3: The DEAR MAN technique

Let's face it: **asking for what we need can be...awkward**. Whether it's a deadline extension, help with a task, or asking someone not to interrupt you again while you're trying to focus. Many of us with ADHD struggle to assert ourselves without either apologizing too much or coming in too hot.

That's where DEAR MAN comes in.

DEAR MAN is a communication tool from Dialectical Behaviour Therapy (DBT). It's designed to help you express your needs clearly and effectively, without trampling over anyone else's feelings (or your own).

It can be especially helpful for people with ADHD who:

- struggle with emotional regulation or rejection sensitivity
- tend to people-please until they snap
- avoid asking for things because it feels too risky or uncomfortable.

Let's break it down.

What does DEAR MAN stands for?

Letter	What it means	In practice
D	**Describe** the situation	'When I'm working at my desk and get interrupted.'
E	**Express** how you feel	'...I lose my train of thought and feel really stressed.'
A	**Assert** what you need	'I need uninterrupted blocks of time in the morning.'
R	**Reinforce** the benefit	'That way I'll be more productive and less snappy later.'
M	**Mindful** of your goal	Stay on track. Don't get pulled into side arguments.
A	**Appear confident**	Try to sound sure of yourself, even if your insides disagree.
N	**Negotiate** if needed	'Could we try this for a week and see how it goes?'

The 'M' and 'A' stages don't have to be included in a communication but are guard rails to help keep you on track and to retain control.

Let's look at protecting focus time at work:

> You need an hour of quiet time each day, but your chatty coworker keeps popping by 'just for a sec'.
>
> Here is DEAR MAN in action:
>
> 'Hi Tom, can I talk to you about something quickly? **(D)** When I get interrupted in the middle of focused work, I lose momentum, and it takes ages to get back into it. **(E)** I've realized I really need uninterrupted time in the mornings to stay on top of my tasks. **(A)** If I can protect that time, I'm much more productive and less stressed. **(R)** Would you mind holding non-urgent chats until after lunch? **(N)** We can still catch up. I just need that particular block of time to be quiet.'
>
> It's calm. It's direct. It leaves room for collaboration. And crucially, you've stated your needs without sounding like a diva or a doormat.

Why this can work:

- **Structure helps us stay on track:** No rambling, spiralling, or giving in halfway through.
- **Planning in advance reduces overwhelm:** Try writing your DEAR MAN out beforehand if you're nervous.
- **It builds self-advocacy:** Many of us didn't get to develop that muscle while we were constantly masking or trying to be 'easy'.

You can use DEAR MAN for many situations, such as when asking for flexible deadlines or accommodations, setting a boundary with a friend or partner, explaining why you can't take on another task, or requesting a change in routine or environment.

Using DEAR MAN doesn't guarantee a yes. However, it can significantly increase your likelihood of being heard and taken seriously without resorting to passive-aggression or burnout.

Chapter summary

For many adults with ADHD, saying no feels impossible, whether due to impulsive yes responses, time blindness, emotional overwhelm or a lifetime of people-pleasing. But boundaries aren't selfish walls; they're scaffolding that keeps us upright. They protect time, energy and focus so we can work and live without constant burnout.

This chapter explored why boundaries matter for productivity and mental health, especially for ADHD brains that leak energy through over-commitment and fear of letting others down.

Clear boundaries help:

- Protect focus by reducing interpersonal and digital interruptions.
- Preserve energy by stopping the emotional drain of constant people management.
- Manage time by avoiding endless task creep and late-night obligations.

We dug into the resistance ADHD creates to saying no, like executive dysfunction (impulsive yeses, forgotten commitments), time blindness (saying yes to 'future you's problem), and emotional hurdles like rejection sensitivity and low self-esteem, which fuel the overcompensation cycle: saying yes > overwhelm > failure > shame > saying yes again.

The chapter also offered practical, ADHD-friendly strategies for building firmer boundaries:

- **The Positive No:** a three-step script (gratitude, honesty, helpfulness) to decline requests without guilt or conflict.
- **The 'If I say yes, what am I saying no to?' pause:** a reality check to avoid impulsive commitments.
- **The DEARMAN method (from DBT):** a structured way to assert needs calmly, from requesting quiet focus time to declining extra work.

The takeaway? Boundaries aren't just being selfish or self-care; they're a vital productivity tool. Each no you say is a yes to your priorities, your brain's limits and your long-term well-being. Start with the area where your time, energy or peace feel most under siege and build from there.

Every boundary you set isn't a rejection of others; it's a commitment to yourself.

Chapter 15

THE PRODUCTIVITY CRASH

Transitions, task switching and getting started again

Transitions, task switching and getting started again are some of the biggest barriers to Sam getting shit done. It takes their brain a long time to task switch, so they have to allow time for transitioning from one thing to the other, because getting started again (or in the first place) can take the longest time, usually involving lots of procrastination! They will delay going to the toilet for hours because they know that if they stop doing something (like writing this book right now!), even for a second, they will find it incredibly difficult, if not impossible sometimes, to get back into it.

If you've ever found yourself staring at an email for 20 minutes, too overwhelmed to reply, or bouncing between ten tabs without actually doing anything, you've met the trio of ADHD's most frustrating productivity saboteurs: task initiation, task switching and transitions. Let's break them down in an easier-to-understand way.

Getting started is a task in itself

Starting a task, aka task initiation, isn't just doing it. It's more like mentally dragging yourself uphill in the rain, wearing socks made of cement. Task initiation means:

- mentally preparing to begin something
- deciding how and when to start
- overcoming the invisible resistance screaming 'Not now!'

This is yet another executive function, so, as you might expect, it takes brainpower. If you've ever avoided a task you actually wanted to do, needed a deadline, a timer, or another person to kick you into action, or felt paralysed by the size of a task, even if you knew the first step, then you'll be familiar with task initiation issues.

The sheer mental load of getting ready to act, the pre-action brain work of deciding, planning and emotionally wrangling yourself, can be exhausting. That's why strategies such as the 5-minute rule or body-doubling can work so well for some people. They can help to sneak you past the resistance and get you moving before your brain notices what's happening.

Switching tasks is not a free action

We've all heard that multitasking is a myth, and here's why: **what we call multitasking is actually usually rapid task switching. And every time you switch tasks, your brain pays a toll.**

Switching tasks actually involves multiple stages: not only stopping a task but mentally letting go of it, then the energy of initiating a new task, or catching up where you left off with an existing task.

Each switch costs time and mental energy, especially with ADHD. Studies show it can take the human brain 15–25 minutes to fully shift focus to a new task. **During that time, the brain (and the person whose cranium it sits in) are not fully engaged with the new task *or* the old one.** It's a kind of mental no-man's land, a fog called 'attention residue'.[1]

And it gets worse. **The more different the tasks are, the harder it is. Even tiny interruptions (a notification ping, a chat, a thought) create micro-switches, and over the day, these add up to serious brain-drain.**

So no, you're not imagining it, just checking your phone for a second can totally derail your focus. That's why strategies like batching similar tasks, turning off notifications and using 'deep work' blocks are so important. They reduce the number of times your brain has to reboot.

Transitions are the hidden battleground

Transitions are more than just finishing one task and starting the next. They're everything that happens in between. And with ADHD, this space can become a sinkhole.

There are three kinds of transitions:

- physical (moving places or shifting environments)
- mental (changing your focus or thinking style)
- emotional (dealing with how you feel about what's next).

Let's see what getting stuck in a transition can actually look like.

Let's say you finally finish writing a report you've been putting off for a week. You click save, stretch, and then...nothing. You just sort of...hover. You're not sure what's next, so you go to tidy your desk, but in the process of moving a notepad, you notice a half-finished spreadsheet. Oh yeah, that thing! You open it to just check something, and an hour later, you're deep into fixing formatting errors that aren't needed and that no one asked for.

Then you look at the clock, feel a wave of guilt and suddenly the idea of starting your next actual task makes your stomach twist. It feels... emotionally too much. You don't even know why, but the thought of diving into a new thing makes you want to cry or hide.

That, right there, is transition trouble. You finished one task, but your brain didn't get the memo about what to do next. So, it defaulted to a distraction, then slammed into emotional resistance when asked to switch gears.

These shifts are where ADHD brains often freeze. Why? Because **transitions demand cognitive and emotional flexibility**, something that doesn't come easily when your executive functions are astray.

And when it comes to productivity it means that:

- Starting tasks is hard because your brain does so much work before anything even happens.
- Switching tasks burns energy, increases errors and leaves mental clutter behind.
- Transitions are where productivity goes to die, unless you plan for them.

Why can't I just start the thing? Task paralysis, procrastination and that weird stuck feeling

For many of us with ADHD, getting started is one of the hardest parts of being productive. And it's not because we don't care or aren't trying. It's because we face **task initiation challenges, which can lead to task paralysis.**

What does task paralysis really feel like? You know you have stuff to do. You might even want to do it. But when you try to start, it's like your brain says, 'nope'. You freeze. You stall. You open a new tab and Google 'Why am I like this?'

Task paralysis is that sticky, uncomfortable in-between state where you can't start, even when you know what needs doing, you care about the outcome and you might already be late.

Sound familiar? Here's what it can look like in real life:

- Putting off important projects, even as the deadline looms.
- Avoiding job applications or admin, even when they really matter.
- Rewriting your to-do list ten times without ticking anything off.
- Feeling completely overwhelmed by a particular task that seems too much.
- Trying to start, getting hit by a wave of anxiety and giving up.

From the outside, task paralysis can look like laziness or procrastination. But that's not what's happening. **What's really going on is a combination of cognitive overload (too many moving parts to hold in mind), emotional overwhelm (anxiety, guilt, frustration, shame) and executive dysfunction.**

In ADHD, the brain's motivation system works differently (as we covered in Chapter 5). We often need a stronger or more immediate reason to get going, especially if the task is boring, difficult, or emotionally loaded.

And to make things more exasperating, the more overwhelmed we feel, the harder it gets to start...which makes us feel more anxious... which makes it even harder to start. It becomes a self-reinforcing cycle of paralysis:

emotion + executive function = stuck

Let's break that down:

1. You're facing a task.
2. Your brain goes into overload; there are too many steps and you're unclear about where to begin.
3. That triggers emotional distress: panic, shame or dread.
4. Those emotions then further block your ability to start.
5. You stay stuck. The task doesn't go away. The feelings get worse.

This is **a cognitive-emotional loop**, and it's exhausting. To break the cycle, we need to work with both parts:

- **The thinking part:** break things down, simplify decisions, reduce overload.
- **The feeling part:** manage the emotional reaction and self-judgment that comes with it.

Wait, I thought I was born to switch tasks?

There's a stereotype that ADHDers can't stay on task. But here's the truth: **switching tasks can be just as hard as staying on task, *especially when it's not on our terms.*** We generally struggle with letting go of something we're focused on, picking up something we don't feel ready for and coping when plans or priorities suddenly change.

Signs that task switching is hard for you can include:

- You panic when plans change or new tasks are added at the last minute.
- You find it difficult to adapt or think on your feet.
- You resist stopping something, even to go to the loo, because you might lose your flow.
- You get distracted by small things and forget what you were just doing.
- You dread transitions between tasks, roles, or environments.

Underneath all this is something called **cognitive flexibility**, your brain's ability to shift gears. **In ADHD, that flexibility is often reduced. In AuDHD it can be much worse. Combined with poor working memory and a high sensitivity to distractions, this creates a kind of mental friction any time you try to change direction.**

The hidden cost of every switch

The 15–25 minutes to fully refocus after switching tasks statistic from earlier was taken from research in the general population. **For ADHD brains, this time is longer, and the energy cost is higher.** One study found that even children with ADHD experienced larger switch costs than their peers; their performance dropped more when switching.[2]

That invisible delay and mental effort adds up. It not only slows you down, it drains your energy and so increases your risk of forgetting what you were doing or missing something important.

And that's not just with big work tasks. This applies to everything from switching tabs to making lunch to answering a message. **We're constantly using brainpower just to keep up with everyday transitions.**

This means:

- We often feel more tired than others, even if we haven't done much.
- We miss deadlines, not because we didn't care, but because the switching and starting and restarting was too much.
- We may over-focus on one thing and under-focus on another, without intending to.

Some experts call it an invisible tax, a constant background cost that's rarely acknowledged.

Strategies to tackle transitions and maintain momentum

ADHD brains may not handle starts and switches on autopilot, but different strategies can help support task initiation and transitions.

Strategy 1: Tips for starting tasks

There are many approaches that can help. Reflect on what might have worked in the past, or what you haven't tried from this list:

- **Plan and preview:** Mentally picture what starting looks like (if you are able to). Not finishing, *starting*.
- **Define the first step:** Instead of 'clean the kitchen', try 'put the plates in the dishwasher'.
- **Break it down:** Smaller chunks = smaller dread.
- **Use external prompts:** Timers, check lists, visual cues, because your brain's internal alarm system hits snooze too often.
- **Try the 5-minute rule:** Just do 5 minutes. If you want to stop after that, you can. (You probably won't.)
- **Automate the boring bits:** Create routines for repetitive stuff so your brain can save energy for the hard stuff. We cover automations in Chapters 4, 11 and 13.
- **Reward yourself:** Even small wins deserve celebration. That little dopamine hit matters.
- **Make it personal:** Connect the task to something meaningful or make it mildly fun.
- **Let go of perfect:** Done is better than perfect and never finished. Or, as Anna, one of our podcast listeners from Edinburgh, put in a card to us: 'half-arsed is better than f*ck all' (Sam uses this almost every day as a mantra to help her to battle her perfectionism!).

There are exercises on 'automating the boring stuff' and 'building a transition ritual' in our online resources (see p.343).

Strategy 2: Tips for task-switching

So, you got started, but now you have to switch to a different task, which can be just as difficult as starting a task. Have a look at the list below, and see which one of these you could try first:

- **Group similar tasks together:** It's easier for your brain to go from email to email than from email to budgeting spreadsheet.
- **Prioritize before you start:** Know what's important, so your brain doesn't try to do everything at once.
- **Pre-plan the next thing:** Before you finish one task, decide what you'll do next. This cuts down on mental flailing.
- **Try Pomodoro:** 25 minutes of focus, 5-minute break (or whatever intervals work for you). Rinse and repeat. (And *actually* take the break.) Sam does something fun, calming or enjoyable in between work tasks. This feels like a palate cleanser between courses; it helps them with task switching but also gives their brain a reward.
- **Micro-pauses:** Even 30 seconds to stretch or breathe can help your brain reset.
- **Transition rituals:** Create a mini routine to signal 'this task is done, time to switch'. Close tabs, stand up, take three deep breaths.
- **Change your environment:** A different chair, room or browser window can help shift your mental gears.
- **Cut distractions:** Turn off pings, pop-ups and pet squirrels (where possible).

There is an exercise to help with task switching in our online resources (see p.343).

Strategy 3: Tips for transitions

Transitioning from the desk to the printer, from home to work, or work to break time can be challenging. Here are some approaches you might try:

- **Again, group tasks in advance:** Know what you're doing in this block of time, not just 'work'.
- **Again, use rituals to shift gears:** Shut your laptop, stretch, tidy your desk, or literally say, 'OK, next task'. (Yes, out loud works.) Go a short walk before and/or after work to help with the transition and to give you processing time. The drive to and from the office is great for this too. Changing clothes can help to signal that the working day is starting/ending. Having a safe sensory space or using a sensory kit (more on this in Chapter 13) can also help.
- **Build transition time into your routine:** Even five minutes between tasks can help your brain catch up. You don't have to do nothing; you could do something calming (Sam lies under their weighted blanket and watches their chasing lights) or energizing (looking at bees in the garden for five minutes can really energize Sam!) – whatever works for you.
- **Practice mindfulness:** A short breathwork or grounding exercise helps clear the mental clutter.
- **Use timers:** Let an alarm cue the end of one task or the start of the next, so you don't have to keep checking the clock. Although if you're in flow and don't want to stop then keep going if you need to!
- **Create physical boundaries:** Have different workspaces (or even different mugs) for different tasks to signal a shift.
- **Acknowledge the emotions:** Switching tasks isn't just mental, it's emotional. Letting go of one task and facing another can feel weird. That's OK.

Chapter summary

For many adults with ADHD, the real productivity drain isn't just distraction, it's getting started, switching gears and navigating the messy in-betweens. This chapter explored why these invisible taxes hit so hard and how to reduce the toll.

We looked at three big challenges:

- Task initiation – starting feels like pushing a boulder uphill, thanks to executive dysfunction, emotional overload and a brain that needs extra cues to kick into gear.
- Task switching – every switch drains time and energy, with attention residue and mental lag slowing us down, especially when interruptions pile up.
- Transitions – those limbo moments between tasks (physical, mental, or emotional) often lead to derailment or procrastination, or spiral into low-value busywork.

These struggles are a mix of neurological wiring, cognitive overload and emotional weight. And they add up, making ADHD brains feel more exhausted, scattered and behind than other people's, even when we're working just as hard (or harder).

The chapter also outlined practical strategies to break through:

- For task initiation: break tasks down, visualize starting (not finishing), use external cues, the 5-minute rule, routines and rewards to bypass resistance.
- For task switching: batch similar tasks, plan the next thing before you finish the current one, use the Pomodoro

technique or micro-pauses and create mini rituals to signal 'done, now move on'.

- For transitions: build in buffer time, use mindfulness or breathwork to clear mental clutter, shift environments or cues, and acknowledge the emotional weight of changing gears.

The key takeaway? ADHD brains don't handle starts and switches on autopilot. But with the right scaffolding, external cues, structured rituals and realistic planning, you can reduce the switch tax, escape paralysis and build momentum without burning out.

Chapter 16

PERMISSION TO BE HUMAN

Sam often says that the most difficult thing about their ADHD is that whatever tools, systems, routines, etc., they put in place, they will generally only work for a short amount of time before they have to scrap them and start again. It can be exhausting mentally, physcally and emotionally. As much as they *love* starting a new system – and they *really* do! – having that system not work or stop working, and then trying to build a new system, can be soul-destroying if they're not in a good headspace. They find it easy to get caught up in chastising themselves and feeding their self-loathing (and that's a pretty big part of them already, so it doesn't need feeding!).

To help to combat this, they try to think of a system that is no longer working as an opportunity to learn and make the system better next time. Occasionally, if they're in a good place mentally and emotionally, this can work really well! Most of the time their brain rejects that though, and actually they've learned that the system doesn't always need tweaking. Sometimes they can try it again another time and it works! What works today is very unlikely to work for ever and what doesn't work today might work tomorrow.

Accepting that whatever approaches we take and systems we put in place may not work, or, if they do, may only work for a limited time, can help to alleviate some of the constant pressure we put ourselves under. Sam and James try to lighten the shame and hate spirals that can occur when things don't go as planned (and they rarely do!) with humour. They value humour *so much*. So now for Sam, when something goes wrong, that initial disappointment, anger, shame, regret, whatever...is usually replaced quickly with excitement that they now have a new self-deprecating story to tell, and those are their favourite types of stories!

Why it's so hard to stick with things

Let's start with the obvious: staying consistent is hard. Staying consistent with ADHD can feel like trying to hold water in your hands. You have every intention of keeping it together, then, whoops, you blink, and a month has passed, and your planner is buried under laundry and regret.

This isn't a personal flaw. Remember, your ADHD brain is battling:

- Executive dysfunction: the invisible glitch that makes starting, switching and finishing tasks unpredictable.
- Time blindness: meaning just ten minutes can turn into three hours of phone scrolling.
- Emotional dysregulation: where one bad day can derail a whole week of good habits.

Sometimes, if a system that worked once, such as a habit tracker, an app or a fancy timer, suddenly stops working, with no warning and no refund, you wonder, 'Why can't I just keep going?'

The answer? Because ADHD isn't a disorder of not knowing what to do. It's a disorder of not doing what you know. **Your struggle is with execution, not intelligence or effort.**

The shame spiral: when trying again feels pointless

If you've ever thought, 'What's the point? I always screw this up,' you're not alone. Most adults with ADHD carry some version of the same script:

- I should be better at this by now.
- Other people don't have to keep restarting.
- What's wrong with me?!

Let's name what's happening here: Rejection Sensitive Dysphoria (RSD), perfectionism and a lifetime of internalized messages that framed inconsistency as laziness.

But here's the reframe: ***you* didn't fail. *Your system* did.** That's not a moral judgment, it's just data. **If your plan fell apart when life got chaotic or your sleep worsened, it doesn't mean you're broken. It means that the setup wasn't flexible enough for your brain.**

Shame says, 'You're hopeless.' Compassion says, 'Let's look at what happened.'

Choose compassion.

Reframing what progress looks like

Perfection tells us that real progress is clean, linear and Instagramable. Reality looks more like three good days, two confusing weeks, one terrible crash and a sudden urge to reorganize your entire sock drawer.

Let's stop grading ourselves solely on consistency.

Try this instead:

- **Productivity as a practice:** Like meditation or exercise, it's something you return to. Not something you nail every time.
- **Messy wins still count:** Half-done is still progress. Done late is still done. Doing something is better than doing nothing. Showing up counts.
- **Tiny restarts are powerful:** You don't have to relaunch the whole routine. Just do one small thing. That's enough.

Resetting (again)

You will fall off track. That's not a failure; that's baked into ADHD for pretty much all of us. So, let's build a reset toolkit that's kind, flexible and ADHD-friendly.

Here are some gentle ways to restart without self-flagellation:

- **The 5-minute jumpstart:** Set a timer. Pick one small task. Do just that. If it snowballs, great. If not, you still did something.
- **The try-again-tomorrow list:** Instead of rewriting your whole plan, jot down one or two things you'd like to try again tomorrow. Keep it realistic. Keep it light.

- **Compassionate self-check-in:** Ask 'What made this difficult for me?' not 'Why am I like this?' You'll get more useful answers.
- **Dopamine anchors:** Pair your restart with something enjoyable. Light a candle. Play a song. Wear a costume or your favourite hoodie. **Make restarting rewarding.**
- **Habit tweaks, not overhauls:** You don't need a new system every time you struggle. Just ask, 'What's one thing I can adjust to make this easier?'

Celebrating imperfect effort

You know what deserves praise? Showing up at all. Starting again yet again. Taking a deep breath and deciding to be kind to yourself instead of spiralling.

Here are some ways to reframe your inner monologue:

- Instead of 'I failed again,' try 'OK, that didn't work for me today. Let's try a different approach tomorrow.'
- Instead of 'I'm behind,' try 'This might be taking longer than expected, but I'm making progress.'
- Instead of 'I should be doing more,' try 'I'm doing what I can with the brain I have.'

One important note: **self-kindness isn't the opposite of accountability.** It's what makes accountability sustainable. **Beating yourself up won't build momentum, but self-respect might.**

Final reflection

If you're reading this, whether at the end of the reading journey or if you skipped to the end (just in case that's where all the good stuff is), you've already done something powerful. **You showed up. You read. You thought about your brain. You tried.**

Sure, you might forget some of it or even all of it. That's OK.

You don't have to finish every chapter to be changed by this book. You don't have to apply every option perfectly. You don't have to become a productivity ninja. **You just have to keep circling back, in whatever way you can.**

You're allowed to take breaks without guilt.

You're allowed to start over without shame.

You're allowed to be a work in progress. For ever.

Because the truth is, so are we.

Try again tomorrow.

Or Thursday.

Or next March.

The point is...You can.

NOTES

Chapter 1: What even is ADHD?

1 The specific version of the American Psychiatric Association's handbook that we are referring to here is the Diagnostic and Statistical Manual version 5 (or DSMV-TR for short).

2 Diamond, A., (2013). Executive functions. *Annual Review Psychology*. 64:135–68. doi: 10.1146/annurev-psych-113011-143750.

3 Barkley, R.A. (2012). The important role of executive functioning and self-regulation in ADHD. *The ADHD Report*, 20(2), 1–5.

Chapter 2: ADHD and productivity challenges

1 Mark, G., Gudith, D. and Klocke, U. (2008). The cost of interrupted work: more speed and stress. *Proceedings of the SIGCHI Conference on Human Factors in Computing Systems.* New York: ACM, pp.107–110.

2 Mark, G., Gonzalez, V.M. and Harris, J. (2005). No task left behind? Examining the nature of fragmented work. *Proceedings of the SIGCHI Conference on Human Factors in Computing Systems.* New York: ACM, pp. 321–330.

3 https://www.gallup.com/workplace/653711/great-detachment-why-employees-feel-stuck.aspx.

4 https://www.gallup.com/workplace/236927/employee-engagement-drives-growth.aspx.

5 van den Bosch, R., and Taris, T.W. (2014). Authenticity at work: Its relations with worker motivation and well-being. *Frontiers in Psychology*, 5, 1–10.

6 Jangmo A., Kuja-Halkola R., Pérez-Vigil A., Almqvist C., Bulik C.M., D'Onofrio B., *et al.* (2021). Attention-deficit/hyperactivity disorder and occupational outcomes: The role of educational attainment, comorbid developmental disorders, and intellectual disability. *PLoS ONE* 16(3): e0247724.

7 https://www.sciencedaily.com/releases/2008/05/080527125324.htm.
8 https://www.akiliinteractive.com/workplacesurvey.

Chapter 3: ADHD-friendly goal setting

1 Jeong, Y.H., Healy, L.C., and McEwan, D. (2021). The application of Goal Setting Theory to goal setting interventions in sport: a systematic review. *International Review of Sport and Exercise Psychology*, 16(1), 474–499.
2 Doran, G.T. (1981). There's a SMART Way to Write Management's Goals and Objectives. *Journal of Management Review*, 70, 35–36.
3 Pietsch, S., Riddell, H., Semmler, C., Ntoumanis, N., and Gucciardi, D.F. (2024). SMART goals are no more effective for creative performance than do-your-best goals or non-specific, exploratory 'open goals.' *Educational Psychology*, 44(9–10), 946–962. https://doi.org/10.1080/01443410.2024.2420818

Chapter 4: Automating life

1 https://www.verywellmind.com/the-importance-of-keeping-a-routine-during-stressful-times-4802638.
2 Lanza H.I., Drabick D.A. Family routine moderates the relation between child impulsivity and oppositional defiant disorder symptoms. *Journal of Abnormal Child Psychology*, 2011 Jan;39(1):83-94. doi: 10.1007/s10802-010-9447-5.
3 https://www.bps.org.uk/psychologist/self-control-moral-muscle. *See also* Vohs, K.D., Baumeister, R.F., Schmeichel, B.J., Twenge, J.M., Nelson, N.M., and Tice, D.M. (2008). Making choices impairs subsequent self-control: A limited-resource account of decision making, selfregulation, and active initiative. *Journal of Personality and Social Psychology*, 94(5), 883–898.

Chapter 5: Finding motivation

1 Deci, E.L., and Ryan, R.M. (2008). Self-determination theory: A macrotheory of human motivation, development, and health. *Canadian Psychology / Psychologie canadienne*, 49(3), 182–185.
2 Smith, Z.R., Langberg, J.M., Cusick, C.N., Green, C.D. and Becker, S.P. (2020). Academic motivation deficits in adolescents with ADHD and associations with academic functioning. *Journal of Abnormal Child Psychology*, 48(2), pp. 237–249. —Oram, R., Rogers, M. and DuPaul, G. (2020). Explaining the relationship

between ADHD symptomatology and amotivation in the undergraduate population: the role of basic psychological need frustration. *Canadian Journal of School Psychology*, 35(2), pp. 139–153.

3 Volkow, N.D., Wang, G.J., Newcorn, J.H., Kollins, S.H., Wigal, T.L., Telang, F., Fowler, J.S., Goldstein, R.Z., Klein, N., Logan, J. and Wong, C. (2011). Motivation deficit in ADHD is associated with dysfunction of the dopamine reward pathway. *Molecular Psychiatry*, 16(11), pp. 1147–1154.

4 Girija Kadlaskar, Ana-Maria Iosif, Burt Hatch, Leiana de la Paz, Annie Chuang, Makayla M. Soller, Jocelynn Morales-Martinez, Kimberly G. Tena, Jenna P. Sandler, Sally Ozonoff and Meghan Miller. (2024) Delay of Gratification in Preschoolers with Autism and Concerns for ADHD. *Journal of Clinical Child & Adolescent Psychology* 0:0, 1–13.

5 Sonuga-Barke, E.J.S. (2003). The dual pathway model of AD/HD: An elaboration of neuro-developmental characteristics. *Neuroscience & Biobehavioral Reviews*, 27(7), 593–604. https://doi.org/10.1016/j.neubiorev.2003.08.005.

6 Pelham W.E. Jr, Fabiano GA. (2008). Evidence-based psychosocial treatments for attention-deficit/hyperactivity disorder. *Journal of Clinical Child & Adolescent Psychology*. 2008 Jan;37(1):184–214. doi: 10.1080/15374410701818681.

7 Sindiani, M., Korman, M., and Karni, A. (2022). Time-of-day matters in text learning and recall: Evening lessons are advantageous for adults with ADHD though not for typical peers. *Learning and Instruction*, 80, 101630.

8 Frisch C., Tirosh E., and Rosenblum S. (2003). Children with ADHD Symptomatology: Does POET Improve Their Daily Routine Management? *Children* (Basel). Jun 20;10(6):1083. doi: 10.3390/children10061083.

Chapter 6: Which fire to put out first?

1 de Zeeuw, P. and Durston, S. (2017). Cognitive Control in Attention Deficit Hyperactivity Disorder. In *The Wiley Handbook of Cognitive Control*, T. Egner (Ed.). https://doi.org/10.1002/9781118920497.ch33.

2 Schwabe L and Wolf O.T. (2013). Stress and multiple memory systems: from 'thinking' to 'doing'. *Trends in Cognitive Sciences*. Feb;17(2):60–8. doi: 10.1016/j.tics.2012.12.001. Epub 2013 Jan 2.

Chapter 7: Tackling procrastination

1 Sirois, F.M., van Eerde, W. and Argiropoulou, M.I. (2015). Is procrastination related to sleep quality? Testing an indirect effect model of bed-time procrastination. *Journal of General Psychology*, 142(4), 275–287.

2 Sirois, F.M., Melia-Gordon, M.L. and Pychyl, T. A. (2003). 'I'll look after my health, later': An investigation of procrastination and health. *Personality and Individual Differences*, 35(5), 1167–1184.

3 Minister, C. *et al.* (2025). Understanding the relationships between ADHD symptoms and cannabis-related consequences among young adults. *Cannabis*, 8(1).

—Groenman, A. P. *et al.* (2017) Substance use disorders in adults with attention deficit hyperactivity disorder: prevalence and associations. *Psychological Medicine*, 49(1), 1–10.

Chapter 8: Managing distractibility

1 Schneidt, A., Jusyte, A., Rauss, K., and Schönenberg, M. (2018). Distraction by salient stimuli in adults with attention-deficit/hyperactivity disorder: Evidence for the role of task difficulty in bottom-up and top-down processing. *Cortex*, 101, 206–220. https://doi.org/10.1016/j.cortex.2018.01.021.

2 Osborne, J.B., Zhang, H., Carlson, M., Shah, P., and Jonides, J. (2023). The association between different sources of distraction and symptoms of attention deficit hyperactivity disorder. *Frontiers in Psychiatry*, 14, 1173989. https://doi.org/10.3389/fpsyt.2023.1173989.

3 Zhang, H., Miyake, A., Osborne, J., Shah, P., and Jonides, J. (2023). A *d* factor? Understanding trait distractibility and its relationships with ADHD symptomatology and hyperfocus. PLOS ONE, 18(10), e0292215. https://doi.org/10.1371/journal.pone.0292215.

Chapter 9: Time management for the time-blind

1 Macan, T.H. (1994). Time management: Test of a process model. *Journal of Applied Psychology*, 79(3), 381–391. https://doi.org/10.1037/0021-9010.79.3.381

2 König, C.J., and Kleinmann, M. (2007). Time management problems and dysfunctional self-regulation. *Time & Society*, 16(2–3), 329–346.

3 Britton, B.K., and Tesser, A. (1991). Effects of time-management practices on

college grades. *Journal of Educational Psychology*, 83(3), 405–410.

4 Prevatt F. and Yelland S. (2015). An Empirical Evaluation of ADHD Coaching in College Students. *Journal of Attention Disorders*. Aug; 19(8):666–77. doi: 10.1177/1087054713480036.

Chapter 10: Dealing with the feels

1 Etkin, A., Büchel, C. and Gross, J. (2015). The neural bases of emotion regulation. *Nature Reviews Neuroscience*, 16, 693–700.

2 Gross, J.J. (2015). The Extended Process Model of Emotion Regulation: Elaborations, Applications, and Future Directions. *Psychological Inquiry*, 26(1), 130–137.

3 Shaw, P., Stringaris, A., Nigg, J. and Leibenluft, E. (2014). Emotion dysregulation in attention deficit hyperactivity disorder. *American Journal of Psychiatry*, 171(3), 276–293.

4 Modestino, E. J. *et al.* (2024). Rejection Sensitivity Dysphoria in Attention-Deficit/Hyperactivity Disorder: A Case Series. *Acta Scientific Neurology*. 7–8. 23–30. 10.31080/ASNE.2024.07.0762.

Chapter 11: Forget me not

1 Baddeley, A. (2012). Working memory: theories, models, and controversies. *Annual Review of Psychology*, 63, pp. 1–29. *See also* Baddeley, A. and Hitch, G.J. (2010). Working memory. *Scholarpedia*, 5(2): 3015, http://www.scholarpedia.org/article/Working_memory.

2 Kofler M.J., Singh L.J., Soto E.F., Chan E.S.M., Miller C.E., Harmon S.L., Spiegel J.A. (2020) Working memory and short-term memory deficits in ADHD: A bifactor modeling approach. *Neuropsychology*. Sep;34(6):686–698.

3 Alderson, R.M., Kasper, L.J., Hudec, K.L., & Patros, C.H.G. (2013). Attention-deficit/hyperactivity disorder (ADHD) and working memory in adults: A meta-analytic review. *Neuropsychology*, 27(3), 287–302. https://doi.org/10.1037/a0032371.

Chapter 12: Progress, not perfection

1 Harari D., Swider, B.W., Steed, L.B. and Breidenthal, A.P. (2018) Is perfect good? A meta-analysis of perfectionism in the workplace. *Journal of Applied Psychology*. Oct;103(10):1121–1144.

Chapter 13: When ADHD meets autism

1 Rong, Y. *et al.* (2021). Prevalence of attention-deficit/hyperactivity disorder in individuals with autism spectrum disorder: A meta-analysis. *Research in Autism Spectrum Disorders,* 83.

2 Elwin, M. *et al.* (2020). Psychiatric comorbidities in children and adolescents with suspected ADHD. *Nordic Journal of Psychiatry,* 75(2), 1–9.

3 Antshel, K. M. and Russo, N. (2019). Autism spectrum disorders and ADHD: Overlapping phenomenology, diagnostic issues, and treatment considerations. *Current Psychiatry Reports,* 21(5), 34.

Chapter 15: The Productivity Crash

1 Leroy, S. (2009). Why is it so hard to do my work? The challenge of attention residue when switching between work tasks. *Organizational Behavior and Human Decision Processes,* 109(2), 168–181.

2 Hung C.L., Huang C.J., Tsai Y.J., Chang Y.K., Hung T.M. (2106). Neuroelectric and Behavioral Effects of Acute Exercise on Task Switching in Children with Attention-Deficit/Hyperactivity Disorder. *Frontiers in Psychology.* Oct 13;7:1589. doi: 10.3389/fpsyg.2016.01589.

RESOURCES AND FURTHER READING

Here are a few books, apps, websites and exercises you can try to help with the areas we've discussed in the book.

You'll find all our exercises online at jbhd.uk – just follow the QR code below to take you there.

Chapter 1: What even is ADHD?

Barkley, R.A. (2010) *Taking Charge of Adult ADHD*. New York: Guilford Press

Conner, A. and Brown, J. (2025) *ADHD unpacked: everything you need to know to survive and thrive as an adult with ADHD*. London: Bloomsbury Tonic.

ADHDadultUK – www.adhdadult.uk

ADHDUK – https://adhduk.co.uk/

Russell Barkley's Official Site: https://www.russellbarkley.org/

Chapter 2: ADHD and productivity challenges

Value Assessment – https://personalvalu.es/

Burnout assessment tool – https://burnoutassessmenttool.be/start_eng/

Goblin Tools – https://goblin.tools/

Chapter 3: ADHD-friendly goal setting

Keller, G. and Papasan, J. (2013) *The One Thing: The Surprisingly Simple Truth Behind Extraordinary Results.* Austin: Bard Press.

SMART Goals – https://www.mindtools.com/a4wo118/smart-goals

Strides app – https://www.stridesapp.com/

Goblin Tools – https://goblin.tools/

Exercise: *Build your master task list*

Chapter 4: Building routines

Clear, J. (2018) *Atomic Habits: An Easy & Proven Way to Build Good Habits & Break Bad Ones.* London: Random House Business.

Tiimo app – https://www.tiimoapp.com/

Routinery app – https://routinery.app/

Exercises:

Build your meta-routine

The 'Zuckerberg Approach'

Hook a new habit to an anchor

Chapter 5: Finding motivation

Pink, D.H. (2009) *Drive: The Surprising Truth About What Motivates Us.* New York: Riverhead Books.

Body Doubling services – Focus Mate https://www.focusmate.com/ and Deepwrek https://www.deepwrk.io/

Habitica app – https://habitica.com/

Exercises:

Diagnose your motivation block

Gamifying your unrewarding tasks

Chapter 6: Which fire to put out first?

Allen, D. (2001) *Getting Things Done: The art of stress-free productivity.* London: Piatkus.

McKeown, G. (2014) *Essentialism: The Disciplined Pursuit of Less.* New York: Crown Business.

Todoist app – https://www.todoist.com/

TickTick app – https://ticktick.com/

Microsoft To Do – https://www.microsoft.com/en-gb/microsoft-365/microsoft-to-do-list-app

Exercise: *The task triage grid*

Chapter 7: Tackling procrastination

Fiore, N.A. (2007) *The Now Habit: A Strategic Program for Overcoming Procrastination and Enjoying Guilt-Free Play.* New York: Penguin Group.

Chapter 8: Managing distractibility

Eyal, N. (2019) *Indistractable: How to Control Your Attention and Choose Your Life.* London: Bloomsbury Publishing.

AppBlock – https://appblock.app/

Endel app (music for focus) – https://endel.io/

Freedom app – https://freedom.to/

Exercises:

Workspace optimization

Park your thoughts (internal distractions)

Clear the runway (external distractions)

Chapter 9: Time management for the 'time-blind'

Burkeman, O. (2021) *Four Thousand Weeks: Time Management for Mortals*. London: The Bodley Head.

Motion app – https://www.usemotion.com/

Time Timer – https://www.timetimer.com/

Exercises:

Where does the time go?

Plan backwards from the deadline

Chapter 10: Dealing with the feels

Rosier, T. (2021) *Your Brain's Not Broken: Strategies for Navigating Your Emotions and Life with ADHD*. Grand Rapids: Revell.

How We Feel app – https://howwefeel.org/

Bearable app – https://bearable.app/

Exercises:

Label and challenge emotions with DESC

Calm your system with breathing

Chapter 11: Forget me not

Otter.ai transcription service – https://otter.ai/

Due app – https://www.dueapp.com/

Exercise: *Automating the boring stuff*

Chapter 12: Progress, not perfection

Szymanski, J. (2011) *The Perfectionist's Handbook: Take Risks, Invite Criticism, and Make the Most of Your Mistakes.* Hoboken: Wiley.

Self-Compassion (Dr Kristin Neff) – https://self-compassion.org/

Positive Psychology article – https://positivepsychology.com/how-to-overcome-perfectionism/

Exercises:

Practise 'good enough'

Challenge the perfectionist thought

Chapter 13: When ADHD meets autism

Price, D. (2022) *Unmasking Autism: The Power of Embracing Our Neurodivergent Brains.* London: Monoray.

AuDHD UK – https://www.audhduk.org/

AuDHD Online Community (Meetup) – https://www.meetup.com/topics/audhd/

Exercise: *The energy audit*

Chapter 14: Learning to say no

Tawwab, N.G. (2021) *Set Boundaries, Find Peace: A Guide to Reclaiming Yourself*. London: Piatkus.

Nedra Glover Tawwab – https://www.nedratawwab.com/

Exercises:

Delegating tasks to free up mental space

The 'If I say yes...' reality check

Practicing the Positive No

Chapter 15: The productivity crash

Newport, C. (2016) *Deep Work: Rules for Focused Success in a Distracted World*. London: Piatkus.

Opal app – https://www.opal.so/

The 5 Second Rule (Mel Robbins) – https://melrobbins.com/

Exercises:

Smoother task switching

The transition time-out

ACKNOWLEDGEMENTS

Thank you to our families and friends for standing by us and supporting us, and not just through the unsurprising challenge of writing a book – we are so grateful to all of you.

To Alex, our co-host of *The ADHD Adults Podcast* and friend, thank you for being part of this journey. A small part, just to clarify.

And to the listeners of *The ADHD Adults Podcast*, people who have come to see us at James's little talks, everyone who helped us build a thriving online support network through our charity's Discord group, and especially our Patreon family: thank you for your patience, love, trust, support, and questionable sense of humour. We love and appreciate you all.

INDEX

5-4-3-2-1 method 220
5-minute jumpstart 332
5-minute rule 317, 324

A
ABCDE method 132–3
Acceptance and Commitment Therapy (ACT) 256, 257
accountability 108–9, 157, 190, 283
action 24, 57
  emotions and 207–8
  intention-action gap 141
  opposite action 221–2
ADHD (Attention-Deficit Hyperactivity Disorder): diagnosis 11–15, 19–20
  what it is 9–26
  why it occurs 16–18
agnosia *see* time blindness
AI (Artificial Intelligence) 108
  dynamic dashboards 95
  meta-routines 90–1
  organizational support 238
  perfectionism strategies 257–8
  prioritization tools 133–4, 282
  task automation 286–7, 241
  time management 198, 199
  working memory toolkit 236
aids, strategic use of 234, 236
alarms 240
alexithymia 159
amnesia, future 193–4
amotivation 104, 105
amygdala 121, 209, 216, 267, 268
analysis paralysis 148–9, 251
anchors 238–41
anterior cingulate cortex (ACC) 210
anterior insula 210
anxiety 76, 185
  about saying no 303, 304
  and ADHD 42, 43
  effective time management 189
  fear of success 147
  intention-action gap 141
  intrusive thoughts 174
  and perfectionism 244, 247, 248, 255
  performance anxiety 62
  and priorities 117
  and procrastination 144, 154
  racing thoughts 173
attention 53, 169, 229

attention paradox 272
attention residue 317
bottom-up attention 165–6, 169
how the brain regulates 164–7
inattention 38–9
maintaining 24
and perfectionism 247
re-anchoring your attention 184
sustained attention 213
time-blocking to contain attention 183
top-down attention 120, 165–6
working memory and 231
AuDHD 261–88
attention paradox 272
the AuDHD tug-of-war 268
biology of 266–7
and the brain 267
diagnosing 263–4
and productivity 269–70, 274–7
routines 270–1, 274
strategies to help 277–87
what it is 263–6
autism, and ADHD 261–88
automations 73–98, 238–41, 285, 286, 324

B
Barkley, Dr Russell 23, 24
basal ganglia 81, 82, 121, 124–5, 193, 195, 228
Baumeister, Roy 78
body doubling 100, 108–9, 157–8, 283, 317
boundaries 46, 289–315
different types of 293–4
difficulty of setting with ADHD 300–3
emotions and 303–7
and productivity 294–5, 296–7, 298–300
psychological pay-off of 295–6
strategies for building healthy 307–14
task switching 326
what boundaries are 291–3
box breathing 220
the brain: ADHD brain 11, 25, 265–6, 267, 277
attention regulation 164–7
and AuDHD 267–8, 277
autistic brain 265–6, 267
building routines 80
development of 16–17, 18–19
dopamine 87
emotional regulation 208–13
executive functions 20–2
externalizing your brain 182
how the brain tells time 192–3
neurotransmitters 16, 17, 18
priorities and 120–2, 124–7
time management 190–1, 195, 202
see also individual parts of the brain
breathing techniques 220
Brown, Thomas 24
burnout 41, 43–7
and AuDHD 277
avoiding 46–7
and boundaries 290, 292–3, 295, 305, 307
daily toll of living with ADHD 41
definition of 43–4
early warning signs 45
hidden cost of saying yes 297–8
and hyperfocus 273
and perfectionism 244, 247, 250, 251, 255
prevention and recovery from 46
and productivity 29–30, 32–3, 34

C
cerebellum 121, 125, 193, 228, 267
cerebral cortex 193
children: development of ADHD in 17
importance of routines 77
task switching 322–3
chunking 234, 235, 284–5
cingulate cortex 228
circadian rhythms 76
clocks 199
coaching 219
Cognitive Behavioural Therapy (CBT) 219, 256–7

cognitive control 122, 123
cognitive demand 176
cognitive distortions 148
cognitive distraction 164
cognitive-emotional loop 321
cognitive flexibility 22, 85, 123, 213, 319, 322
cognitive off-loading 77, 79
cognitive overload 184, 320
cognitive reappraisal 216
commitment 52, 156–7
communication 31, 237, 238, 292, 295, 299
compassion, self- 46, 151, 159, 255–6, 287, 331, 333
Conner, Dr Alex 307
consistency 84, 239, 330
control, inhibitory 22
coping mechanisms 9–10, 20, 250
cortisol-dopamine cocktail 150
creativity 35, 62

D
the d-factor 175–6
deadlines 55, 60, 83, 119, 149, 150–1, 195, 305, 323
DEAR MAN technique 311–14
decision-making 41, 78, 125, 193, 230–1, 250, 274, 310
  decision paralysis 308
  decisional procrastination 148–9
  externalizing decisions 280
  using AI to help 134
decluttering 61–2, 181
default mode network (DMN) 167, 168, 169, 172
delay aversion 106–7
delegation 285–6
depression 42, 43, 244, 247
DESC method 220–1
Dialectical Behaviour Therapy (DBT) 219, 221–2, 312
dichotomous thinking 148
digital distractions, blocking 179–80
discordant pleiotrophy 266–7
distractibility 59, 124, 322, 325
  ADHD and 169–70
  blocking digital distractions 179–80
  cognitive distraction 164
  the d-factor (general distractibility) 175–6
  external distractibility 170–1, 175, 176, 177–81
  externalizing your brain 192
  filtering 163–4, 169
  frictionless focus 179
  internal distractibility 171–2, 175, 176, 182–5
  interrupting the mind-wandering loop 183–4
  intrusive thoughts 174–5
  managing 161–86
  manual distractions 164
  mental distractions 164
  mind-wandering 172
  minimizing 234, 235, 283–4
  racing thoughts 173–4, 176
  reducing cognitive overload 184
  staying focused 167–8, 180–1
  strategies for managing internal distractibility 182–5
  strategies for manging external distractibility 177–81
  supporting emotional distractions 184–5
  time-blocking to contain attention 183
  visual distractions 164, 177–8
  what it is 169
dopamine 16, 17, 18, 87, 121
  and ADHD brains 111
  boosting 202
  cortisol-dopamine cocktail 150
  digital distractions 179
  dopamine anchors 333
  habits and 82–3
  and motivation 96, 106, 121–2
  and prioritization 121–2, 125
  routines and 91, 92
  and time management 195
  and working memory 229–30, 232

Doran, George 54
dorsal attention network (DAN) 165–6, 168, 170
downtime, and burnout 45, 46

E
Eisenhower matrix 130
emotions 24, 85
  cognitive-emotional loop 321
  and decision-making 125
  emotional boundaries 293
  emotional distress 35
  emotional dysregulation 206, 214–23, 253, 303, 330
  emotional flexibility 319
  emotional incentive 100
  emotional intensity 60
  emotional regulation 76, 78, 153, 206, 208–14, 216, 217, 312
  emotional side of productivity 204–23
  emotional symptoms 19
  and perfectionism 247
  prioritization and 121
  and procrastination 144–6, 152, 158–9
  and productivity 32
  Rejection Sensitive Dysphoria (RSD) 217–18, 304
  and setting boundaries 303–7
  supporting emotional distractions 184–5
  task switching and 326
  what emotions are 206–8
energy 53, 278–80, 285, 294
environmental factors 17–18, 177
executive dysfunction 22–5, 37, 57, 153, 253, 320, 330
  and AuDHD 269–70
  boundaries and 300
  routines 84–6
executive functions 20–2, 23, 77, 89, 122, 123, 317
  and AuDHD 269–70
  boundaries and 300
  and emotional regulation 213–14
executive overload 44
exhaustion, and productivity 29–30
expectations 32, 42
exposure therapy 257
external hard drives 280–1

F
fear 99–100, 147, 149
feedback 52–3
feelings, labelling and challenging 220–1
flexibility, helpful 281
flourish or fail thinking 148
focus 24, 76, 103, 124, 125
  and AuDHD 273
  boundaries and 294
  frictionless focus 179
  hyperfocus 194, 197, 200, 262, 272–3, 275
  improving 202
  managing distractibility 161–86
  setting up a 'launchpad' for 180–1
  top-down attention 120
  working memory and 231
frontoparietal network (FPN) 163, 166–7, 168, 170
fronto-striatal circuits 267
frustration 19, 34

G
gamification 109–10, 281–2
genetics 16–17, 18, 266–7
goals 120, 124, 137
  ADHD-friendly goal setting 49–72, 123
  AI tools 70–1
  emotional dysregulation 215
  execution and persistence 59–60
  flex points and recovery plans 69–70
  formation and planning 59
  Goal-Setting Theory (GST) 51–4, 55, 57
  learning goals 56, 65
  making goals visible 66–7
  master task lists 68–9, 90
  monitoring and self-regulation 60
  open goals 56–7, 63–4, 65

optimising goal setting for ADHD 61–3
and perfectionism 247
performance 53–4, 56
power of goal setting 51–4
SMART goals 54–72
stages of goal setting 59–60
starting small 65–6
strategies for improving goal setting 64–71
using to start habits and routines 63
golden hours 112, 201
Goldman, Dr Rachel 76
gratification, delayed 22, 106–7
Gross, James 211
grounding 184, 219–20
guilt 19, 29

H
habits: dopamine and 82–3
the habit loop 80–1, 86, 96
starting using goals 63–4
tweaking 333
hippocampus 121, 193, 210, 229
hobbies 62
hyperactivity 11–12, 13–14, 15
and productivity 38, 39–41
self-monitoring and impulse control 24
signs of 40
hyperfocus 194, 197, 200, 262, 272–3, 275

I
imperfect effort, celebrating 333
imposter syndrome 115
impulsivity 11–12, 13–14, 15, 125
impulse control 24, 78, 214, 300
reacting on impulses 22
and productivity 38, 39–41
verbal 40–1
inattention 11, 12–13, 15, 38–9
INCUP model 58
inhibition 22, 123
insular cortex 193
intentions 57
intention-action gap 141
interference control 22
intrusive thoughts 174–5

J
Jobs, Steve 79

L
laziness 42, 47, 143, 144, 320
learning 56, 65, 190, 231, 232–3
life: automating life 73–98
lifestyle 234, 236
lighting, tweaking 178
limbic system 121, 125, 146
lists 68–9
master task lists 90, 94–5, 128–30, 134, 280, 281
ta-da lists 53, 67
to-do lists 182, 200
try-again-tomorrow list 332

M
masking 9–10, 44
meetings 31
memory 24
boundaries and working memory 300–1
daily life with poor working memory 232–3
externalizing memory 280
how working memory works 227–8
long-term memory 226
memory burden 239
short-term memory 226
strategies for supporting working memory 234–41
working memory 21, 24, 59, 77, 85, 93, 127, 153, 166, 224–41, 300–1, 322
working memory impairment 231–2
working memory toolkit 234–6
mental health 16, 24, 32, 43
midbrain 228
mind-wandering 172, 183–4
mindfulness 183–4, 216, 219–20, 326
mistakes, making 38

momentum, maintaining 323–6
monotropism 272, 273
mood repair 145
MoSCoW method 131
motivation 24, 82, 87, 153
  accountability with body doubling 108–9
  amotivation 104, 105
  body doubling 283
  boosting 53
  creating structure around tasks 112–14
  and delayed gratification 106–7
  and dopamine 96, 106, 121–2
  extrinsic motivation 104, 108
  finding motivation 99–114
  gamification 109–10
  impact of ADHD on 105–6
  impact of dysregulation of dopamine 58
  increasing motivation 107–14
  interest vs importance 57–9
  intrinsic motivation 104, 105
  making rewards immediate and visible 111
  motivation fade 60
  prioritization and 121
  and productivity 33
  response to 25
  Self-Determination Theory (SDT) 104–5
  understanding 101–2
  and values 35
  what it is 102–4
multitasking 33, 162, 166, 317

N
neural gain 230
neurotransmitters 16, 18
'no': learning to say no 41, 289–315
  the 'Positive no' 307–9
noise, blocking 177
noradrenaline 121–2, 125, 195, 229–30, 232

O
Obama, Barack 79
organization 39, 85, 120, 153, 249
organizational support, asking for 236–8
overcompensation cycle 305–6
over-scheduling 127
overwhelm 23, 39, 44, 85, 121, 125, 185
  effective time management 189
  emotional dysregulation 215
  and lack of boundaries 296, 305, 307
  minimizing 283–4
  and procrastination 153–4, 155–6
  reducing 258
  and task initiation 320, 321

P
pacing 46, 285
PAG (periaqueductal grey) 209
parietal lobes 228
people-pleasing 289–315
perfectionism 183, 243–60, 270, 296, 324, 331
  adaptive perfectionism 245–6, 247, 252
  ADHD and the pressure to be perfect 252–4
  burnout 244, 247, 250, 251, 255
  covert perfectionists 248
  emotional dysregulation 215
  healthy vs harmful 245, 250
  impact on productivity 249–50
  maladaptive perfectionism 246–7, 250, 251
  non-perfectionists 248
  overt perfectionists 248
  and procrastination 148, 149, 245, 250
  reframing 332
  spectrum of 248
  strategies to help 254–8
  what it is 244, 248–9
  when perfect becomes paralysis 250–1
performance: performance anxiety 62
  performance goals 56
persistence 53, 103

planning 85, 120, 153, 167, 191, 230, 270, 301, 324
Pomodoro technique 113–14, 183, 325
positive illusory bias 42, 126–7
predictability 75–7, 274
prefrontal cortex 22, 81, 120, 124, 146, 193, 195, 216–17, 228, 229, 268
prenatal exposure 17
prioritization 153, 301, 310, 325
  ABCDE method 132–3
  and the brain 120–2, 124–7
  the challenge of in ADHD 122–4
  common prioritization pitfalls 127
  definition of prioritization 117–19
  how people prioritize 119–20
  importance vs urgency 119–20, 124, 127, 130
  the master task list 128–30, 134
  the MoSCoW method 131
  picking 115–38
  strategies that work 128–37, 281
  the task matrix approach 130
  traffic light system 134–5
  two-minute win 136–7
  using AI to help 133–4
problem-solving 54, 230–1
procrastination 33, 35, 66, 87, 102, 194, 270, 320
  ADHD and 151–9
  body doubling 283
  and decision-making 280
  effect on productivity 149–50
  and emotions 144–6
  mood repair 145–6
  and perfectionism 245, 250
  psychological drivers of 146–9
  reducing procrastination by being busy 150–1
  strategies to tackle 155–9
  tackling 139–60
  what procrastination is 142–3
  what procrastination isn't 143–4
  working under pressure 150
productivity 82, 332
  and AuDHD 269–70, 274–7
  and boundaries 294–5, 296–7, 298–300
  challenges to 27–48
  common barriers to 30
  daily life with poor working memory 232–3
  definition of personal productivity 28–9
  effect of procrastination on 149–50
  and emotional regulation 213–14
  emotional side of 204–23
  fear and 100
  and goal setting 51
  impact of perfectionism on 249–50
  internal challenges 32–4
  and motivation 102–3, 105
  and prioritization 122
  productivity crash 316–28
  systemic challenges to 30–2
  and time management 189, 190
  and values 34–7
  why 'time spent' doesn't equal 'value' 29–30
  working memory and 224, 230–1
progress 243–60, 332

R
racing thoughts 173–4, 176
reactivity 122
recharge rituals 46
Red/Yellow/Green day plan 279
reframing 333
rejection sensitivity 19, 303, 312
  Rejection Sensitive Dysphoria (RSD) 217–18, 253, 304, 331
resetting 90, 332–3
resilience 35, 53
restlessness, internal 40
reviews, weekly 90
rewards 58, 67, 69, 141, 324
  ADHD brain and 106–7
  dopamine and 82, 106, 110, 121
  the habit loop 80–1, 86

making obvious and immediate 95–6, 111
response to 25
temporal discounting 87
time management 201
routines 73–98, 190, 194, 268, 270, 324
building with factored-in wiggle room 201
consistency tax 84
cues and rewards 95
dopamine and 82–3
executive dysfunction 84–6
externalizing everything 93–4
flexible 285
from new to automatic 81
the habit loop 80–1, 86, 96
how the brain builds 80
meta-routines 89–91
power of predictability 75–7
the routine trap 274
routine vs novelty 270–1
and saving brainpower 77
small wins, big impact 79
starting small and building gradually 91–2
starting using goals 63
strategies for building routines 88–96
time blindness 86–7
transition time 326
why routines are hard with ADHD 83
why routines matter 75
and willpower 78
and working memory 238–41
the 'Zuckerberg approach' 78–9, 92–3

S
salience network (SN) 165–6, 168, 170
schedules, visual 199
self-awareness 60, 201
self-care 45, 289–315
self-compassion 46, 151, 159, 255–6, 287, 331, 333
self-control 22, 78, 124
self-criticism 248, 250, 255–6
Self-Determination Theory (SDT) 104–5
self-efficacy 52, 79, 190
self-esteem 42, 43, 83, 246, 292, 304
self-monitoring 214
self-regulation 60, 143
senses 220
minimizing sensory stress 283–4
sensory overwhelm 44
sensory regulation 45
shame 19, 27, 125
about saying 'no' 304, 306
distractibility and 167
intention-action gap 141
and perfectionism 252
procrastination and 151, 155, 250
and productivity 33, 42
shame spiral 331
side quests 68, 101, 129–30, 281–2
skill acquisition 231
sleep 45, 46, 76, 155, 174, 234, 236
SMART goals 54–72
smart speakers 200
social overwhelm 44
stress 44, 202, 250, 274
boundaries and 295
and productivity 32, 33
minimizing stressors 283–4
striatum 228
success, fear of 147

T
'ta-da' lists 67
tasks: automating 286–7
breaking down to reduce overwhelm 155–6
choosing at random 281–2
chunking 234, 235, 284–5
complexity 53
creating structure around 112–14
difficulty in picking one 271
emotional dysregulation 215
emotional regulation and 213
master task lists 94–5, 128–30, 134, 280, 281

micro-tasks 284–5
poor task initiation 87
prioritizing 115–38
procrastination 139–60
task aversion 146–7, 153, 154
task initiation 85, 87, 92, 112–13, 153, 213, 283, 317, 319, 320
task management and planning 200, 230
task matrix approach 130
task paralysis 320–1
task rituals 113
task switching 161–2, 316–28
templates to help 282–3
visual task management tools 113
technology 200–1, 238, 239–41
templates, task 282–3
temporal discounting 87
temporal fog 301–2
therapy 219, 256–8
thoughts: intrusive 174–5
naming 257
racing 173–4, 176
train of thought 226, 312
time: perception of time 152, 191–3, 195
time-blocking to contain attention 183
time-bound goals 55
time boundaries 293, 294
time management 187–203
time sinks 201
using AI to calculate 134
time blindness 60, 86–7, 126–7, 153, 291, 301–3, 309–10, 330
ADHD, time blindness and future amnesia 193–4, 195
effect of 195–8
strategies for tackling 198–202
time management for 187–203
timers 198–9, 326
traffic light system 134–5
transitions 316–28
strategies to tackle 323–6
supporting 284
types of 318

U
urgency, vs importance 119, 120, 124, 127, 130

V
values 34–7, 120, 257
how to spot (and use) 35–7
identifying 36
losing 34–5
misaligned 35
ventral attention network (VAN) 165–6, 168, 170
ventral striatum 209
visual cortex 228
visualization 234, 235

W
willpower 78, 101, 143, 191, 239
work: asking for organizational support 236–8
boundaries at 298–300
daily life with poor working memory 232–3
distracting work environments 31–2
pacing issues 194
performance at 24
procrastination in 149–50, 154
and productivity 30–48
setting boundaries 32
and time blindness 190, 195, 196–8
workspaces: decluttering 61–2, 181
making it yours 178
workspace optimization 158
World Health Organization 42, 43–4

Y
'yes', hidden cost of saying 297–8

Z
Zuckerberg, Mark 78–9

Dear Reader,

We'd love your attention for one more page to tell you about the crisis in children's reading, and what we can all do.

Studies have shown that reading for fun is the **single biggest predictor of a child's future life chances** – more than family circumstance, parents' educational background or income. It improves academic results, mental health, wealth, communication skills, ambition and happiness.[1]

The number of children reading for fun is in rapid decline. Young people have a lot of competition for their time. In 2024, 1 in 10 children and young people in the UK aged 5 to 18 did not own a single book at home.[2]

Hachette works extensively with schools, libraries and literacy charities, but here are some ways we can all raise more readers:

- Reading to children for just 10 minutes a day makes a difference
- Don't give up if children aren't regular readers – there will be books for them!
- Visit bookshops and libraries to get recommendations
- Encourage them to listen to audiobooks
- Support school libraries
- Give books as gifts

There's a lot more information about how to encourage children to read on our website: **www.RaisingReaders.co.uk**

Thank you for reading.

[1] OECD, '21st-Century Readers: Developing Literacy Skills in a Digital World', 2021, https://www.oecd.org/en/publications/21st-century-readers_a83d84cb-en.html

[2] National Literacy Trust, 'Book Ownership in 2024', November 2024, https://literacytrust.org.uk/research-services/research-reports/book-ownership-in-2024